Christian
Philosophy

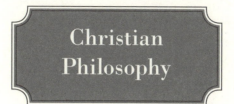

Christian Philosophy

A Systematic and Narrative Introduction

Craig G. Bartholomew
Michael W. Goheen

Baker Academic

a division of Baker Publishing Group
Grand Rapids, Michigan

© 2013 by Craig G. Bartholomew and Michael W. Goheen

Published by Baker Academic
a division of Baker Publishing Group
P.O. Box 6287, Grand Rapids, MI 49516-6287
www.bakeracademic.com

Printed in the United States of America

Library of Congress Cataloging-in-Publication Data
Bartholomew, Craig G., 1961–
    Christian philosophy : a systematic and narrative introduction / Craig G. Bartholomew and Michael W. Goheen.
        p.   cm.
    Includes bibliographical references and index.
    ISBN 978-0-8010-3911-9 (pbk.)
    1. Christian philosophy. I. Goheen, Michael W., 1955– II. Title.
BR100.B25 2013
230.01—dc23   2013017852

13   14   15   16   17   18   19   7   6   5   4   3   2   1

To Bob and Elaine Goudzwaard:
good friends and scholarly examples,
always ready for a stimulating
philosophical discussion.

Contents

Preface

Mission—real mission—involves a deep encounter of the gospel with our culture(s). In our view, one indispensable element in any such encounter is Christian philosophy. We are thus delighted to present this book and hope that it will inspire you to take philosophy seriously even if you are not called to be a philosopher.

While *Christian Philosophy* is a separate book in its own right, it is also a companion to our *Drama of Scripture: Finding Our Place in the Biblical Story* and *Living at the Crossroads: An Introduction to Christian Worldview*, both published by Baker Academic.

Readers and professors should note that we have kept references to a minimum. Secondary sources and teaching resources can be found at www.biblicaltheology.ca and www.paideiacentre.ca/resources/teaching/christian-philosophy.

Our thanks go to Jim Kinney and his team at Baker Academic for their sterling work. In addition, we are grateful to Elaine Goudzwaard-Botha, Bob Goudzwaard, Harry van Dyke, Bruce Ashford, Heath Thomas, Robert Mac-Larkey, Josh Walker, Adam Harmer, and others who have read the manuscript and helped us improve it. Defects remain, of course—our responsibility! Craig is grateful to Redeemer University College for the exhilarating opportunity to teach Christian philosophy as the occupant of the H. Evan Runner chair, and we are both grateful to The Paideia Centre for Public Theology for its support in our writing of this book.

Introduction

Readers of *The Drama of Scripture* will remember that at the outset of that book we introduced Abby and Percy, who were just starting to get to know each other. Much water has passed under the bridge since that momentous encounter, and we wish we had time to tell you the whole story. To cut to the chase, they have now been going steady for a year and are deeply involved in their local church. Shortly after their memorable coffee together, a new pastor took over at their church, and his ministry has turned their lives around.

He has introduced them to a life-changing way of reading the Bible as the true story of the whole world. Whereas before they had known the Bible piecemeal, now they have a growing sense of its unity and of how they are called to indwell the story and to live it out. Their pastor loves to quote Eugene Peterson's saying that "we are all in holy orders," and Abby and Percy have come to see that they too are full-time servants of Christ and that discerning their vocation and training for it is serious business.

After lots of soul-searching and long conversations with their pastor, their parents, friends, and each other—to say nothing of a lot of prayer—Abby has registered at a prestigious Christian school named Long Obedience College and is majoring in psychology, and Percy thinks he may be called to medicine and has enrolled at Brighton Secular University, internationally known for its sciences and premed training. Alas, pursuing their vocations seriously has meant that they are now separated by some seven hundred miles. Email and Skype have been a great help, as we will see. During the Christmas break, each having survived the first semester, Abby and Percy were comparing notes about what lay ahead. Abby had really enjoyed the first semester but wondered about the value of some of the core courses she had to take in the second semester. "Next semester," she sighed to Percy over a glass of hot cider, "I'm signed up for Introduction to Philosophy! Why on earth as a psychologist would I need to do that?"

Percy was sympathetic but pointed out that he too had to do a course in philosophy, and he decided to see if he could also take it in the next semester

so that he and Abby could do it at the same time and compare notes. A quick
check online confirmed that he could and that it would fit well with his schedule.
Abby felt much better. "But still," she said to Percy, as they went for a walk in
the snow, "what possible value could philosophy have to our 'holy orders'?"

To answer Abby's question, we think there is great value in philosophy.
There are different ways to introduce philosophy. Our approach is a combination of systematic philosophy and close attention to the history of philosophy.
After two introductory chapters looking at the value of philosophy and its
relationship to faith, in the next several chapters we attend to the narrative
of philosophy as it has unfolded since its origin among the ancient Greeks.
As we will stress repeatedly, the way you tell the story of philosophy is never
neutral, and our goal is to tell the story from a Christian perspective. Having
a sense of this narrative is indispensable to studying philosophy.

In recent decades there has been an astonishing renaissance in Christian
philosophy, particularly in the United States of America. We will tell this
story, examine contemporary Catholic philosophy, and then look in more
detail at the work of two (Reformed) Christian philosophers who have made
major contributions to this renewal—namely, Alvin Plantinga and Nicholas
Wolterstorff.

In the twentieth century, another Reformed Christian philosophy, commonly called *Reformational philosophy*, developed out of the work of Dutch
philosopher Herman Dooyeweerd. We are most in tune with this tradition
of philosophy, and in conclusion we will explore its contours and note the
many areas of agreement with the Reformed epistemology of Plantinga and
Wolterstorff.

Part 1

Approaching
Christian Philosophy

1

Why Philosophy?

Introduction

In many Christian circles today, philosophy gets bad press or, even worse, is simply ignored. Abby's response to hearing that she needed to take a course in philosophy is far too common. There have been times in the history of the church when a good knowledge of philosophy was regarded as indispensable, but now is not such a time. Bible study and knowing how to evangelize are indispensable, but it would be regarded by many Christians as strange indeed if their local church announced a course in philosophy as a vital part of the church's mission.

However, we believe that a working knowledge of Christian philosophy *is* a vital ingredient in mission, if by mission we mean facilitating a deep encounter of our culture with Christ. Philosophy, from our perspective, is the attempt to discern the structure or order of creation, and to describe systematically what is subject to that order. The difference that a *Christian* philosophy makes is that the whole of life, apart from God, is studied as *creation*. The Apostles' Creed sums up the biblical doctrine of creation when it states, "We believe in God the Father Almighty, creator of heaven and earth." As Genesis 1:1–2:3 and the creed inform us, creation involves God not just ushering the world into existence but *ordering* it in a particular way so that there is heaven and earth; night and day; seasons; earth, sea, and sky; and plants, animals, birds, and human beings. Much of the order in creation we simply take for granted. We just know that it is normal for human beings to walk upright, and we would be astonished and disturbed if someone came into church doing the sort of leopard crawl that soldiers learn in their training. We can pretend that gravity

does not exist, but step out of the window of a high building and the order
of creation will manifest itself in no uncertain terms.

But God's ordering of creation is more complex than this kind of natural
order. Genesis 1–3 teaches us that God's order extends to things like gender
(male and female), marriage, farming, and how we relate to God and to the
animals. Indeed, the doctrine of creation teaches us that just as the whole of
creation comes from God, so it is *all* subject to his order for it. As Abraham
Kuyper, the nineteenth-century Dutch prime minister, theologian, journalist,
and churchman, saw so clearly, "there is not a square inch in the whole domain
of our human existence over which Christ, who is Sovereign over all, does not
cry: 'Mine!'"[1] Although curiosity is a major motive in philosophy, the primary
emotion driving Christian philosophy will be wonder. The mind-blowing
implication is that with creation comes God's order for things like

- what it means to be human;
- history and historical development;
- culture, in the sense of how we organize the societies we are part of;
- art;
- business and economics;
- politics;
- sport and leisure;
- friendship;
- and so on.

As if this comprehensive range of God's order were not challenge enough,
the fall into sin opened up the catastrophic possibility of humans *misdirecting*
God's good order for creation. The possibility of family life is a great gift written
into the fabric of creation, but we know from Genesis 4 that outside of Eden
brotherly love can become fratricide. Humans have the God-given ability to
build cities, and these can be places of delight and human flourishing and full
of God, but they can also be like Babel, monuments to idolatry (see Gen. 11).

Despite being fallen, humans retain the God-given ability to shape God's
world in which we live in accordance with the complex order of creation;
constant misdirection means that in many areas of life, hard work is required
to understand God's order for his creation today. The Bible, as we will see,

---

1. Abraham Kuyper, "Sphere Sovereignty," in *Abraham Kuyper: A Centennial Reader*, ed.
James D. Bratt (Grand Rapids: Eerdmans, 1998), 488. At about the same time C. S. Lewis wrote,
"There is no neutral ground in the universe: every square inch, every split second, is claimed
by God and counter-claimed by Satan" ("Christianity and Culture," in *Christian Reflections*
[Grand Rapids: Eerdmans, 1967], 33).

gives us indispensable clues to such a journey of discovery—but it gives us the *clues*, not all the answers! The great twentieth-century missiologist Lesslie Newbigin perceptively noted that "Jesus is the clue to history, its goal and source."[2] We commit the worst sort of folly if we *ignore* that clue which is Christ, but we are also fools if we fail to *pursue* that clue in all areas of life as God has made it. Take any of the above topics and you will see that the Bible addresses these issues, but in not one case does it provide us with a detailed analysis of the sort we need if we are to live effectively for God in his world today. Philosophy is precisely the quest for that *detailed analysis* of the order of creation as it relates to the many different aspects of life under the sun.

The Importance of Philosophy for Christian Mission

Apologetics

The minute we come to Christ and start to live for him, we find our neighbors asking questions about our faith. This has always been so, and it is why Peter tells us that we need to be ready to give an account of the hope within us (1 Pet. 3:15). Such an account will range from the narrative of our conversion and what Christ has come to mean to us to a rigorous defense of the faith. So it was with the early church: as their numbers and influence grew, accusations were leveled against them and questions asked. In order to respond to these, early Christians had of necessity to give an account and defense of their faith in terms that their non-Christian neighbors could understand. Inevitably early Christian thinkers reached for concepts from the philosophies of the day in order to provide a robust articulation of their faith.

Increasingly in the West today, Christians are in a minority amid an often hostile culture, and in this situation it is vital that we are able not only to live out our faith but also to account for it. We should never underestimate the compelling power of a life lived in Christ and of a conversion narrative, but the credibility of our faith will still depend to an extent on our being able to provide a logical account of it.

Apologetics cannot by itself convert a person to Christ; that is the work of the Spirit. But it can be used by God to clear the ground for conversion in what is sometimes called preevangelism. One thinks of the long process whereby C. S. Lewis came to faith in Christ. The final step was experiential and not as a result of having Christianity proved true to him. In *Surprised by Joy*, the story of his conversion, Lewis movingly describes how he got on a bus in Oxford not a Christian and disembarked a believer. His actual conversion

---

2. Lesslie Newbigin, *The Gospel in a Pluralist Society* (Grand Rapids: Eerdmans, 1989), 123.

was *far more* than logical, but a great deal of thinking and discussion with Christian friends preceded his conversion.[3] And Lewis of course went on to become one of the greatest Christian apologists of our time. It is less well known that Lewis took a first in philosophy at Oxford University, and he used this to great effect in developing his apologetics.

Francis Schaeffer, who with his wife founded L'Abri in the tiny village of Huemoz in Switzerland, exercised an international ministry as Christian and non-Christian students flocked from around the world to ask their questions and seriously discuss them with Schaeffer and his coworkers. The extraordinary story of L'Abri is told by Edith Schaeffer in her book *The Tapestry*. At the heart of Francis Schaeffer's ministry was a welcoming community and apologetics. Schaeffer's preevangelism and evangelism necessitated that he immerse himself in the culture of his day and in philosophy. Many came to Christ through L'Abri's ministry, and many Christians awoke to the need to take culture and philosophy seriously.

Clearly there will be a variety of levels of apologetics, ranging from witnessing to what Christ means to you, to answering a neighbor's queries, to academic defense of the Christian faith at the most rigorous level. A robust apologetic requires Christians to operate at all levels. An example of academic defense of the faith at the highest levels is Alvin Plantinga's *Warranted Christian Belief*, the third volume in his magisterial trilogy on epistemology. Of course not all Christians are called like Plantinga to be a philosopher, and even among those who are, few can rise to his level of excellence. But a basic introduction to Christian philosophy will help in answering your neighbor's queries, and those like Plantinga who are called to be Christian philosophers have a crucial role in making the case for the credibility of Christianity at the highest academic level.

Missional Cultural Engagement

Once we see that mission involves an engagement of the gospel with the whole of our culture and that mission takes place at the crossroads of the biblical story and our cultural story, it becomes clear that serious mission requires a deep understanding of our culture(s).

Here again philosophy can be an enormous help.[4]

Take the issue of homosexuality for example. In our opinion it is clear from Scripture that homosexual practice is unbiblical and not according to

---

3. Whenever asked about his conversion, Lewis always stressed its strongly philosophical component. We are indebted to Adam Barkman, Craig's colleague in philosophy, for this information.

4. Augustine's *City of God* and Thomas Aquinas's *Summa Contra Gentiles* were both written in response to requests from missionaries. See Curtis Chang, *Engaging Unbelief: A Captivating Strategy from Augustine and Aquinas* (Eugene, OR: Wipf and Stock, 2000), 13–18.

God's design for human life. In this we are in wholehearted agreement with conservative Christians. But how does one engage *society* from this perspective? It is one thing to believe that homosexuality is clearly wrong, but what does this mean for our diverse societies? What sort of legislation should Christians push for, and how do we actively protect the civil rights of homosexuals while preserving the sanctity of marriage between a man and a woman? These are crucial but complex issues, and many Christians are lost when it comes to engaging them. Such engagement requires far more than an understanding of the biblical view of homosexuality; it requires a *philosophy* of society, an understanding of the role of politics (philosophy of politics), and gracious but determined resistance to political correctness in a variety of ways.

Many orthodox Anglicans who are being forced to face up to the direction of mainstream North American Anglicanism find themselves wondering how on earth they got to the point where church leaders are moving away from the gospel. It is a good question. To answer it, one needs to know what has happened in Western culture and the philosophies that have shaped it over the past several centuries and the philosophies shaping Western culture at present. Only in this way will we be able to understand what time it is in our culture and the forces manifesting themselves in issues like homosexuality and many others. And only from such a deep understanding will we be able to discern the spirits at work and how to engage them missionally.

Lesslie Newbigin tells the story of attending a major conference on mission, where he was sitting next to an Indonesian general. At a certain point in the conference Newbigin heard the general mutter under his breath, "Of course, the number one question is, Can the West be converted?" After spending some forty years as a missionary in India, Newbigin and his wife returned to the United Kingdom. In the remaining years of his life, Newbigin did his best to rouse Western Christians from their slumber to attend to the mission on their doorsteps. The problem with culture is that it is like the water the fish swims in: we get so used to it that it appears normal, until we enter a very different culture and start to see that what we assumed was normal and "Christian" is not necessarily so.

Western Christians urgently need a deep understanding of the culture they live in with all its strengths and weaknesses. Newbigin worked to provide such an understanding, and a cursory perusal of his important writings will indicate the central role of philosophy in such a missional approach to and analysis of Western culture.

Philosophy and Christian Scholarship

Universities play a formative role in preparing students for their life's work, whatever form that may end up taking. Central to modernity is the view that universities provide neutral, objective scholarship and teaching. Despite this view being savaged in recent decades, it remains dominant in popular culture among Christians and non-Christians alike. What modernity calls a neutral, objective approach to academia is anything but. In any discipline, as you go deeper and deeper into a subject, finally you reach those really fundamental questions that we usually take for granted. That is philosophy. At the foundation of *every* subject are foundational questions like:

- How do we go about knowing in this subject area such that we can trust the results to be truthful? This is the question of *epistemology*.
- What does it mean to be human? This is the question of *anthropology*.
- What is the nature of the world around us? This is the question of *ontology*.

These are foundational philosophical questions. We like to call them *launchpad questions* since they are the base from which any subject is launched. And the answers to them are normally taken for granted. Indeed, modernity has had a vested interest in concealing these questions and the impact of modernity's answers on scholarship. It doesn't take much reflection to realize that the gospel has major implications for how one might answer these three fundamental questions, and a Christian answer will shape a subject differently than non-Christian answers.

Of course, once we see this, the hard work begins. How *does* a Christian view of the person shape a contemporary psychology? And what does the gospel mean for economics or law or medicine or education or, for that matter, religious studies? The university was a Christian invention of the Middle Ages, but along the way something major happened to most Western universities: they became thoroughly secular in line with cultural developments. In the typical Western university there *may* be a place for faith in the religion department, but it is generally considered absurd to want to engage with other disciplines from a Christian perspective.

It is not surprising therefore that several years ago the church historian George Marsden wrote a provocative book with the title *The Outrageous Idea of Christian Scholarship*. It is not that Marsden thinks Christian scholarship is outrageous, but he knows only too well that most scholars do. If we are serious about mission and genuinely concerned that Christian students are trained for a lifetime of service to Christ in whatever area of life he calls them to, then we urgently need to recover a vision for Christian scholarship. Sending the best and brightest young Christians to study at the feet of the best secular scholars of the day simply will not do.

We need top-rate Christian scholars in every discipline, and we need students to study at their feet—or at least to be prepared for the secular university so that they can excavate the big questions operating in their subjects—and take the good while leaving the bad and developing a Christian understanding of their chosen field. Christian philosophy alone will not produce this, but it is a fundamental ingredient in the recipe for such cultural engagement. Philosophy attends precisely to the sort of fundamental questions noted above, and a Christian philosophical framework will go a long way toward inoculating a student against secularism and provide a basis for developing a Christian perspective in his or her subject area. A university subject is like an iceberg. Generally what is taught is what lies above the water, and few professors have the expertise or inclination to alert their students to the formative mass under the water. Christian philosophy is a great help in learning to spot the launchpad questions—and answers—informing a subject and the way it is taught.

Philosophy and Christian Life

Some people say that philosophy is not practical. Nothing could be further from the truth.[5]

As we noted above, not everyone should become a professional philosopher, just as not every Christian should become a professional theologian. But just as a basic knowledge of Christian doctrine is indispensable, so a basic understanding of Christian philosophy is of enormous practical value. Our societies are shaped according to particular philosophies, and the result is that, no matter what areas of life we serve in, an understanding of philosophy is helpful.

Take nurses and doctors, for example. In countries like Canada and the United Kingdom where there are national health systems, medical professionals are being stretched to the limit and becoming increasingly mechanical and impersonal. How is it that Western health care has become this way, and how should Christians operate within it? What does a doctor do when his or her Christian faith conflicts with a course of treatment a patient wants and perhaps demands? A Christian *philosophy and history of health care* are key elements in beginning to orient oneself in this system. At the very least, they will alert one to the fact that it does not have to be this way.

Athletics and sports are great gifts, and many of us enjoy the entertainment they provide. But in our world they are also locales of idols, and many young people find themselves pushed into living for their sport and making winning everything. A *philosophy of sport* will provide a healthy orientation toward the values and limits of sport and orient the Christian healthily in what is often a distorted area of our world.

5. Phil Washburn, *Philosophical Dilemmas: Building a Worldview* (New York: Oxford University Press, 1996), 11.

An energetic youth pastor is wondering how best to develop the youth ministry in his growing church. Numbers at Friday night meetings range from fifteen to sixty. Does he try to compete with alternative entertainment, or what exactly does he do to build a lasting youth ministry? A *philosophy of the institutional church* and its distinctive characteristics, as well as its relationship to other spheres of society, will help this youth pastor in discerning the biblical focus of youth ministry.

Some recent converts are worried about their children, who are attending a local government school. The children's language and behavior are becoming more and more uncontrollable. What should the parents do? Again, a basic understanding of *philosophy of education* is of enormous help to such parents as they seek to form the lives of their children.

As a professor of philosophy, Craig is often asked by students why they should consider a major in philosophy. What will they do with it, and how will it help them get a job after university? It is unfortunately true that philosophers are not in great demand in our societies. In ancient Greece, the sophists were like the rock stars of the day and could charge considerable sums for their instruction. How times have changed! Of course, if you plan to become a philosopher, then a major in philosophy is essential, but a good plan for other students is to pursue majors in their subject of choice and minors in philosophy, provided they have access to a good, Christian philosophy department. Jean Vanier is world renowned for his founding of L'Arche, whose communities are now spread throughout the world. It is less well known that Vanier holds a doctorate in philosophy on Aristotle and well into his L'Arche work published a book on the value of Aristotle's philosophy.[6] We have also found that students who go on to graduate school with a grounding in Christian philosophy tend to cope better than those without such training.

And so we could continue. Because God is the Creator and because his order is comprehensive in that it relates to all of life, there is not an area of practical human life for which a Christian philosophy will not provide helpful insight.

The Way Ahead

We hope this has made you excited about the potential of Christian philosophy. It certainly had that effect on Abby. Back at Long Obedience after the short Christmas break, Abby wrote excitedly to Percy, explaining how her philosophy prof addressed the importance of philosophy head-on in the very first lecture. The prof's emphasis on apologetics had not surprised her, but

6. Jean Vanier, *Made for Happiness: Discovering the Meaning of Life with Aristotle*, trans. Kathryn Spink (Toronto: Anansi, 2001).

seeing philosophy within a missional context was a revelation. "The gospel just keeps getting bigger and bigger," she wrote to Percy. "Now I'm starting to see how indispensable philosophy may be for my work as a psychologist. The most obvious connecting point for me was anthropology, the view of the person. Clearly, how we think of the human person impacts one's psychology, but I had never thought that Christian philosophy could help me develop a honed view of anthropology that can help orient my psychology and counseling in the right direction. This stuff really matters!"

Having sent her email off to Percy, Abby took a sip of her piping hot coffee and pressed the refresh button on her email, reflecting on how much she missed Percy. What—a reply from him already? No, not a reply but a new message headed "HELP!" Abby hurriedly clicked on the email. What could be wrong?

Percy too had just had his first class in philosophy, but what a different experience than that of Abby. His prof had started out by explaining the difference between philosophy and religion. Religion was based on faith, but philosophy was a science based on reason alone. In philosophy you are justified in believing something only if it can be established by reason. The prof acknowledged that many in the class might be believers, but in his class they were to leave their faith at the door—only reason was an acceptable criterion in their discussions. The prof went on about the importance of rational, human autonomy in the quest for truth and explained how philosophy emerged as certain ancient Greeks abandoned belief in the gods and sought natural explanations for the state of the world. One brave student asked if religion had no place in philosophy, to which the prof replied, "It does as a subject for analysis, but it is valid only if it can be shown to be true by reason."

"What do you make of this, Abby?" wrote Percy. "I was quite shaken when I left the class. It all sounds so logical, but as I reflect upon it, isn't human autonomy the great temptation to which Adam and Eve succumbed in Genesis 3? This is going to be one tough class. Any suggestion as to how to survive this course, or do you think I should just drop it for now? I'm not sure my faith is ready for this."

Abby quickly replied: "I see my prof again on Thursday. Let me get his advice and see if he can help."

In the next chapter we will examine the relationship between the Bible, a Christian worldview, and a Christian philosophy, making sure that we take the authority of Scripture with full seriousness. This will enable us to examine the far-too-common view that Percy was encountering in his introduction to philosophy.

2

Faith and Philosophy

After her Thursday philosophy lecture, Abby shyly waited for the prof to ask if she could meet with him sometime to discuss a few questions. "Sure," he answered. "Let's grab a coffee, and we can talk in my office right away."

Comfortably seated in the prof's office with her cappuccino nestled in her lap, Abby explained the very different experiences of philosophy she and Percy were having. "You are stressing that we need to engage the full resources of our faith in doing philosophy, whereas Percy is being told that faith must be left outside the philosophy class and that philosophy must be based on autonomous reason alone. His prof's approach sounds so *rational*, but I just can't imagine exploring the big questions of philosophy apart from my faith."

A long discussion ensued, but when Abby reviewed her notes later in her room so that she could convey the discussion to Percy, she saw that her prof had stressed two major points.

1. To understand the position that Percy's prof was insisting on, you have to know the story of the history of philosophy. While his view has ancient roots, it really became mainstream after the eighteenth-century Enlightenment, which largely rejected religion and tradition as the path to truth and insisted instead on human autonomy and rationality as *the* royal road to truth.
2. Some sort of faith is unavoidable in philosophy. Faith in human autonomy and reason is *as much* a type of faith as is faith in God. Neither can be proved; both have to be believed. This is increasingly being recognized today thanks to "postmodernism" but sadly the old, neutral, objectivist view persists.

Finishing off yet another coffee, Abby clicked open her email account and began, "My dear Percy . . ."

Introduction

"Some sort of faith is unavoidable in philosophy." In practice it is not a question of *whether* to allow faith to shape philosophy but rather *which* faith. Once we accept that our faith should play a formative role in our philosophy, the question becomes, *how* exactly should it do so? Faith is directed toward Jesus, who is authoritatively revealed for us in Scripture. Faith has at least two dimensions to it: an affective disposition—faith involves belief in God, not just assent to propositions—and a cognitive dimension. Both elements are important in doing philosophy, but it is the cognitive or doctrinal element of faith that comes to the fore in the question of the relationship between faith and philosophy. Not surprisingly, therefore, the relationship between faith and philosophy soon expands into the relationship between Scripture and philosophy, between worldview and philosophy, and between philosophy and theology, as we will see below. It is to these questions that we now turn.

Scripture

An effect of believing faith is that we come to see the Bible as God's fully trustworthy (infallible) Word for all of human life. A challenge is to hear it as the unified Word that it is. In *The Drama of Scripture* we argued that a really helpful way to grasp the unity of the Bible is to approach it as a sprawling, capacious narrative.

In recent decades scholars have increasingly recognized how important story is to human life and that at a very deep level human beings live out their lives in the context of a basic, foundational story. The technical word for this is *metanarrative*; a metanarrative is a grand story that aims to tell the true story of the world. Individuals and societies may be unconscious of the story they indwell, but always it is some particular grand story that an individual or community is living out.

There are different ways that the unity of the Bible can be articulated, but we think that it is particularly helpful to approach the Bible as a drama in six acts, a drama that really does tell the true story of the world. We identify the following six acts in the drama of Scripture:[1]

---

1. See Craig G. Bartholomew and Michael W. Goheen, *The Drama of Scripture: Finding Our Place in the Biblical Story* (Grand Rapids: Baker Academic, 2004).

1. God Establishes His Kingdom: Creation
2. Rebellion in the Kingdom: Fall
3. The King Chooses Israel: Redemption Initiated
4. The Coming of the King: Redemption Accomplished
5. Spreading the News of the King: The Mission of the Church
6. The Return of the King: Redemption Completed

In this way the Bible not only tells us the true story of the world but also invites us to make the story our own. It positions us clearly in act five of the drama—the mission of the church—and invites us to become active participants in God's journey with his creation as the drama continues to unfold and moves toward its conclusion (act six).

The Bible is the deposit—like the silt that settles at the bottom of a river—of God's journey with the people of Israel and of the life, death, and resurrection of his Son and of the early church that sprang up after Pentecost. The New Testament is not written in the polished literary Greek of the day but in the Koine Greek of the marketplace and of everyday people. Even in the time of the early church some found this scandalous, but we find it quite wonderful. The Bible is not an academic textbook but a book for Christians on the journey of life. Of course our understanding needs to be fully engaged when we read the Bible, but the Bible is not given to us first of all to analyze; rather it is God's Word to us as whole human beings and is the primary means whereby God wants to give himself to us again and again. The Bible is primarily directed at our hearts—the center of our beings—not at our heads. Its primary mode of reception is through the open heart, allowing God through the preaching of the Word or through private meditation upon it, to draw us into his very life.

In terms of understanding the Bible, we believe, as do all orthodox Christians, in the clarity of Scripture—its major truths are not hard to discern; they are there on the surface for all to see. Especially because of the different cultural contexts the Bible was written in, however, parts of it remain hard to understand, and that is why we appoint pastors in our churches; their job is to work hard to understand the Bible and to continually make more and more of the Bible clear to us so that we can receive it all as God's Word and allow it to guide our lives.

As we consider the relationship between Scripture, worldview, and philosophy, it is important to take note that the Bible is neither a doctrinal confession like the Belgic Confession or Catholic Catechism, nor is it a philosophy book. Now don't get us wrong. We are *not* saying that the Bible is not authoritative for doctrine and philosophy—it surely is—but the Bible is not, and was never intended to be, a doctrinal confession or a philosophical treatise.

Take the doctrine of the Trinity, for example. In essence it is on every page of the New Testament, but nowhere will you find a careful, logical statement of it, as you will in the church confessions. Indeed, it took centuries for the church to hammer out the details of this doctrine. All the raw material of the major doctrines is present in abundance in the Bible, but this material has to be systematized into logical doctrines. Beyond that, theologians reflect in greater depth on the meaning and implications of these doctrines.

It is the same with philosophy. In chapter 1 we alluded to the important clues the Bible provides for a Christian philosophy, but these are never developed into one in the Bible itself. Take the question of epistemology, for example. There are major clues to the proper acquisition of knowledge in the Bible that we ignore to our folly. Commenting on the wisdom literature of the Old Testament, Gerhard von Rad notes that

> the thesis that all human knowledge comes back to the question about commitment to God is a statement of penetrating perspicacity. . . . It contains in a nutshell the whole Israelite theory of knowledge. . . . There lies behind the statement an acute awareness of the fact that the search for knowledge can go wrong . . . because of one single mistake at the beginning. To this extent, Israel attributes to the fear of God, to belief in God, a highly important function in respect of human knowledge. She was, in all seriousness, of the opinion that effective knowledge about God is the only thing that puts a man into a right relationship with the objects of his perception.[2]

In the New Testament, John's use of *logos* to refer to Christ in chapter 1 of his Gospel is highly significant. The *logos* was a central concept in Greek philosophy used to refer to the rational principle of the universe.[3] It would certainly have caught the attention of any readers of John who knew some Greek philosophy. The real scandal would have come in verse 14—the logos became flesh and dwelt among us. In this way John connects with his audience but fills the Greek concept with the new wine of the gospel.

In our view, a Christian philosophy needs to take these—and the many other—clues seriously and make such insights foundational to its work. The fact remains, though, that the Bible is not a philosophy book, and just as doctrine has to be developed from the Bible, so too a Christian philosophy will have to negotiate carefully its relationship with the Bible so that it bows willingly before its authority while being genuinely philosophy. In our view, the concept of worldview plays a vital mediating role between Scripture and philosophy.

2. Gerhard von Rad, *Wisdom in Israel*, trans. James D. Marton (London: SCM, 1972), 67–68.
3. It is particularly associated with Heraclitus and the Stoics.

Scripture and Worldview

> Worldview is an articulation of the basic beliefs embedded in a shared grand story that are rooted in a faith commitment and that give shape and direction to the whole of our individual and corporate lives.[4]

All worldviews originate in a grand story of one sort or another. As Ecclesiastes 3:11 says, God has put eternity—a sense of beginning and end, a sense of being part of a larger story—in our hearts, in the very core of our beings, so that we require some larger story within which to situate, to make sense of, the smaller stories of our lives and cultures.[5] God intended us to find meaning in our lives through being part of a larger story that gives us purpose and direction and explains our world. It is important to note, therefore, that one who rejects the Christian story will not simply live without a grand story but will find an *alternative* grand story to live by. Even the postmodern view—that there *is* no grand story—is itself a whopper of a grand story!

As Ecclesiastes 3:11 signifies, all humans appropriate a grand story of one form or another because we are creatures and not the Creator. Our hearts—the religious core of our beings—are directed either toward the living God or toward an idol, and the grand story we indwell is an expression of the direction of our hearts. Grand stories and worldviews are, as a result, always rooted at their deepest level *in religious faith*, whether that is in the living God, in human ability, in some other aspect of God's creation, in an impersonal spirit pervading the universe, or in any of the multitude of other idols that humans manufacture.

Embedded in all grand stories are fundamental beliefs about the world and answers to questions of ultimate significance: What is life all about? Who are we? What kind of world do we live in? What's wrong with the world? How can it be fixed? The answers to these great questions are *not* philosophical concepts; they are *beliefs*, often not clearly articulated, embedded firmly in the particular grand story we hold. They achieve coherence precisely because they are merely elements of a single, unified vision of the world that arises from that story.

These beliefs give shape and direction to the whole of our lives, both individual and corporate. A worldview not only describes the world for us but also directs our lives in the world. It not only gives us a perspective on how the world *is* (its *descriptive* function) but also acts as a guide for how

---

4. Michael G. Goheen and Craig W. Bartholomew, *Living at the Crossroads: An Introduction to Christian Worldview* (Grand Rapids: Baker Academic, 2008), 23.

5. See Craig G. Bartholomew, *Ecclesiastes*, Baker Commentary on the Old Testament Wisdom and Psalms (Grand Rapids: Baker Academic, 2009), 158–74.

the world *ought to be* and how we ought to live in the world (its *normative* function).

In philosophical terms we would say that the move from the Bible to the articulation of a Christian worldview is an *abstraction* from the biblical story. In other words, we establish a worldview by drawing out or abstracting the key building blocks or beliefs in the biblical story and showing how they fit together to constitute a worldview. In *Living at the Crossroads* we explained why establishing a worldview is necessary and the dangers inherent in the process. It is necessary because we need a basic framework or Christian mind if we are to think and live effectively as Christians. It is dangerous because it is a move "beyond" Scripture and must never be allowed to usurp the authority of Scripture itself.

Thus in terms of developing a Christian worldview, although the process is more complex than this, there are three basic levels.

1. The Bible itself.
2. The story the Bible tells, which we sought to articulate in *The Drama of Scripture*. Among biblical scholars this is commonly referred to as a form of *biblical theology*—an attempt to express the unity of the Bible *on its own terms*.
3. The development of the biblical story into a Christian worldview.

A worldview is more doctrinal and more logical in its arrangement than the biblical story, but it still lacks the careful logic of a systematic analysis of a doctrine—the doctrine of God, for example—or the systematic rigor of philosophy. Both doctrine and philosophy are present in a Christian worldview in an early phase—in seed form, if you like—but they are not developed or carefully defined. How then might a worldview relate to philosophy?

Worldview and Philosophy

Al Wolters has examined the different ways in which a worldview has been thought of in terms of its relationship to philosophy in the history of Western thought. He identifies five major models for the relationship of worldview to philosophy.[6]

The first model is that worldview and philosophy *repel* each other, in the sense that an unavoidable tension exists between a scientific philosophy and

6. Albert M. Wolters, "On the Idea of Worldview and Its Relation to Philosophy," in *Stained Glass: Worldviews and Social Science*, ed. Paul Marshall et al. (Lanham, MD: University Press of America, 1983), 14–25.

an existential worldview. Both are necessary, and we should not try to resolve the tensions between them.

The second model is that worldview and philosophy *flank* each other and are to be kept apart lest the scientific nature of philosophy be compromised. This view stems from the desire for philosophy to be thoroughly "scientific" and thus based on reason alone. Bertrand Russell's definition of philosophy makes this clear: "Like theology, it [philosophy] consists of speculations on matters as to which definite knowledge has, so far, been unascertainable; but like science, it appeals to human reason rather than to authority, whether that of tradition or revelation. All definite knowledge—so I should contend—belongs to science; all *dogmas* as to what surpasses definite knowledge belongs to theology."[7]

If all definite knowledge belongs to science because it is based on reason, then a philosophy we can trust will also need to be based on reason and thus be as scientific as possible. There is indeed a rational element to a worldview, but a worldview is far more than rational, involving faith, tradition, trust, and so on. It is easy to see that if knowledge we can trust as true must be based finally on reason, then a scientific philosophy will need to keep well away from worldview and do its best to make reason its final arbiter.

The third model is that a worldview *crowns* philosophy—that is, it is the crowning achievement of a philosophy to be able to articulate a unified worldview. From this perspective one simply cannot start from a unified worldview, but philosophy can slowly work toward articulating the contours of a unified view of the world. A clear example of this is found in Phil Washburn's *Philosophical Dilemmas: Building a Worldview*. Washburn states that "the *goal* of philosophy is to build a coherent, adequate worldview."[8] He defines a worldview as "a set of answers to questions about the most general features of the world and our experience of it."[9] For Washburn, philosophy enables the individual to construct his or her own worldview; it is a long and challenging endeavor.

The fourth is that a worldview *yields* a philosophy—that is, a worldview can be developed into a philosophy. Since this is the view we espouse, we will leave elaboration of it to the end of this chapter.

The fifth model is that worldview *equals* philosophy.

How do we judge between these approaches? Intriguingly, the view you take will be determined by your worldview and your view of philosophy! This is apparent, for example, from Washburn's guidelines for constructing a worldview.

7. Bertrand Russell, *A History of Western Philosophy* (New York: Simon and Schuster, 1945), xiii.

8. Phil Washburn, *Philosophical Dilemmas: Building a Worldview* (New York: Oxford University Press, 1996), 6 (italics added).

9. Ibid.

He suggests three guidelines for such construction:[10] one's worldview should be based on human experience in the widest possible sense; one should attend closely to how the different parts of one's worldview are interconnected and ensure their compatibility; and one should only accept answers to the basic worldviewish questions that are clear and understandable. He acknowledges that "the guidelines are based on the nature of philosophy itself."[11] It would be more accurate to say that his guidelines are based on *his* view of the nature of philosophy. For Washburn, the individual constructs his or her own worldview, and the guidelines reveal that experience and reason are the key criteria. This reveals a typically individualistic, modern view of philosophy based on human autonomy.

If you adopt a view of the world according to which humankind—and in particular humankind's reason—is the measure of all things, then you will clearly opt for one of the first three models, since in different ways they all assume the autonomy of philosophy. The autonomy of philosophy involves a belief that one can step outside of one's worldview and operate in a neutral, autonomous way in search of the truth about the world.

The crucial question is whether a worldview, with its religious underpinnings, can be set aside in this way. In the history of philosophy it is Wilhelm Dilthey (1833–1911) who argued that this is just not possible because our reasoning always emerges *out of* our worldviews. For our present purposes, two aspects of Dilthey's thinking about worldview deserve particular attention. First, worldview is for Dilthey an *underlying* set of beliefs about the world that serves to shape all of our subsequent thinking. Thus worldview cannot simply derive from the exercise of reason: "World-views are *not* products of thought. They do not originate from the mere will to know. The comprehension of reality is an important factor in their formation, but only one. They emerge from our attitude to, and knowledge of, life and from our whole mental structure."[12] A worldview, then, is *deeper* than either philosophy or science; indeed, philosophy and science stand on the foundation of one's worldview. As Sander Griffioen puts it, "Philosophy itself is dependent on worldview. Dilthey attributed the metaphysical search for ultimate unity to worldviews, which in turn underlie philosophies."[13]

In our opinion this is correct. Not only is a worldview unavoidable but so too is some kind of religious faith underlying a worldview. But, you might object, how can this possibly be the case when so many people, and especially

10. Ibid., 7–9.
11. Ibid., 7.
12. W. Dilthey, *Selected Writings*, trans. H. P. Rickman (Cambridge: Cambridge University Press, 1976), 141 (italics added).
13. Sander Griffioen, "The Worldview Approach to Social Theory: Hazards and Benefits," in Marshall et al., eds. *Stained Glass*, 87.

philosophers, are not religious? Again it all depends on what you mean by
"religious." Clearly multitudes of secular philosophers do not attend church
regularly or pray to the Father or indulge in any overtly "religious" activities.
However, from a Christian perspective we know that humans are creatures—
and *religious* creatures—by design. Because we are creaturely and not the
Creator, we always depend on something as the ultimate source of meaning.
We are made for God, and if we will not have him, then inevitably we find a
replacement, what the Bible calls an idol.

The key to understanding how pervasive idolatry remains today is to avoid
thinking of idolatry only as the worship of other gods. In his acute analysis of
the nature of religion, the philosopher Roy Clouser defines a religious belief
as a belief on which everything else depends but which itself does not depend
on anything.[14] An idol can be a belief in wealth or the material world as basic
reality or in human reason as the source of meaning and truth. From this
perspective a Marxist is as religious as an evangelical Christian or an atheist;
the difference is (only) in what they depend on as divine.

Worldview and Christian Doctrine

The relationship between theology—systematic reflection on the major doctrines of the faith—and philosophy is a controversial and tricky one. According
to our articulation, a Christian worldview involves identifying the central *beliefs*
of the biblical story and showing their interrelationship. Beliefs indicate the
doctrinal component of a Christian worldview, but is this theology?

It all depends on what you mean by "theology"! If by theology you mean a
systematic, logical examination of the key Christian doctrines, then the answer
is no. A basic belief remains fuzzy at the edges, and one can and should hold to
such biblical beliefs whether or not one has a logical, systematic understanding
of them. A helpful way to understand the relationship between a Christian
worldview and Christian doctrine is to recognize that there are a variety of
levels of ever-increasing complexity in theology. These include

a. basic doctrinal affirmations hammered out in the early centuries of the
   life of the church such as the belief that Jesus is fully God and fully man
   and that God is triune;
b. basic creeds like the Apostles' Creed and the Nicene Creed;
c. denominational confessions such as the Belgic Confession and the Catholic Catechism; and

14. Roy A. Clouser, *The Myth of Religious Neutrality*, 2nd ed. (Notre Dame, IN: University
of Notre Dame Press, 2005), 9–42.

d. systematic theology proper, which involves theoretical reflection on the doctrines of the faith (one thinks of Thomas Aquinas's *Summa Theologica*, Karl Barth's *Church Dogmatics*, Louis Berkhof's *Systematic Theology*, G. C. Berkouwer's *Dogmatics*, and so on).

Especially at level d, systematic theology, like any other subject, has philosophical foundations that it ignores at its peril. Explorations of such foundations are generally called "prolegomena (or introduction) to theology." To be true to the gospel, a Christian theology therefore requires Christian philosophical insight.

Levels a and b undoubtedly and rightly inform the development of a Christian worldview, and certainly in this respect basic Christian doctrine will play an important role as a Christian worldview is developed into a Christian philosophy. But does a Christian philosophy also require input from systematic theology, or is it more foundational than systematic theology? In our view, while both need to develop from a Christian worldview, ideally a healthy, organic *partnership* needs to develop between these disciplines. A Christian philosophy will attend to the order of creation as a whole and to foundational academic issues like epistemology, ontology, and anthropology, which systematic theology requires. At the same time, systematic theology will reflect on the core doctrines of the faith that are embedded in the biblical story and that are foundational *in* a Christian worldview and thus *for* the development of a Christian philosophy.

Not only do we urgently need healthy interaction between Christian theologians and philosophers, but it must not be forgotten that both have a responsibility to take the authority of Scripture into sustained account. Our larger model looks like this:

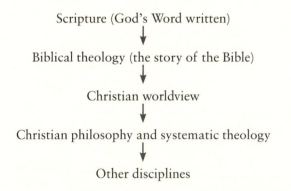

We do think that this indicates the major direction in which one should move—from the Bible outward. But, like a fountain, the higher levels also feed back into the other levels, and we do *not* think that once one has articulated a worldview that Scripture gets left behind. In our view a good philosophy and a good theology will lead back into *greater* engagement with Scripture rather than away from it.

Worldview Yielding Philosophy

One's decision about how worldview relates to philosophy will depend to a large extent on how one conceives of faith/religion and its relationship to reason—and thus to philosophy. Central to modernity is the autonomy of reason and a suspicion of the validity of knowledge arising from a religious commitment. However, it is precisely this autonomy of reason and its supposed neutrality that needs to be challenged. In recent decades there has been a growing acknowledgment that there is no one, neutral rationality.

For example, the Catholic philosopher Alasdair MacIntyre has written a well-known book titled *Whose Justice? Which Rationality?* Central to MacIntyre's argument is that rationality always operates within a particular *tradition*, or what we would call a worldview; there is no such thing as an untraditioned, neutral rationality. In the third volume of his trilogy on epistemology, *Warranted Christian Belief*, the Christian philosopher Alvin Plantinga rightly notes that

> what you properly take to be rational, at least in the sense of warranted, *depends on what sort of metaphysical and religious stance you adopt.* It depends on what kind of being you think humans are, what sort of beliefs you think their noetic faculties will produce when they are functioning properly, and which of their faculties or cognitive mechanisms are aimed at the truth. Your view as to what sort of creature a human being is will determine or at any rate heavily influence your views as to whether theistic belief is warranted or not warranted, rational or irrational for human beings. And so the dispute as to whether theistic belief is rational (warranted) can't be settled just by attending to epistemological considerations; it is at bottom not merely an epistemological dispute, but an ontological or theological dispute.[15]

Similarly, the fascinating twentieth-century French philosopher Simone Weil observes that "man always devotes himself to an *order*. Only, unless there is supernatural illumination, this order has as its centre either himself or some particular being or thing (possibly an abstraction) with which he has identified

---

15. Alvin Plantinga, *Warranted Christian Belief* (New York and Oxford: Oxford University Press, 2000), 90 (italics added).

himself (e.g., Napoleon, for his soldiers, Science, or some political party, etc.). It is a perspective order."[16]

The question then is not *whether* philosophy should be rational but *which* rationality it should be governed by. MacIntyre has worked tirelessly to revive rationality in the tradition of Aristotle; in our opinion—although we will say more of this later—the tradition that follows Augustine in which rationality is understood as *faith seeking understanding* holds far more promise. Ultimately it comes down to the question of whether or not the Bible tells the true story of the world.

If it does, then it is a gross distortion of Christian faith to try to analyze the order of the world from a so-called neutral, autonomous base that merely serves to conceal its non-Christian presuppositions. Rather, all the insights of Scripture and a Christian worldview need to be harnessed in developing a logical, systematic understanding of the order of creation. Alvin Plantinga uses the example of mountain climbing, a pursuit that he enjoys. One can try to climb the mountain of knowledge with one's feet shackled (a perilous undertaking), or one can do so free of such encumbrances. Hence our view that the relationship between philosophy and a Christian worldview is by far best understood as that of *a worldview yielding or being developed into a Christian philosophy*. This can be illustrated by the following drawing of the tree of knowledge.

Does this mean that Christians should have no contact with non-Christian philosophers or have nothing to learn from them? By no means! As Augustine noted, all truth is God's truth, and Christians must be open to the truth wherever it may be found,[17] including among the most secular of philosophers. Al Wolters has helpfully noted that when we encounter non-Christian philosophies, we need to do two things: firstly, note the idolatry at work, but secondly, note that it is precisely at the point of idolatry that the most poignant insights will be found.[18] The hard task of Christian philosophy is to appropriate those insights without taking on the ideological baggage in which they are embedded. And it should be noted that we will have no chance of doing this if we have not first attended to the development of a Christian philosophy. Nor will we be in a position to dialogue genuinely with non-Christian philosophers and the diversity of Christian philosophers if we have not honed our own philosophy to a significant extent.

16. Simone Weil, *Gravity and Grace*, trans. Marion von der Ruhr (London: Routledge, 2002), 61.

17. Augustine, *On Christian Teaching*, trans. R. P. H. Green (Oxford: Oxford University Press, 1997), 2.72.

18. Al Wolters, "Facing the Perplexing History of Philosophy," *Tydskrif vir Christelike Wetenskap* 17 (1981): 1–17.

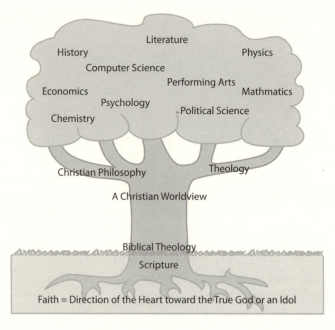

Our Approach

Philosophy is thus never approached neutrally, and it is important that readers are aware of our approach. Broadly speaking, we work in the Augustinian tradition of Abraham Kuyper and his followers.[19] Central to this tradition is the view that redemption involves the recovery of God's purposes for all of creation and that no area of life, including philosophy, is neutral and exempt from religious presuppositions. In our view, it is a serious mistake to try to do philosophy on the basis of autonomous human reason. Rather, we should employ the full resources of our faith—revelation *and* reason—in order to develop a Christian philosophy. Our strategy as we narrate the history of philosophy will therefore be as follows.[20]

Throughout our narrative we work hard first to understand on their own

19. You can find a one-page summary of what we understand by this on the following websites: www.missionworldview.com and www.paideiacentre.ca. Chapters 13–14 and especially 15 set out the Augustinian approaches to philosophy in which we position ourselves.

20. Herman Dooyeweerd (see chapter 15) identifies three types of philosophical critique: (1) transcendent critique, which simply compares "the" Christian view with another one and notes the differences; (2) immanent critique, which enters into the philosophy being examined and notes contradictions within the perspective of that philosophy; and (3) transcendental critique, which examines the (ultimately religious) presuppositions of a philosophy. All three of these are important and will feature in our narrative.

terms the many philosophies that we examine. In his excellent book on Augustine's *City of God* and Thomas Aquinas's *Summa Contra Gentiles*,[21] Curtis Chang describes this strategy as "entering the challenger's story."[22] Augustine and Aquinas were responding to challenges to the Christian faith. Likewise many philosophies we deal with—but not all—will present such a challenge. And so, we try to understand and do justice to the philosophies we examine on their own terms before turning to critique. Especially in the footnotes, readers will find references to current scholarship.

Our critique takes two forms. The first is to attend to contradictions internal to particular philosophies. Chang refers to this as retelling the story from the inside.[23] As Chang notes of Augustine and Aquinas, "They reinterpret the challenger, again by appealing to the challenger's own terms. In fact, they will argue that their rendition is the truer one by the challenger's own terms."[24] Herman Dooyeweerd (1894–1977) refers to this as *immanent* critique—critique from the inside of a particular philosophy.

The second is to place the work of a philosopher within the context of the grand story of the gospel. In regard to Augustine and Aquinas, Chang articulates this as follows: "Augustine and Aquinas handcraft their versions of the gospel metanarrative to take in the retold shape of the challenger's tale. Like sanded pegs falling into the holes of a massive woodwork, all the reworked aspects of the challenger's story—whether they are the desires of its characters, the flow of its plot or the direction of its dramatic action—now find their final and true place in the gospel."[25]

It should be noted that to perform this second critique, more than the gospel metanarrative is required. We are busy with *philosophy*, and some sense of the shape of a Christian philosophy is required in order to critique other philosophies. This puts us in something of a chicken and egg situation; we need a Christian philosophy, but that only emerges out of engagement with the story of philosophy. Our philosophical framework is discussed in chapter 15 in particular, but it guides our analysis even as we narrate the history of philosophy. Some readers might prefer to read chapter 15 first, and that is fine with us. However, having covered some of the important introductory issues to philosophy in chapters 1 and 2, we think it better to start with the story of philosophy before looking more closely at major options

---

21. See chapters 5 and 6.
22. Curtis Chang, *Engaging Unbelief: A Captivating Strategy from Augustine and Aquinas* (Eugene, OR: Wipf and Stock, 2000), 26.
23. Ibid.
24. Ibid.
25. Ibid., 27.

in systematic Christian philosophy. For now, it is useful to bear in mind the three questions that Dooyeweerd rightly asserts that every philosophy has to provide an answer to.[26]

1. Since philosophy is concerned with the whole of reality, the first question is, where does the philosopher stand or on what does he or she depend in order to gain an understanding of reality?
2. Second, how does a philosophy account for the rich diversity in creation?
3. Third, how does a philosophy account for the unity in creation?

So much work is now being done on individual philosophers that it is often hard to discern the wood from the individual trees. As noted above, we work hard to do justice to the trees, but a major concern of ours is to map out a Christian telling of the narrative of philosophy *as a whole*. Our major building blocks in this respect are as follows:

1. The origin of philosophy in its pagan form among the ancient Greeks.
2. The Christ event as the fulfillment of the Old Testament with its major implications for philosophy.
3. The synthesis of the gospel—for better and worse—with pagan Greek philosophy in the centuries following the time of Jesus and the establishment of the early church, as evidenced particularly in the works of Augustine (Plato) and Aquinas (Aristotle).
4. The unraveling of this synthesis in the late Middle Ages and following centuries.
5. The emergence of modern, autonomous, humanist philosophy in the Enlightenment.
6. The development of distinctively Christian philosophy.

From: abby@longobedience.edu
To: percy@secular.edu
Subject: Worldview, worldview, worldview

Dear Perc,
Hope you have had a good week. I miss you so much! Philosophy gets more interesting by the day. After looking at the main models for relating worldview to philosophy in history, our prof argued that *all* philosophy develops out of a worldview and that Christians should self-consciously allow their worldview to be developed into a Christian philosophy. Your prof's view sounds like the second model we looked

---

26. See chapter 15 for a detailed discussion of these three questions.

at—namely, worldview flanks philosophy. This view acknowledges that people have worldviews and live out of them, but asserts that they are unscientific and not to be trusted. True philosophy must reject worldviews and develop on the basis of reason alone. Our prof went on to argue that such a view actually assumes a worldview, which, however, it tries to conceal. Fascinating stuff!

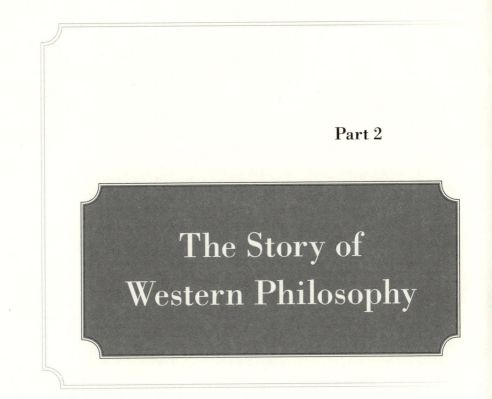

Part 2

The Story of
Western Philosophy

3

Ancient Pagan Philosophy

The Pre-Socratics to Socrates

From: abby@longobedience.edu
To: percy@secular.edu
Subject: History of philosophy: pre-Socratics

Well, this week we start on an overview of the history of philosophy. What a strange bunch. I can see why Tertullian, the early church father, was so wary of philosophy. We'll see what the prof has to say about this lot. Hope your work is going well.

Love, Abby

Introduction

Amid our changing world, Western philosophers are increasingly becoming aware of the importance of alternative, ancient traditions of philosophy, and in particular Indian and Chinese philosophies. Many of these originated around the same time as Greek philosophy, and nowadays a fertile dialogue is under way between these different traditions. Insightful as these alternative traditions may be, on the whole they failed to develop with anything like the depth or rigor of Western philosophy as it emerged from ancient Greece, and thus they are often categorized as religions rather than philosophies.

Ancient Greece is thus rightly considered to be the cradle of philosophy. If we ask ourselves how it is that we have subjects today such as epistemology, metaphysics, ethics, political philosophy, social philosophy, aesthetics, and so on—standard fare in a philosophy curriculum—the answer is that they are a gift from the ancient Greeks. To allude to the *structure/direction* distinction,[1] we can say that we owe the emergence of the structure of philosophy to the Greeks without necessarily affirming the direction they gave to this good structure, as we will note below.

We begin therefore with the pre-Socratic philosophers, a group of Greek philosophers who lived during the seventh to the fifth centuries BC. They gave birth to Western philosophy as they began to examine the world and its natural order through observation and reason. A group of Sophists emerged in Athens in the latter half of the fifth century BC. They were skeptical that anyone could really know the truth and so advocated a relativism that regarded truth claims as relative to a place and time in history. During the fourth and fifth centuries three philosophers arose to counter this skepticism—Socrates (469–399 BC), Plato (428–348 BC), and Aristotle (384–322 BC). Plato and Aristotle developed comprehensive philosophies that have exercised an extraordinary influence on the history of Western thought. In those two men, Greek philosophy reached its climax, and thus they will be dealt with in a separate chapter.

While many historians of philosophy describe Greek philosophy with the word *classical*, we use the word *pagan* in order to carefully distinguish the structural from the directional aspect of philosophy. *Classical* implies a positive value judgment of this period of philosophy as a model to follow. Richard Tarnas discerns the legacy of Greek philosophy in the belief that "the final measure of truth was found not in hallowed tradition, nor in contemporary convention, but rather in the autonomous individual mind."[2] Modern philosophy has placed great emphasis on human autonomy as the road to truth and thus far too comfortably links the emergence of the structure of philosophy with its—in our view—autonomous *misdirection*. A comparable mistake is made by Christians who reject all philosophy because of its pagan roots, once again confusing direction with structure. *Pagan* thus simply indicates that the tradition of Greek philosophy developed apart from the light of the gospel and the Word of God, a light that is essential in answering the questions of order, of the nature of humanity, of evil and salvation, of social ethics, of the nature of knowledge, of origins, of the nature of God—questions that drove the Greek philosophical tradition.

From a Christian perspective we should acknowledge the gift of the ancient Greeks but insist on contextualizing the emergence of philosophy in the context

---

1. See Albert M. Wolters, *Creation Regained: Biblical Basics for a Reformational Worldview* (Grand Rapids: Eerdmans, 1985), 72–95. Basically this distinction maintains that the order and potentials given in creation are good but that after the fall they are subject to being misdirected. Sexuality, for example, is a good structure or part of creation, but, as with pornography, it can be badly misdirected.

2. Richard Tarnas, *The Passion of the Western Mind: Understanding the Ideas That Have Shaped Our World View* (New York: Ballantine, 1991), 71.

of the metanarrative of creation-fall-redemption. Philosophy is a good gift of God, and we should see it as a development of the creative potentials built into God's creation. In his providence God chose to have philosophy emerge from the ancient, pagan Greeks; a good gift but one they often misdirected, uninformed as they were about God's revelation to Israel and in Christ. Thus we will continually need to ask, given their worldviews, what are they seeing truly about God's world and what are they distorting? This indeed is the hard work of Christian philosophy.

Pre-Socratic Philosophers

Since Socrates is a turning point in the Western philosophical tradition, and since the philosophical project of those who preceded him was similar, the pre-Socratic philosophers are usually treated together. The primary concern of these early philosophers was to find unity and order in the midst of a world of variety and constant change. Was there an *archē*, a basic principle, that both made up the basic stuff of the world and gave it order?

We have only fragments of these philosophers' writings preserved for us,[3] and so sometimes understanding exactly what they meant is like constructing the whole picture with just a few pieces of the puzzle. Although in what follows we will concentrate on their ideas, as is typical in philosophy, it is important to remember that a person's philosophy is always an expression of his or her life. What we "know" of the lives of the pre-Socratics makes for interesting reading. As soon as Thales, for example, was of age, he embarked on a series of voyages between Egypt and the Middle East. It was thus the Egyptian and Chaldean priests who educated him. He never married, and when asked about this always replied "It is not yet time," until the day came when he changed tack and replied "It is too late!" When asked why he had no children he replied, "because he loved children."[4]

The first stream of pre-Socratic thought was Ionian naturalism.[5] *Naturalism* is a term that refers to an understanding and explanation of reality solely in terms of natural causes. Rather than believing the myths about the gods, these philosophers employed empirical observation and reasoning to discover natural explanations for the world. Nevertheless, they also invoked mythological

3. In English, see G. S. Kirk, J. E. Raven, and M. Schofield, eds., *The Presocratic Philosophers*, 2nd ed. (Cambridge: Cambridge University Press, 1983).

4. Diogenes Laertius, *The Lives and Opinions of Eminent Philosophers*, trans. C. D. Yonge (London: Henry G. Bohn, 1853), book 1, "Life of Thales," iv.

5. The first three of these philosophers hailed from the Ionian city of Miletus, which is on the east coast of the Aegean Sea (present-day western Turkey).

forces and properties. The first of these philosophers was Thales (624–546 BC), who believed that reality could be explained in terms of the first principle or primary substance of water. He regarded water as the most beautiful thing in the world and observed that there is water in every living thing. He thought of the earth as floating like a raft on a huge expanse of water and famously said, "All is water, and the world is full of gods." It is clear from this fragmentary statement that Thales was far from a consistent naturalist; his emerging naturalistic approach was still suffused with mythological assumptions. Water was the basic stuff of the universe, at once a material substance and a living substance that was divine, capable of changing into various forms. By gods, Thales did not, of course, refer to a personal god but to a powerful life force, a world soul, at work in the world, a power that was more than human and not subject to death but everlasting.

Anaximander (610–546 BC), a pupil of Thales, also posited a first principle or elementary substance to explain the world, something even more basic than water. The original stuff of the world is not some ingredient we see around us but exists eternally as a large imperceptible mass of everlasting stuff—*apeiron*—that is indefinite and boundless in nature but possessing its own inherent power to give rise to elements that constitute the world as we know it. This primary stuff brings our world into existence by a motion that separates the opposites of heat and cold, wet and dry, air and earth.

Following in this path, Anaximenes (585–528 BC) posited air as the primary substance that changed form by expansion and contraction, stating, "Air is God."[6] Like his forebears, Anaximenes did not cast off his mythological past; air as the fundamental substance in the universe and in humanity retains divine properties. All these philosophers tried to understand the variety and change in the world in somewhat naturalistic terms—identifying some first substance and principle as the explanation of the ultimate nature of things— but continued to rely on mythological explanation to explain how and why the world is as it is.

The last and most famous of these Ionian philosophers was Heraclitus (ca. 535–475 BC). "The enormous influence he has exercised on philosophers ancient and modern is a matter for astonishment."[7] While the Milesian natural philosophers were interested in discovering some fundamental principle, Heraclitus focused on a new issue, the problem of constancy and change in the world. He compared the world to an ever-flowing and constantly changing stream. He said that "you cannot step twice into the same river"; the river

6. Cicero, *De Natura Deorum* I, 10.
7. Anthony Kenny, *Ancient Philosophy*, vol. 1 of *A New History of Western Philosophy* (Oxford: Clarendon, 2004), 16.

has changed by the time you step into it again. "All things are in flux"—that is clear—but it also seems that there is constancy, since one can speak of a different river while at the same time recognizing continuity.

Heraclitus also spoke of the world as an ever-living fire. Fire is also a picture of constant change, always being kindled and fueled on the one hand, but also being quenched and going out on the other. In both the picture of the stream and the fire, the original substance is never lost but continuously changes its form; indeed that is its essence. Yet this change is not haphazard but orderly and directed by *logos*, an impersonal yet divine principle of rational order that permeates the universe and also gives humanity its reasoning power. Order in the world directed by *logos* is the coincidence and conflict of opposites—good and bad, strife and peace, young and old, and so on—that brings a harmonious rhythm to the world. Human beings often do not discern this order and thus live in a dream world. Their task is to face this rational order and conform their lives to it. This world ordered by *logos* also means that there is a divine law for human societal and political life that stands above all human laws. According to Heraclitus, "all the laws of humans are nourished by a single law, the divine law."[8] This idea—of a universal intellectual principle regulating the universe to which humankind, who shares in it, is to conform—was to become widespread in succeeding centuries in Greek philosophy and endures into the modern age in various notions of natural law.

Pythagoras (570–490 BC) was born on the island of Samos, not far from Miletus. Like many of the pre-Socratics, he traveled a great deal and then founded a school that in many ways was more like a religious sect. Members had to adhere to a set of strict rules that included such strange regulations as never to eat beans and never to look into a mirror beside a light. Pythagoras taught every evening, and people flocked to hear him. In line with the secrecy of his sect, he allowed no one to see him but spoke from behind a curtain. Even in the ancient world, Pythagoras's view of the reincarnation of the soul was mocked—Pythagoras claimed to have already lived four times[9]—but the influential heart of his thought was that numbers were the *archē* of the universe. What Thales declared to be water, Anaximander *apeiron*, and Anaximenes air, Pythagoras asserted to be number.[10] He argued that in the beginning there was Chaos and then the Monad (the number One) created the numbers, which gave rise to points and lines until Harmony arrived to regulate right relationships everywhere, resulting in the ordered cosmos.

8. Ibid.

9. Diogenes Laertius, *Lives and Opinions*, book 8, "Life of Pythagoras," iv.

10. This view stems from Aristotle, *Metaphysics* A, 5, who understands the Pythagorean emphasis on number as an examination of the formal cause of the universe.

Philolaus (ca. 470–385 BC) was the first Pythagorean to write a book, fragments of which have now emerged. He distinguished between unlimited stuff and limiters that constitute the world order. Water and earth, for example, become limited by shapes to lakes and stones.[11] Carl Huffman notes that "here we have a bold first step toward the matter-form distinction."[12] As we will see in the next chapter, this distinction is central to Plato's and Aristotle's philosophies. It is also the unresolvable polar tension that Herman Dooyeweerd discerns as underlying ancient Greek philosophy, what he calls its "ground motive."[13]

Another path of pre-Socratic thought was taken in the Greek colony Elea (present-day Italy), in the way of rationalism. *Rationalism* refers to confidence in human reasoning to come to the ultimate truth about the world. Parmenides (born 515 BC) stood in antithetical contrast to Heraclitus. One cannot trust the senses, which seem to disclose a changing and transient world. If something *is*, it cannot change to become something that *is not*. Similarly, what *is not* cannot become something that *is*. If something *is*, it cannot change or pass away, since it exists. If something *is not*, it cannot come to be, because it does not exist. The very notion of change as it appears to the senses defies logic. Thus Parmenides argued that one cannot trust the senses but must trust human reason and abstract logical argument to judge what is real. Parmenides's pupil Zeno (born in 489 BC) further developed deductive arguments and paradoxes to demonstrate the truth of his master's conclusions—while there appears to be change, it opposes logic. In the final analysis, logic and reason are the most trustworthy guides to truth.

The attempt characteristic of emerging naturalism to find the primary substance of reality, along with discussion of change articulated by Heraclitus and the Eleatic rationalists, generated increasingly nuanced theories to explain order, constancy, and change in the world. For example, Empedocles (490–430 BC) believed the problem stemmed from reducing reality to one primary substance (monism); in fact, he believed, there were four constant and basic elements—earth, air, fire, and water (pluralism). Parmenides was correct, Empedocles believed: there is no coming to be or passing away. Rather, coming to be is the temporary mixture of enduring elements, and passing away is their dissociation. But to understand change one must also recognize semimythical forces like "love," which draws the basic elements together, and "strife," which separates them.

Two thinkers, Leucippus (early fifth century BC) and Democritus (460–370 BC), followed along this same line of thought, which distinguished between

11. See Carl A. Huffman, "The Pythagorean Tradition," in *The Cambridge Companion to Early Greek Philosophy*, ed. A. A. Long (Cambridge: Cambridge University Press, 1999), 78–83.
12. Ibid., 80.
13. See chapter 15.

a primary *substance* and a fundamental *force* that acted on the substance to bring about order and change. These two thinkers are known as *atomists* because they argued that the fundamental stuff of the universe is unchangeable, consisting of indivisible particles called atoms. The atoms move around randomly in an empty void moved by the impersonal force of necessity or fate. These atoms take different forms (plants, animals, and people, for example) as they cluster together. A particular entity can dissolve and cease to exist, but the atoms themselves continue their existence. They disperse and combine together in new ways to form something else. In the atomists the semi-personal forces of love, strife, and mind are demythologized and replaced by a more impersonal and mechanical power of fate. This description explained the constancy of being as well as change in the world.

What are we to make of the pre-Socratics? At first blush, many of their views sound quite absurd. And indeed, while few nowadays would affirm their *answers*, many rightfully detect a major breakthrough in their *method* of inquiry. Ernest Renan referred to the fundamental shift from mythical to natural explanations, from superstitious belief to rational analysis, as "The Greek Miracle."[14] Whether or not one can affirm such a glowing depiction—it is doubtful, for example, that the pre-Socratics ever really did escape religion—it is clear that important insights were discovered. We have gained much from those first rudimentary steps taken twenty-six hundred years ago.

The origin of a discipline is *always* important, since it is in the origin that the basic questions and possibilities of a discipline are often articulated. For example, the pre-Socratics foreground a vital question—namely, does reality originate from one source or two or more? Those who reduce it to one are *monists*, whereas those who discern two or more sources are *dualists* or *pluralists*. The trend among the pre-Socratics is, as we have seen, toward monism, but there are important exceptions. The atomists, for example, distinguish between "the full," consisting of atoms, and "the void." As we will see in chapter 15, the distinction between monism and dualism recurs throughout the history of philosophy.

A characteristic of a pagan worldview is to absolutize some part of the creation and then seek to explain everything from it. This is characteristic of the pre-Socratics. Most of them find the ordering principle for the world *in this world*. Again there are exceptions. Anaximander, as we saw, sought an origin for our world in *apeiron*, an eternal substance separate from our world. Thus the pre-Socratics foreground the question of the origin of our world: is it to be found in our world or outside of it? From our scientific, sophisticated point of view, it understandably sounds ridiculous to locate the origin

14. Ernest Renan, *Recollections of My Youth* (London: Chapman and Hall, 1883), 51.

of everything in air or water. However, we should not forget that paganism is alive and well today; evolutionary naturalism, for example, which seeks to explain the origin of everything out of some primal matter apart from God, is one significant example.

A third important issue that emerges with the pre-Socratics is whether philosophy should focus on *the structure* or *the genesis* of the world. Some of the pre-Socratics focus on the process by which the world comes into existence, whereas others are more attentive to the order of reality. Again, this is an issue that resonates down the centuries of philosophy.

Calvin Seerveld (1930–), reflecting on the pagan ethos of pre-Socratic philosophy, contrasts it with what was going on among God's people at this time:

> When you realize that Heraclitus was figuring these things out in the dark of Asia Minor shortly after Daniel was given dreams from Yahweh in Babylon about the fall of civilizations foreign to His Rule, and at about the same time as Zechariah was receiving visions at night straight from the Lord and Nehemiah was building up the little tumble down wall of Jerusalem . . . then you understand why the apostle Paul, after passing through Heraclitus's home-town 600 years later could refer to such patterns as *atheoi* [without God] (Eph. 2:11–22) and plead with Christians not to lose their minds that way but to get their whole consciousness truly new in Jesus Christ (Eph. 4:1–24).[15]

If the world is as the Bible narrates it, then the order in our world comes from a God whose presence and Word faithfully uphold the creation. Neither self-animating matter like water or air, nor semimythic personalized forces like reason, mind, or love, nor more impersonal and mechanical forces of fate bring an underlying order and structure to our world. These are inventions of the pagan imagination to "explain" the regularity of the world in which we live. Second, all idolatry leads to problems. No such idol can support the weight of our deepest faith and so will finally collapse. Growing confidence in autonomous human rationality and observation to understand the nature of the world inevitably led to problems. Among the pre-Socratics there was a growing confusion and consequent skepticism with regard to knowledge. Many different theories were being advanced to explain the world. How does one judge which is true? These growing problems found expression in the Sophists and in Socrates during the fifth century BC.

The great insight of the pre-Socratics was that observation and reason can discover an orderly world of constancy and change, and there is a constant

---

15. Calvin Seerveld, "The Pedagogical Strength of a Christian Methodology in Philosophical Historiography," *Koers* 40 (1975): 227.

order because God is faithful. These philosophers helped to recover and to develop these creational gifts, and Western culture is the better for it. We find a similar insight in Old Testament Wisdom literature, according to which the fear of the Lord is *the beginning* of wisdom and knowledge (cf. Prov. 1:7). An awareness of the wonder of God and his creation should lead us to explore, examine, and understand the world. It was, however, these early Greeks who started to ask the foundational questions and to explore them in a new spirit of inquiry, a spirit that would give rise to philosophy. Thales's place in the history of philosophy is important not so much for his answers but for the questions he asked in the first place. Of course, as Proverbs 1:7 reminds us, such questioning should be done *starting* with the fear of the Lord.

The Sophists and Socrates

The primary project of the pre-Socratics was to understand the natural world. With the Sophists (fifth century BC) and Socrates (469–399 BC) philosophy took an ethical and political turn. The interest became how human beings should live as individuals (ethics) and as community (politics). Indeed, this focus was the major contribution of the Sophists. The context of the Sophists and Socrates is the individual citizen in the city-state of Athens where Socrates lived and many of the Sophists spent their careers.

The best-known Sophists are Protagoras (490–420), Prodicus (465–395), Gorgias (485–380), and Thrasymachus (459–400). Much of our knowledge of them comes from a negative portrayal in Plato's dialogues. So, for example, if you want to study Plato's philosophy of language and thus turn to his dialogue the *Cratylus*, you will discover that Thrasymachus is one of the dialogue partners, the other two being Socrates and Cratylus. The Sophists were professional teachers who plied their trade in Athens, where the opportunity for participation in the life of the city-state was increasing. Their importance in the history of philosophy arises from the fact that Socrates and Plato formulated their distinctive philosophical emphases in direct response to the danger that the Sophists represented.

The Sophists were secular humanists.[16] The gods held no final authority in the life of human beings. Protagoras says, "About the gods, I am not able to know whether they exist or do not exist, nor what they are like in form; for the factors preventing knowledge are many: the obscurity of the subject, and

---

16. There are very limited primary sources for the Sophists, and there is considerable debate about what they believed. Recent scholarship tends to be skeptical of Plato's representation of the Sophists and to stress the diversity of views among them.

the shortness of human life."[17] Thus the ultimate judge of truth is humanity itself. Protagoras further affirms that "man is the measure of all things."[18]

Yet the problem is that different human beings experience this world in different ways and make different claims to truth. We have access only to our experience of the world—appearances (*doxa*)—and not the essence of unchanging truth (*alētheia*). For the Sophist, that meant that truth was relative.[19] They believed that not only Greek religion but also all claims to true knowledge were in the final analysis human conventions. Since all of these men had lived and traveled in different countries and had experienced many different customs, they came to Athens with a critical eye. Moreover, the previous two centuries of Greek philosophy had not only brought about doubt in pagan religion, it had served to undermine philosophy itself. Thus the Sophists were skeptical about the possibility of discovering ultimate truth about the world, society, or morality.

This skepticism issued in the Sophists' *pragmatism*: if there is no ultimate truth, then knowledge is judged simply in terms of its practical utility. What was useful at the time in Athens was the ability to use logic and rhetoric (the art of using language to communicate persuasively) to advance in Athenian political life. The Sophists were willing to teach these skills to anyone who would pay for their services. Indeed, one could employ these skills to present plausible arguments to convincingly advocate any position. This is what gave rise to the term *sophistry* as a specious argument for deceiving someone.

For Socrates the Sophists' position was positively dangerous. If the Sophists were right, then there was no possibility of the knowledge of truth or standards of justice for political life or of morality. Socrates set himself against the Sophists' epistemological and ethical relativism with the goal of uncovering transcendent norms for true knowledge and behavior.

What we know about Socrates comes from various conflicting sources.[20] He never wrote anything, and there is disagreement about the reliability of the various extant descriptions of his life and character. Nevertheless, we can construct a relatively reliable portrait of his life and thought, especially from the writings of Plato and Aristotle.

Socrates found the work of the pre-Socratics unsatisfying and irrelevant to human life. He turned from cosmological concerns to concrete issues. Cicero

17. Walther Kranz and Herman Diels, eds., *Die Fragmente der Vorsokratiker*, 5th ed. (Weidmann: Berlin, 1934), 80b4.

18. Ibid., 80b1.

19. This point is debated. Kenny, *Ancient Philosophy*, 29, agrees that Protagoras's saying about man being the measure of all things encapsulates a "relativist epistemology."

20. See *Socrates: A Source Book*, comp. and trans. John Ferguson (London: Macmillan, Open University Press, 1970).

said that Socrates "was the first to call Philosophy down from the skies, and establish her in the towns, and introduce her into people's homes, and force her to investigate ordinary life, ethics, good and evil."[21] How could one live a good and happy life? This was his philosophical project. To answer such a question, one must ask about the nature of what it means to be human. For Socrates, what mattered was the soul, the core of humanity. The soul is fundamentally rational and moral, and so the clue to a happy and satisfying life is the development of a rational and virtuous character. As Plato has Socrates say in the *Apology*, "For I go around doing nothing but persuading both young and old among you not to care for your body or your wealth in preference to or as strongly as for the best possible state of your soul."[22] Socrates believed that if one knew what the good was, what virtue was, what justice was, that person would inevitably pursue it.

Aristotle describes two elements central to Socrates's philosophy that would enable a person to know and live the good life—"inductive arguments" and "general definitions."[23] To live the good life a person must know the unchanging essence or universal definitions of virtue, courage, piety, justice, and the good. Over against the Sophists, Socrates believed that the good and virtuous were not simply a matter of social convention but universal standards that transcended particular historical circumstances.

The question is *how* one can discover those universal standards. For Socrates it is by means of a vigorous discussion, a way known as the Socratic method. Socrates would ask his discussion partner a question about the meaning of justice or goodness. His interlocutor might offer a definition of goodness or justice, or a particular example of a just or good act. If a definition was offered, Socrates would expose the weaknesses of that definition and ask questions to elicit a more adequate definition. If an act or particular instance of goodness or justice was offered, he would pursue an inductive argument—an argument, that is, from the particular acts of justice to the universal definition of justice. What was it in the particular instance of justice that made it just? Thus truth emerged by way of a *dialectical method*—careful reasoning and rigorous dialogue that would move beyond inadequate definitions and particular instances to abiding and universal definitions of goodness. Socrates manifested a deep confidence in human reason to discover universally valid norms for human life and was thus a rationalist, one who trusts in reason to arrive at the truth.

21. Quoted in Paul Johnson, *Socrates: A Man for Our Time* (New York: Viking, 2011), 81–82. However, he was at least partially indebted to the Sophists in this respect.

22. Plato, *Apology* 30, in *Plato: Complete Works*, ed. John M. Cooper (Indianapolis: Hackett, 1997), 28.

23. Aristotle, *Metaphysics*, trans. Hugh Lawson-Tancred (London: Penguin, 1998, 2004), Book Mu, 4 = 1078b 27–29.21.

In this process, the intellect is the "divine faculty by which the human soul could discover both its own essence and the world's meaning."[24]

Socrates saw himself as a gadfly. A gadfly bites, provokes, and annoys livestock; this is what Socrates did with his questions and critiques in an attempt to unsettle people in their false sense of security and push them toward universal truth. Gadflies are a major nuisance—and we all know what one wants to do to an annoying gadfly! Indeed, Socrates made many enemies, and he was finally sentenced to death by an Athenian court, ostensibly for atheism and corrupting the youth. Committed to the justice of his cause, he refused any way of escape and drank the hemlock.

Socrates is exceedingly important for the history of Western philosophy. There are at least two important philosophical insights Socrates has left us. First, Socrates rightly comprehended that the ethical and happy life must be rooted in the nature of humanity. Moral standards are not arbitrary rules imposed from outside but are in harmony with what it means to be human. Second, Socrates rightly understood the ethical importance of universally valid standards and norms that stand above history.

Yet in Socrates's thought the very rationalism of his ethics remains a problem. These standards must be grounded in something more transcendent than ideas, concepts, and definitions. All definitions, ideas, and concepts, as well as the very process of reasoning by which one arrives at those definitions, are deeply shaped by human culture and history, as the Sophists of old and their contemporary postmodern counterparts clearly understand. The ethical insight of Socrates can only come into its own when we understand both the nature of humanity and transcendent norms in terms of God's revelation. The only ultimate grounding for human nature and norms for human conduct is found in God and his stable creation order. Thus, as Proverbs reminds us, *the fear of the Lord* is the beginning of wisdom.

From: percy@secular.edu
To: abby@longobedience.edu
Subject: New friend, worldview, pre-Socratics

Hey Abby, how is it going there? Through our student Christian group I made a new friend, Damien, who is also in my philosophy class. He's quite the intellectual and plans to major in philosophy. He's already studied quite a lot of philosophy, and today while we went for a long run together—some good weather at last!—I was telling him about your reading about the pre-Socratics. He told me about a good book on worldview by James Sire—*The Universe Next Door*—in which Sire lists seven diagnostic questions you can ask to discern a person's worldview. Apparently the

24. Tarnas, *Passion of the Western Mind*, 38.

first question is "What is prime reality?" Damien explained to me that this means what is at the bottom of everything. He thought that the pre-Socratics were mainly trying to answer this question. Does that sound right?

Percy

From: abby@longobedience.edu
To: percy@secular.edu
Subject: RE: New friend, worldview, pre-Socratics

Dear Perc,

Glad to hear about Damien. I rushed off to the library and found Sire's book. A great insight! I think Damien is absolutely right. On the whole the pre-Socratics were trying to answer Sire's first question, whereas Socrates was trying to answer different questions in Sire's list, questions such as what does it mean to be human and how do we know what is right and wrong.

Wonderful—many thanks.

Weather here remains grim; glad you were able to get out for a long run.

Yours as ever,
Abby

4

The High Point
of Greek Philosophy

Plato, Aristotle, and Their Legacy

The high point of Greek philosophy was reached with Plato and Aristotle. Additional important schools of thought include Stoicism and Epicureanism. In the final portion of this chapter, we will also examine the most important tradition to emerge prior to the Middle Ages, the Neoplatonism of Plotinus (AD 205–70), a remarkable synthesis of the different schools of Greek thought that played a significant role in the ongoing story of Western philosophy.

Plato

The twentieth-century English philosopher Alfred North Whitehead noted Plato's abiding importance in the history of philosophy when he wrote that the "safest general characterization of the European philosophical tradition is that it consists of a series of footnotes to Plato."[1] Not only has Plato exercised tremendous influence on the history of philosophy; his thought has also permeated the Christian tradition through the church fathers. It is thus vital to grasp the main contours of his thought.

Plato was born into a wealthy Athenian family during the fifth century BC. His Aristocratic upbringing exposed him to a broad education and acquaintance with the Greek philosophical tradition. Aristotle tells us that during this

1. Alfred North Whitehead, *Process and Reality* (New York: Free Press, 1978), 39.

formative period in Plato's life he was exposed to the Heraclitean philosopher Cratylus and perhaps learned from him to distrust the world of sense perception that was in constant flux,[2] an emphasis central to Plato's philosophy. Much more important was Plato's relationship with Socrates, of whom he became a pupil at twenty years old. Socrates is the main character and hero in most of Plato's dialogues. Socrates's disquiet over the relativism of the Sophists and the trumped-up charges that led to his untimely and unjust death etched itself in Plato's mind. Urgent foundational questions thus drove Plato's philosophy. Healthy social, political, and individual life was at stake. Plato took hold of Socrates's emphasis on universal standards and later expanded it beyond ethics to develop a whole view of reality (ontology) and knowledge (epistemology).

Plato established a school in Athens called the Academy that boasted some significant alumni, including Aristotle. Plato's philosophy comes to us in the form of dialogues, and although we never hear Plato speak in his own voice in these dialogues, the main contours of his philosophy are clear enough.[3] Plato was the first philosopher to develop a comprehensive philosophy that includes an ontology (theory of reality), an epistemology (theory of knowledge), and an anthropology (theory of humanity).

The most characteristic and important conception of Plato's philosophy is his theory of ideas or forms. This doctrine underlies and permeates his whole philosophy. Plato understands the world in terms of an ontological or cosmological dualism; that is, the world is made up of two worlds—the invisible and eternal world of ideas that can be grasped by reason and the visible and temporal world of matter known by sense perception.

Plato inherited from Heraclitus a distrust of sense perception. Because the particulars of our perception are always in a state of flux and change, our sense perception is not as reliable as our rational capacity that can take hold of unchanging ideas. And so our knowledge must move through the particular object to the universal essence. For example, there are many human beings, but to know what it means to be human, one must go beyond these particular people and ask the question of what constitutes human nature: what is the universal essence of "humanness" that all people possess that makes them human? There must be an unchanging and constant standard to assess these manifold appearances. These unchanging essences transcend this world and can only be grasped by reason.

Plato calls these universal essences "ideas" or "forms." We normally take ideas to refer to conceptual abstractions that we form in our minds as we seek

2. Frederick Copleston, *Greece and Rome*, vol. 1 of *A History of Philosophy* (New York: Image Books, 1946), 128.

3. See Anthony Kenny, *Ancient Philosophy*, vol. 1 of *A New History of Western Philosophy* (Oxford: Clarendon, 2004), 49–56, 205–16, on the development of Plato's thought in this respect.

an understanding of the world. However, this is not what Plato means. These forms or ideas have objective reality in another realm beyond this world and beyond our minds. Forms or ideas actually exist as perfect paradigms of the good, of the beautiful, of white, of justice, of a tree, and so forth that provide patterns for particular objects in this world. For an act to be just, it must imitate the ideal form of justice. To say someone is beautiful means that he or she is a concrete expression or instance of the transcendent form of beauty. Knowledge that merely grasps the temporal appearances of the empirical world with the senses is opinion. Opinion stands on a lower realm than true knowledge, which directly apprehends the eternal forms of the ideal world with reason.

A major insight of Plato's is the recognition that the ordering principle for the world cannot be found within the world itself, and this is one reason that Christians have found his philosophy so attractive. However, it is important to note that Plato's forms are very different from the biblical view of creation order. In Genesis God orders the creation by his Word, and he continues to actively sustain his creation in existence. Creation order stems from the true and living God and calls for a joyful response of obedience. Plato's forms are impersonal and transcend everything so that even the "god" who brought creation into existence is subject to them. The only adequate response to the forms is rational, theoretical contemplation.

Another implication of Plato's ontology is that lived experience cannot be trusted; theory, achieved through contemplation of the forms, is the royal road to truth. Not only is this elitist and provides an obstacle to the development of science, but it is an early form of the exaltation of theory over lived experience that has plagued the modern world.

The Allegory of the Cave

For Plato knowledge and goodness have redemptive power: they actually bring, to some degree, an escape from the evil of this world. Plato's famous allegory of the cave in book 7 of *The Republic* makes this dimension clear. He invites us to imagine an underground cave. Inside there are people who are chained in such a way that they are able only to face the inside wall. The people in that cave have never seen the outside or the light of the sun. Against the wall or screen appear various images and shadows as objects pass in front of a fire behind the prisoners. All the prisoners see are the shadowy images, and so they believe that these are reality. Sadly this is the state of most people in the world, simply believing that the shadows they perceive constitute the only reality that exists. But suppose a prisoner escapes his chains and goes out into the light of the sun outside the cave. He now knows true reality and realizes that what he has seen to this point is mere shadows. He sees the world and all its objects illuminated by the sun. And then with a little more effort he is able also to see the sun itself, which represented for Plato the highest of the forms, the good that is the cause of all that is beautiful and true.

This outside world represents the transcendent world of the forms, and the cave represents our experiential reality. What we sense in the particulars of the empirical world are mere shadows. But if our reason is able to ascend to the transcendent world of ideas, it is able to see the real world in the light of the sun. Reason is capable of grasping the true essences of those objects in the light and their relation to the good, the beautiful, and the true. One can pursue the good life, know the truth, and delight in true beauty.

This allegory opens up the redemptive, religious dimension of Plato's philosophical quest. Reason not only gives us the truth but also is a saving power that brings liberation. One escapes darkness into the light; one is liberated from his or her chains; one finds the life that is truly good.

Plato employs mythological language to describe the origin of the empirical world. The Demiurge employed the ideas in the invisible realm to fashion the world. However, the stubborn irrational "Necessity" (*ananke*) of preexisting material resists the imposition of these rational forms. The Demiurge is a mythological description of the operation of Divine Reason to bring order to the world. The Demiurge is in most cases able to overcome this refractory matter even as it remains obstinately resistant to a rational order. Thus in our world, for the most part, we discern order and beauty. Plato did not view the material world as intractably evil like those gnostics and Neoplatonists who followed him. Reason still permeates the universe, giving it order and purpose. However, this Necessity remains in the material world, and its continuing presence is what accounts for disorder and evil. The Demiurge also created the rational part of the human soul out of the same rational substance that continues to order and govern the world. This is what renders human reason capable of knowing the ideas that give order to the world. Plato's dualism can be depicted as follows:

Higher Realm	Idea	Essence	Being	Truth	Reason
	Changeless	Universal	Eternal	Soul	
Lower Realm	Object	Appearance	Becoming	Opinion	Senses
	Changing	Particular	Temporal	Body	

Plato's Anthropology

Corresponding to Plato's dualistic ontology is a dualistic anthropology. Human beings are made up of two parts: a divine soul that is related to the invisible realm and a body that belongs to the visible world. The soul existed in the invisible world before time, and that is its proper home. However, the soul fell into this visible world and is now imprisoned in the body. The body drags the soul down, polluting it with its impurities, and thus is a hindrance to true knowledge and the pursuit of the soul's true destiny in the invisible world. As Plato puts it: "While we live, we shall be closest to knowledge if we refrain as much as possible from association with the body and do not join with it more than we must, if we are not infected with its nature but purify ourselves from it until the god himself frees us."[4]

The human soul has three parts.[5] The highest is the rational part, which is immortal and distinguishes human beings from animals. This part strives for true knowledge and a return to its original place in the invisible realm. The lowest part is the appetitive part, which is constituted by bodily desires. The rational part of the soul has a passion for truth, a desire to ascend to the world of ideas. The appetitive part corrupts the soul and drags it down. The middle part is the spirited part, which is nobler than the appetitive part and is an ally to reason.

Plato uses a vivid image to describe the conflict between these parts. The rational part is like a charioteer, and the spirited and appetitive parts are like two winged horses. The spirited part wishes to take the soul up to its proper realm in the region of the eternally real. The spirited part drags the soul down, corrupting it with its bodily desires and hindering the quest to return to the invisible realm.

Liberation in this life comes as one cultivates reason and pursues an ethical life, especially in controlling the bodily desires. Then one is able to escape this earth to heaven or the dwelling place of the gods: "That is why a man should make all haste to escape from earth to heaven; and escape means becoming as like God as possible; and a man becomes like God when he becomes just and pious, with understanding."[6] Knowledge of the good and true comes primarily by dialectical reason—that is, argument and counterargument that moves one close to discerning the essence of the good and the true. Thus reason plays a redemptive role in human life, liberating one from the evil of this world.

Plato, like Socrates, clearly discerns that if there is to be a moral life and a just society, there must be standards that transcend the particularities of history. Plato recognizes more fully than Socrates that this is true not only of individual and social ethics but also of knowledge of the world. Further, Plato moves beyond Socrates in recognizing an important distinction between

---

4. Plato, *Phaedo* 67, in *Plato: Complete Works*, ed. John M. Cooper (Indianapolis: Hackett, 1997), 58.

5. See Plato, *Republic* 435c–441c.

6. Plato, *Theaetetus* 176ab, in Cooper, *Plato*, 195.

the knowledge we gain of the empirical world by perception and analytical knowledge that is the product of reason. These are important insights.

Nevertheless these insights are the very problem: Plato's appreciation for and confidence in reason leads him to idolize this dimension of created reality. G. R. F. Ferrari notes of Plato's view of the soul in *The Republic* that "the soul we are considering here is one in which reason is king. . . . Within this little city that the philosopher has founded for himself, . . . reason's word is law. . . . The philosopher's rational part seeks to order those realms whose order is entirely within its rational control. . . . One such realm is the individual soul; another . . . is the whole cosmos."[7]

As the magnified shadow of a person is projected against the clouds and given objective reality beyond the observer, so Plato projects the world of human reason into another world and gives it an objective existence. However, just as the magnified shadow is only the image of the observer, so the world of ideas is only the projection of human reason. Yet as Plato gives an exalted place to human rationality, it begins to answer deep religious questions: it is in reason that he finds the stable order for knowledge, the standards for the good life, the nature of humanity, and the chief end of human life. Moreover, this becomes the key for understanding evil and salvation: evil is the irrationality of the material realm, and redemption lies in escape to reason.

However, these foundational religious questions cannot be answered truly by autonomous reason, for it is one part of the creation. Rather, this kind of knowledge can only come by way of revelation from the Creator, Ruler, and Redeemer of all things. In his analysis of Greek philosophy, Herman Dooyeweerd, for example, discerns the driving religious force—or what he calls its *ground motive*—as that of "form-matter," which he argues has its origin in Greek myth and religion.[8] This ground motive is clearly evident in Plato's dualistic philosophy. Without a biblical understanding of creation, Plato thought in terms of two principles of origin: the Demiurge, Plato's divine reason, and preexistent chaotic matter, to which the Demiurge gave form. The one calls forth its polar opposite and inevitably is in tension with it, as we have seen. Another way of expressing this is that there is a deep tension in Plato's thought between change (matter) and changelessness (form). Amid a sense of constant change, Plato sought an anchor in the realm of forms, but this raises more questions than it solves, not least that of knowing the forms. Not surprisingly, Aristotle, in so many ways the father of science, brought Plato down to earth by locating the forms in actual entities.

7. G. R. F. Ferrari, "The Three-Part Soul," in *The Cambridge Companion to Plato's* Republic, ed. G. R. F. Ferrari (Cambridge: Cambridge University Press, 2007), 199–200.

8. Herman Dooyeweerd, *Roots of Western Culture: Pagan, Secular, and Christian Options*, trans. John Kraay (Toronto: Wedge, 1979), 15–22.

Aristotle

In Raphael's painting *The School of Athens*, many philosophers populate the scene, with Plato and Aristotle at the center. What this painting portrays artistically is certainly true historically: Plato and Aristotle dominated not only Greek philosophy but the whole philosophical tradition of the West. As Samuel Taylor Coleridge expresses it, "Every man is born an Aristotelian, or a Platonist. . . . They are the two classes of men, beside which it is next to impossible to conceive a third."[9] We referred above to Whitehead's statement that all Western philosophy is a footnote to Plato. Jonathan Barnes comments, "A witty apothegm, but false: substitute 'Aristotle' for 'Plato' and the aphorism will be, as it were, less false."[10]

Aristotle arrived at Plato's Academy as a student at the age of seventeen, and he remained there for almost two decades, until Plato's death in 347 BC. He left Athens for twelve years, during which time he continued his philosophical activity and tutored the boy Alexander who would later be called "the Great" and amass a world kingdom, thereby assuring that Greek thought would be spread far and wide. In 335 BC Aristotle returned to Athens, where he established his own school, the Lyceum. His school dealt with a remarkably wide range of subjects beyond philosophy, including many of the natural sciences, music and the arts, politics, psychology, ethics, and even theology. While Plato's philosophy comes to us in literary dialogues, Aristotle's literary legacy is lecture notes and course texts used in his school.

A second observation of Raphael's painting grants us entry into Aristotle's philosophy: Plato, wearing the colors of fire (red) and air (white)—elements that move upward—points to the heavens with his right hand, indicating that truth can be found in another world. Aristotle, clothed in the colors of earth (brown) and water (blue)—elements that move down—holds his palm down parallel to the ground, signifying that truth is found by investigating this empirical world. While we might say that Plato's paradigmatic discipline was mathematics, where we find unchanging universals, Aristotle's was biology, where you must observe, analyze, and classify to understand the universal patterns.[11] Yet Aristotle, like Plato, wanted to move beyond or through the empirical world to gain knowledge or wisdom about the deeper questions of purpose and meaning. While there is a different view of reality at work in Aristotle, there remains a fundamental continuity with Plato.

9. Samuel Taylor Coleridge, *Table Talk of Samuel Taylor Coleridge* (London: George Routledge and Sons, 1884), 102.

10. Jonathan Barnes, introduction to *The Cambridge Companion to Aristotle*, ed. Jonathan Barnes (Cambridge: Cambridge University Press, 1995), xv.

11. See Marjorie Grene, *A Portrait of Aristotle* (London: Faber and Faber, 1963).

Aristotle set out a hierarchical ontology that moves from nonliving things to plants to animals to human beings. Animals and humans are able to understand the world with their sense perception. But only human beings have the ability to think rationally about the world. This is what distinguishes humanity from the rest of the world.

This fundamental structure demonstrates why the senses are important for Aristotle. Our most basic way of knowing and understanding the world is through our senses. While Plato distrusted the senses, Aristotle believed that true knowledge begins with our sensory perception. However, knowledge comes not simply through sensory experience but as we use our reason to clarify, categorize, and analyze the world. Thus for Aristotle knowledge involved empirical observation and logical analysis.

Aristotle developed a host of analytical and logical tools to perform this task of analysis. He was the first to analyze the processes of logic, or formally correct reasoning.[12] He distinguished between *inductive* logic, which draws general conclusions from a collection of specific observations, and *deductive* logic, which demonstrates a conclusion with a compelling argument. He saw the value in both kinds of reasoning for understanding the world, but his embrace of inductive logic shows a far deeper confidence in the senses and the visible world than that of Plato.

Aristotle made a distinction between *essence* and *accidents*. The essence of something is that which distinguishes something and makes it what it is. Accidents are characteristics of a particular thing that are not essential. For example, the essence of a human is the person's human nature or humanness. But there are many accidents that may be attributed to a person—height, weight, color of hair and eyes, and so on. Moreover, Aristotle distinguished between genus, species, and individual. For example, in his view the category of *animal* is a genus that includes many species, such as dogs, cats, mice, and human beings. John Smith would be an individual who is a human being (species), which is part of the broader category of animal (genus). Further, Aristotle distinguished ten categories for analyzing things in the world: substance (true essence of something), quantity (how much or many), quality (what kind), relations (relation to something), location (where), time (when), position (posture or how it lies), state (condition), action (to make or do something), and passivity (being acted upon). All of these analytical tools

12. Graham Priest, *Logic: A Very Short Introduction* (Oxford: Oxford University Press, 2000), 102–4, distinguishes three great periods in the development of logic. The first was in ancient Greece from 400 BC to 200 BC, and its dominant figure was Aristotle. The second was in the medieval universities from the twelfth to the fourteenth centuries with luminaries such as Duns Scotus and William of Ockham. The third occurs in the twentieth century with thinkers such as Gottlob Frege and Bertrand Russell.

equipped Aristotle for using reason to understand the sensory phenomena he observed, and many of these tools remain in the toolbox of scientists down to the present day.

Aristotle was a very observant natural scientist, but he wanted to drive beyond the study of nature (*physis*) to what was after or beyond nature (*metaphysis*). He wanted not simply knowledge but wisdom, to know not simply what the world is like but *why* it is as it is. He referred to this as metaphysics, first philosophy, and even theology. His studies drove him to deeper questions, and his philosophy was an attempt to answer questions of a foundational nature.

The starting point for Aristotle's ontology and epistemology is a particular *substance*. The real world is made up of individual substances, concrete beings that have an unchangeable essence and independent existence. A substance exists as a certain kind of thing and needs nothing beyond itself for its existence. There are people, dogs, tables, trees, just acts, and so on. When we see John or Spot or this particular kitchen table, we can recognize each as a particular kind of thing. Certain characteristics coalesce in each of these creatures, making it what it is—a person or a dog or whatever. Each one of these things has an essential nature different from other things. Metaphysics attempts to grasp the essential nature of these substances.

Aristotle used the word *substance*—his primary category of being—in two ways. The primary substance is a particular thing—this person John Smith or this dog Spot or this kitchen table. Yet Aristotle agreed with Plato that true knowledge could not be simply of particulars but of universals. So substance is understood also in a secondary sense: it is the essential nature or the kind of being that this particular thing is (a human being, a dog, a table).

The universal essence or nature of anything Aristotle calls a form. The universal essence of "dogginess" or "humanness" or "tableness" is the form of a dog, a person, a table. Aristotle recognized that for true knowledge and ethical standards there must be unchanging forms or universal essences as Plato had argued. However, Aristotle believed that Plato had everything upside down.

Aristotle believed that forms or ideas did not have an objective existence of their own and did not stand apart from the matter of the particular object. The form was in the thing itself, in the matter that could be observed, and so this universal essence could be grasped only by observing many particular dogs, people, tables, or acts of justice.

This still leaves the problem of change. If these forms are constant, how can something change? Aristotle accounted for change with a distinction between potentiality and actuality. A fetus has the potential to become an adult human being. The acorn has the potential to become an oak. Sometimes the potential is realized from outside—say, when a person cuts down the tree and makes a table. But potential can also be actualized when something fulfills its own nature, realizes its own essence, and becomes what it is supposed to be. Aristotle believed that the form itself gave a particular substance not only its essential structure but also its developmental dynamic. There is in each form a teleological striving toward fulfillment. Thus with this distinction between potentiality and actuality Aristotle accounted for change in the world.

But diving deeper, the question is, what causes change? Aristotle distinguished four kinds of causes. The first is the material cause: matter provides the potential change. For example, one cannot build a house without bricks and wood. The second is the formal cause: a house is built as the form is realized in its construction. The third is the efficient cause: someone initiates the building of the house and brings about its construction. The fourth cause is the final cause: this is the goal of the particular entity's development. The goal of building a house is so that someone can live in it. There is a teleological structure to Aristotle's world. All things exist with a certain end, a certain purpose, and move toward that purpose.

Aristotle offers a brief sketch of Greek philosophy from Thales to his time.[13] He seeks to show that none of his predecessors had been able to account for constancy and change, because they had neglected the utilization of four causes and especially that of the final cause. This culminates with the question of what constitutes the goal and purpose of the world as a whole. What is the final cause that brings about the unified purpose of all things? What is the final direction of change and development? Aristotle's rigorous logic drove him to posit a Supreme Being, an Unmoved Mover.[14] This Supreme Being is nothing like the God of Abraham, Isaac, and Jacob. It is a pure abstraction created to make sense of the world. Aristotle's god is pure Reason and does not have any kind of material component like all other things. Like Plato, Aristotle is finally compelled to create an idol out of reason. Humanity shares in Divine Reason. Differently than Plato, Aristotle was driven by the teleological nature of the world.

Aristotle has left the West with a rich legacy. Numerous distinctions and observations of the world have deepened our understanding. His hierarchical ontology moves us beyond the reductionism of the philosophers before him. Many of his categorical distinctions and his observations on logic remain helpful in analyzing God's creation. Philosophy can provide a comprehensive

13. Aristotle is thus the first historian of philosophy.

14. Peter A. Angeles, *Dictionary of Philosophy* (New York: Harper & Row, 1981), 305–7, notes the following characteristics of Aristotle's Unmoved Mover: it is eternal, self-moving, self-sufficient, one, a substance; in fact it is the Primary Substance that is the source of all other things—completely actualized, immaterial, good, unchanging, immutable, Divine Thought or Mind.

framework and basic distinctions helpful for various specialized sciences, and
Aristotle's philosophy is a shining example.

Nevertheless, in the end Aristotle was unable to accomplish what he wanted
to do with his metaphysics—gain wisdom by answering the question of the
why. Without recourse to the God of the Bible, Aristotle could not answer the
question of the purpose and meaning of the creation, nor account adequately
for order, constancy, and change. The notion of form to account for purpose,
order, constancy, and change is a product of Aristotle's idolatrous imagination.

Every philosophy of necessity develops a conceptual framework in order
to do the work of analysis. This, of course, is what makes philosophy a challenge, as we have to come to grips with multiple conceptual frameworks and
their technical vocabularies. What is vital to remember is that conceptual
frameworks are not neutral; they inevitably carry with them the baggage—for
better or worse—of the worldview of the individual philosopher and thus
bear close scrutiny. A central concept in Aristotle, which has been hugely
influential, is his doctrine of substance. This doctrine has its complexities in
Aristotle, as we have noted, but to simplify matters let us take a contemporary
definition of substance akin to that of Aristotle. E. J. Lowe notes, "Roughly, an
individual substance is conceived to be an individual object which is capable
of independent existence—one which could exist even in the absence of any
other such object."[15] It is the stress on *independent* existence that Herman
Dooyeweerd rightly criticizes.[16] There is no creature that is a substance—an
independently existing thing. The world is dependent on God's creating and
sustaining Word. Thus Dooyeweerd, in somewhat confusing language, proposes that we avoid the language of substance and think instead of *creation
as meaning*, a way of emphasizing that everything depends for its existence
on God's sustaining creative power and is interdependent with the rest of
creation. There are surely ways to develop a doctrine of substance *without* the
strong stress on independence, as many Christian philosophers continue to
do, but nevertheless it serves as a reminder of what is at stake in the concepts
we adopt in doing philosophy.

Plato attempted to account for the abiding order or law for the various
creatures in God's world with his doctrine of ideas. But ideas remained separate from the various entities of creation, and this was exposed by the relentless critique of Aristotle. Aristotle attempted to explain the orderliness or
lawfulness of the creatures he observed but was unable to account for the
transcendence of this order.

15. E. J. Lowe, "Individuation," in *The Oxford Handbook of Metaphysics*, ed. Michael J.
Loux and Dean W. Zimmerman (Oxford: Oxford University Press, 2003), 79.
16. See Dooyeweerd, *Roots of Western Culture*, 30–31.

The Legacy of Greek Pagan Philosophy in the Hellenistic Era and the Roman Empire

Traditionally, ancient Greek civilization is divided into three periods: the Hellenic age (ca. 800–323 BC), the Hellenistic age (323–31 BC), and the Greco-Roman age (31 BC–AD 476). The Hellenistic age began with the death of Alexander the Great. His empire was divided among his generals into smaller kingdoms until finally all of them came under the sway of Rome in 31 BC. In this last section we will explore the philosophy that has its roots in the Hellenistic era and continued to flourish in the Roman Empire.

During the Hellenic age, when the pre-Socratics, Socrates, Plato, and Aristotle lived, the *polis*, or city-state, was the primary social and political unit. However, the world empire eclipsed the city-state; the *polis* became a *cosmopolis*—a world civilization. The Greek people had to find their way in a world that was much bigger, more complex, more chaotic, and more threatening to their security and way of life.

In this context, philosophical speculation about the good life must take into account the confusion, insecurity, and disorientation that characterized this time period. No longer did autonomous individuals seem to have control of their own destiny. Rather, they were under the sway of much larger forces. Philosophy focused on practical and ethical insight to cope with the uncertainties and disorientation of life. In this section we will deal with how Stoicism, Epicureanism, and Skepticism met this challenge. All three arose in the Hellenistic period.

Stoicism

The most important of these philosophical schools is Stoicism. The founder was Zeno of Citium (335–263 BC), who established his school in Athens. Stoicism remained an influential system for the next five centuries and included among its exponents such eminent Romans as Cicero (106–43 BC), Seneca (4 BC–AD 65), Epictetus (AD 60–117), and Marcus Aurelius (AD 121–80). Stoicism had a major influence on the development of Christianity, including its ethics and views of providence, and is a basis on which Western views of natural law have been constructed.

The goal of Stoic philosophy is human happiness defined in terms of wisdom. Wisdom is conforming oneself to the providential and rational order found in the universe. This requires a dignified resignation when facing difficult circumstances, even serenity when facing death. This is where we get the idea of being "stoic" when facing adversity. One can see the advantage of this kind of philosophy in a turbulent world.

Stoics understood the world as rationally ordered. The basis for a lawful world was found by returning to Heraclitus's idea of the *logos* as a rational fiery substance that permeates the world. Stoic philosophy is deterministic; that is, all events are causally determined in an ironclad inevitability to which all must submit. What will happen will happen; whatever will be will be. The process is not haphazard but providential, as it is guided by a divine and rational substance that pervades and governs all things. The Stoics were also pantheistic: the *logos*, which pervades and gives order to the universe, is equated with god—not a personal god but an impersonal substance.

Human beings are actors in this broader drama. This means accepting the place providence has assigned us with serenity and resignation. The person who is wise will thus live according to nature. Really, one has no choice, since there is a relentless fate that is inescapable and certain. But happiness and wisdom come as one freely adapts oneself to this cosmic natural order, to inexorable fate, to the providential will of god. Epictetus could say: "Seek not that the things which happen should happen as you wish; but wish the things which happen to be as they are, and you will have a tranquil flow of life."[17] Thus the wise man is passionless—free of grief, fear, desire, or pleasure.

Every human being shares in the rational *logos* that orders the world and is able to discern the laws of justice that rule the world. There is a universal natural law of justice that transcends particular communities. Since all people share in reason, all people are to be regarded as members of a common humanity and part of a worldwide commonwealth based on natural justice. This gave a foundation for people struggling to find their roles as world citizens in the drama of a world empire.

The most important insight of the Stoics is the recognition of a cosmic order in creation. Unfortunately, as it was caught up in a pantheistic, rationalistic, and fatalistic web, human freedom was threatened, and notions of normativity were intellectualized.

Epicureanism and Skepticism

Epicurus (341–270 BC) established his school in Athens about the same time Zeno was laying the foundations for Stoicism. According to Epicurus the goal of human life is pleasure. Pleasure by his account is different than hedonism. The primary problem that human beings face is fear of god and anxiety about retribution after death. The goal is to be freed from this fear and anxiety. Pleasure means satisfying natural and necessary needs, being

17. Epictetus, *Enchiridion and Selections from the Discourses of Epictetus*, trans. George Long (Stilwell, KS: Digireads.com, 2005), viii.

content with simple pleasures, and enjoying the company of intellectually stimulating friends.

Like Stoic philosophy, Epicurus retrieved a pre-Socratic understanding of the world and humanity to support this goal. He recycled the thought of Democritus, a materialist who believed all that exists are atoms moved randomly by impersonal forces. The gods have no control over human affairs and are not concerned with this world. Moreover, death is simply a matter of the dissolution of the atoms of the soul. There is no life after death and no retribution; one ceases to exist at death. With this view of the world and human life, a person was liberated from fear of god and death.

Like Stoicism and Epicureanism, Skepticism sought peace and tranquility in the midst of a changing and chaotic world. For Skeptics the problem was the constant frustration and disappointment that comes from the uncertainty that attends the search for infallible truth. Happiness comes as one suspends judgment and approaches life as a seeker with an open mind. Thus Skepticism developed a strategy that harnessed powerful arguments to refute all dogmatic truth claims.

Pyrrho (371–270 BC) is considered to be the founder of Skepticism. The primary targets of the early Skeptics in Athens and for the next few centuries were Stoic philosophers who believed that the senses provided a solid foundation for scientific knowledge. The fact that our senses can deceive us and that they can only give mere appearance of things should lead us to set aside dogmatism. Likewise, the lack of universal agreement and the bewildering number of moral theories should lead to epistemic humility. When one searches for certainty, there is a need to provide a criterion for truth. But to establish that criterion there is a need for another one, and so on, in an infinite regress.

Skepticism was not a philosophical system but a method or a line of reasoning whose goal was to deflate dogmatism and allow one to live a more peaceful life in conformity with prevailing social customs and instinctive feelings. Skeptics did not dogmatically claim that truth was not available, nor did they reject the moral life. They remained seekers using their sharp arguments to puncture the confidence of anyone who presumed to know certain truth.

Plotinus and Neoplatonism

For all their insight these philosophical schools never really satisfied the deepest longings of those living at this time. Instead, it took a new form of philosophy that combined the religious impulse of the mystery religions and the rational philosophies of Greece. This new school is known as Neoplatonism because it revived Plato's legacy in a new time and sought to synthesize the major schools of Greek thought. Philosophers who followed Plato had developed a number of themes within his philosophy, and these themes found expression in Neoplatonism. Neoplatonism became the dominant philosophical school in the late Roman Empire, but its importance reaches beyond its second- and third-century influence. The great Latin church father Augustine synthesized the gospel with Neoplatonism, extending the latter's influence throughout the medieval period and, indeed, right up to the present day.

The founder and primary exponent of Neoplatonism was Plotinus (AD 205–70). He opened a school in Rome, and his most famous student was the celebrated Porphyry (234–305), who wrote a biography of Plotinus and edited his works. Porphyry is also known for his polemic against Christianity, *Against the Christians*. The last words of Plotinus to the physician Eustochius were significant, as they summarized the goal of his philosophy: "I was waiting for you, before that which is divine in me departs to unite itself with the Divine in the universe."[18]

According to the philosophy of Plotinus, the cosmos flowed from god, who was variously called the One and the Good. This god is not the God of the Bible but rather an impersonal transcendent reality who is infinite and beyond all positive description. This is not creation as described in Scripture, which is a free and creative act by a personal God, but the necessary overflow of the infinite One, similar to the necessary illumination that is emitted by light. The first derivation in this series of emanations is the Divine Intellect (*Nous*), which provides the rational order that pervades and structures the universe. The Divine Intellect is the place where one finds the full array of Platonic ideas or forms that provide an intelligible order for the world. From the Divine Intellect comes the World Soul, which animates and gives life to the world. The World Soul is the source of the individual souls of all living things, including humans, and thus connects the spiritual (Intellect) to the material (matter). Matter, the lowest level of being, is the realm of darkness that is furthest from the One. While the material world displays a beauty because of the ordering of the Divine Intellect and World Soul, matter itself is identified with evil as lacking intelligible structure. As Wilhelm Windelband rightly notes, Plotinus's "comprehensive view of nature, however, was under these premises cleft in two."[19]

Human beings are essentially souls that utilize bodies for a temporary embodied existence in this world. In fact, human life is to be lived so as to be freed from this material existence and rise to the level of the Soul and Intellect.

18. Copleston, *History of Philosophy*, 1:464.
19. Wilhelm Windelband, *History of Ancient Philosophy*, 3rd ed. (New York: Charles Scribner's Sons, 1910), 373.

Thus humanity makes its ascent back to the spiritual, and in the final moment is again united with the One.

We see in Plotinus the impulse of Plato: the inferiority and evil of the material realm and the superiority and goodness of the spiritual realm. A spiritual soul trapped in a body is what constitutes humanity. The goal of human life is to throw off the fetters of material existence and reach the heights of a spiritual life. Since spiritual reality is rational, it is precisely through philosophy that one can gain such spiritual heights.

Neoplatonism was the final expression of ancient pagan philosophy and became the most powerful, as it would be primarily in this form that Plato continued to live on in the early medieval period.

From: percy@secular.edu
To: abby@longobedience.edu
Subject: To my *not* Platonic friend

Hi Abby,
Well at last we have got out of logic and are studying some of the big early philosophers. Like you—I think—we have been doing some work on Plato and Aristotle. The main point our prof seems to draw from them is that philosophy is based entirely on autonomous reason. I do find myself asking, why bother with all this pagan stuff when we have the Bible and the gospel? Even the big guns—Plato and Aristotle—hold radically different views of the world, as far as I can work out.

Your frustrated Percy

From: abby@longobedience.edu
To: percy@secular.edu
Subject: RE: To my *not* Platonic friend

Hey Perc,
Yes—I'm really glad you are more than a platonic friend!

I can understand your frustration. Several of my fellow students have expressed similar views. Indeed, your view has an ancient pedigree. As part of the discussion of this issue, our prof had us read chapter 7 of the early church father Tertullian's *Prescription against Heretics*. You should have a read! He rants against philosophy and thinks that Christians should have nothing to do with it since it only breeds heresy! However, as our prof pointed out, Christians such as Tertullian who rejected philosophy ended up being influenced by it, albeit unconsciously. Our prof also alerted the class to how much we take the Greek contribution for granted. It was they, and *not* Christians, who systematically and for the first time put topics such as logic, justice, political philosophy—think of Plato's *The Republic* and Aristotle's *Politics*—biology, philosophy of language, aesthetics, and so on, on the table, as it were. The Western world is unimaginable without the table they set!

From: percy@secular.edu
To: abby@longobedience.edu
Subject: RE: RE: To my *not* Platonic friend

OK, but does that mean we just accept it hook, line, and sinker?
Still frustrated,

Perc

From: abby@longobedience.edu
To: percy@secular.edu
Subject: No, no, no

More to come—have to get a paper done. Will respond ASAP but NO, we don't just accept Greek philosophy.

In haste . . . and with love,

Abby

5

Medieval Synthesis Philosophy
Augustine to Abélard

From: abby@longobedience.edu
To: percy@secular.edu
Subject: Hook, line, and sinker!!

Hey Perc,
Finally some time to continue our previous discussion. I can understand your frustration and feeling there are only two options: to reject philosophy as pagan or to embrace it hook, line, and sinker. In class recently our prof referred us to an article by Professor Wolters—the author of *Creation Regained*—on how to approach pagan philosophy.[1] I found Wolters's advice so, so helpful. You must first spot the idolatry, but then—and for me this was the crucial insight!—you look for the genuine insights that are invariably *close* to the point of idolatry. The hard work of Christian scholarship starts, then, as you take over the insights without the idolatrous baggage. You have to take note of what it is about God's world that these philosophers are seeing correctly, as well as how their *religious orientation* distorts their vision.

Introduction

Defining "Medieval"

An event of enormous significance stands between ancient pagan philosophy and medieval synthesis philosophy—the incarnation, death, and resurrection

---

1. Albert M. Wolters, "Facing the Perplexing History of Philosophy," *Tydskrif vir Christelike Wetenskap* 17 (1981): 1–17.

of Jesus the Christ. The Christian theologians and philosophers who live after this event rightly take as their starting point what happened in the Christ event as decisive for all their thinking. They believed that in Jesus we have the fullest revelation of God and his purpose for the whole world.

Since the gospel offers a comprehensive view of the world, it was inevitable that there would be an encounter between the Christian faith and the Greek philosophy that likewise offered an equally comprehensive vision. So the medieval period is when philosophers began to sort through the Greek philosophical tradition in the light of the Christian faith.

When the term *medieval* or *Middle Ages* or *Dark Ages* is used, we must be alert to the derogatory nature assumed in these designations. "Middle" is an era or time between two more important eras—in this case, the classical and the modern. Characteristic of this scorn of medieval philosophy is the comment by the rationalist Octave Hamelin, who tells us that "Descartes is in succession with the ancients, almost as if . . . there had been nothing in between."[2]

We will at times employ the terms *pagan* to describe the so-called classical era and *synthesis* to describe the "medieval" era. This is because we want to make the gospel, rather than autonomous reason, the "hero of the story." The medieval period is an era of synthesis because the gospel and Greek humanism were merged into a single composite.

In the early synthesis period initiated by Augustine (354–430), philosophy was amalgamated with Platonic and Neoplatonic philosophy in particular. In the late synthesis period it is Aristotelian philosophy that moves to the fore, as it is conjoined to the Christian-Platonic synthesis. The high point of this synthesis is Thomas Aquinas.

The Medieval Period and the Relationship of the Gospel to Greek Philosophy

That the medieval period is a mixture of the gospel and Greek philosophy there can be no question. However, the question of how to interpret and evaluate that synthesis is more controversial. Adolf von Harnack sees in the synthesis a perversion of the Christian faith. By comparison, Étienne Gilson believes that even though Greek philosophy was employed to interpret and defend the Christian faith, medieval thought remains faithful to the authentic teaching of Jesus. The choice we make here is decisive: how we understand the gospel and its relation to Greek philosophy and the Hellenistic worldview into which it was transplanted will determine the way we interpret this period of medieval philosophy.

2. Octave Hamelin, *Le Système de Descartes* (Paris: Felix Alcan, 1921), 15.

There is a fundamental difference in the way that the Christian faith and Greek philosophy understand truth. Ultimate truth for the Christian is located in a story of God's deeds in history that finds its center in Jesus Christ. For the Greek, reliable truth is found in timeless ideas that transcend history and can be accessed by autonomous reason.[3] Since the truth of the gospel is a Person and an event that give meaning to universal history, the gospel need not completely displace other visions of reality; indeed, it may—it must!—be translated into every cultural context. This will be a radical encounter since the gospel is a view of the entirety of the world and human life and so will clash with all other visions. However, while the encounter is radical, it will not completely supplant other life views. Rather, it will embrace the good and the insights in every cultural tradition and will take on the hues of the various contexts of the world.

This means that we cannot agree with Harnack, who sees the translation as a betrayal of the original message. Nevertheless, there is danger in the use of pagan categories. It is our sense that as the early church fathers began to express and articulate the gospel in Greek philosophical terms, much of the pagan thinking of Greek culture was ingested as well. Therefore we cannot entirely agree with Gilson either.

Our point of departure for this era, then, is to acknowledge the validity of a translation of the gospel into Greek categories but to assess that contextualized expression of the Christian faith in terms of both the insights it faithfully harvested and the idolatry that was imbibed along the way.

Roots of Medieval Philosophy: Christian Philosophy in Pagan Rome

The Patristic Era

Christian engagement with Greek philosophy began in the New Testament. In the three centuries that followed (second to fifth centuries) there were at least two impulses for the church to engage Greek philosophy. The first was apologetic: Greek categories were employed to defend the Christian faith against the attacks of pagan thinkers. The second was theological: Greek philosophy offered terms and insights that enabled Christians to articulate and interpret the gospel in the context of classical pagan culture. We do not find in these centuries a systematic approach to Christian philosophy but instead philosophy employed as a handmaiden of theology and apologetics. Thus our approach will be to distinguish the philosophical insights—anthropological, ontological, epistemological—from theology.

3. Lesslie Newbigin, *Proper Confidence: Faith, Doubt, and Certainty in Christian Discipleship* (Grand Rapids: Eerdmans, 1995), 4–5.

The first centuries of Christian thought were dominated by Platonism. "As a rough generalisation, therefore, one may say that the philosophic ideas of the early Christian writers were Platonic or neo-Platonic in character (with an admixture of Stoicism) and that the Platonic tradition continued for long to dominate Christian thought from the philosophic viewpoint."[4] Gilson says of the early medieval period, "Plato himself does not appear at all, but Platonism is everywhere."[5]

There were markedly different approaches to the employment of Greek thought. For Tertullian (155–220) Greek philosophy was, in Paul's terms, the foolishness of the world. "What does Athens have to do with Jerusalem?" he queried, with a clear "Nothing" implied in his rhetorical question. For Clement of Alexandria (150–215), on the other hand, Greek philosophy was God's gift for theological and evangelistic purposes. Tertullian was concerned about the idolatry of Greek philosophy, while Clement recognized the insight of those same philosophical reflections. Thus the church struggled to embrace the insights while rejecting the idolatry. No doubt some did it better than others, but generally all embraced Platonism more uncritically than did the biblical authors.

The earliest Christian thinkers to engage Greek philosophy were the apologists who defended the Christian faith against various pagan accusations. The earliest apologists wrote in Greek, and of these Justin Martyr (103–165) is the most important. Justin Martyr synthesized the gospel with Platonic philosophy in a way that had a widespread impact. The goal of Greek philosophy was to seek after and know God, and so Justin sought out one philosopher after another to satisfy this quest. He approached a Stoic, a Pythagorean, and finally a leading Platonist. It was this Platonic philosopher that enabled him to realize his goal, because Plato's philosophy is oriented to the perception of spiritual reality and its ultimate goal—to look upon God. Yet later Justin encountered an old man who pressed him on the inadequacy of Platonic thinking. The old man offered a more adequate alternative in Holy Scripture, and as Justin puts it, a flame was kindled in his soul for Scripture. Revelation had answered the quest of philosophy, and therefore Justin said, "I am a philosopher," and he continued to wear his philosopher's cloak as a symbol of Christianity as the true philosophy.

As can be seen in Justin's journey, philosophy is seen as a preparation for Christ, who is the fulfillment of the philosophical longing. Philosophy asks the right questions, but revelation answers them. Christianity offers true

4. Frederick Copleston, *Medieval Philosophy*, vol. 2 of *A History of Philosophy* (New York: Image Books, 1950, 1985), 14.
5. Étienne Gilson, *History of Christian Philosophy in the Middle Ages* (New York: Random House, 1955), 144.

philosophy. But how can the gospel answer the questions of pagan philosophy? It is the result, Justin believed, of the fact that the *logos*—the Word, which is Jesus (John 1:14)—enlightens every person who comes into the world (John 1:9). This view is still widely held today. In his foreword to Thomas Woods's *How the Catholic Church Built Western Civilization*, Cardinal Antonio Cañizares, for example, asserts that

> the prologue of St. John's Gospel affirms that Reason (Logos) is intrinsically a part of the divine nature. What's more, the very use of the term Logos proves that the incorporation of Revelation with Greek philosophical thought was no mere accident. Rather there is a natural affinity between the living God of Abraham, Isaac, and Jacob and the pursuit of truth by the earliest Greek thinkers. We discover this connection in a definitive manner in the Resurrection of Jesus Christ, true God and true man. For our purposes, the Risen Lord is also a true Greek.[6]

In our view, as Justin's case reveals, it is more complex than this. Justin collapsed John's notion of the *logos* with its pagan understanding in Greek philosophy. For him, the Word that enlightens every man is a spark of divine rationality that permeates the world; *logos* is the natural light of reason that indwelt every person. The philosopher who follows reason has already begun to share in the truth revealed by the incarnate *logos*. Jesus, who is the true Word, then answers the philosopher's quest for salvation and a vision of God. He mediates the soul's ascent to spiritual reality.

Justin's understanding of the Christian faith was deeply indebted not only to Platonic terminology but also, to some degree, to its content. This is seen in his dualistic ontology (spiritual and material realm), his dualistic anthropology (humanity as soul in a body), his view of salvation as escape to a spiritual realm, and his rationalistic understanding of *logos* in contrast to a more biblical understanding.

Irenaeus (125–202) is more cognizant of the dangers of pagan philosophy than Justin; his thought displays a stronger sense of the historical and cosmic character of the Christian faith. This is partly due to his battle with gnosticism, which posits a dualism between God and matter. Irenaeus battled gnosticism by stressing the goodness of creation as a work of the good and free Creator who creates out of nothing, salvation through faith in Jesus, evil as a result of freedom of the will, the teaching of the apostles' gospel as the only true "gnosis," an emphasis on the unity of salvation history in the Bible, and the historical activity of Jesus as the second Adam who undoes the work of the first Adam.

---

6. Cardinal Antonio Cañizares, foreword to *How the Catholic Church Built Western Civilization*, by Thomas E. Woods (Washington, DC: Regnery, 2012), xiv.

Of the early Christian thinkers, Origen (185–254) is the least critical of Platonic philosophy. Here the synthesis with Platonic philosophy significantly compromises the gospel. God creates the world in eternity by necessity of his goodness. He uses the *logos* as a pattern for creation, and so we can say that by the Word all things are created. Humans are created as spirits with the destiny of being full participants in the divine life of God. But as a result of the fall into sin we are now clothed with bodies. One day all souls will arrive at a spiritual union with God.

With this brief sketch we can see a number of things about this early synthesis between the Christian faith and Platonic philosophy. First, we do not find any philosophical system among these early Christian thinkers. Second, while Platonism negatively impacts all these writers to some degree, there is a significant difference between Origen's fatal accommodation, Justin's and Clement's significant appreciation, Irenaeus's more discerning appropriation, and Tertullian's rejection.[7] Third, a number of Platonic themes are grafted onto the Christian faith that continue to encumber the church: a synthesis between the idolatrous notion of the rational *logos* with the Jewish notion of God's creative Word made flesh in Jesus; a diminishment of the historical, collective, and cosmic dimensions of salvation; salvation as a spiritual escape from this world; the inferior place of the material creation; and a dualism of body and soul that devalues the body and bodily life in the world. Fourth, Greek philosophy in general and Platonic philosophy in particular offer a number of insights (e.g., the knowledge of God as the supreme goal of human life) and a number of analytical tools for the defense and elaboration of the gospel in theology.

Augustine

Augustine (354–430) is by far the greatest of the early Christian philosophers, even one of the greatest in history. Scott MacDonald notes that "he was not the first to defend Christianity as the true wisdom sought by philosophy. But he was the thinker who, above all, and at a critical historical moment demonstrated that Christianity could be mined for philosophical insight, made to answer philosophical questions in philosophically sophisticated ways, and presented as a philosophically satisfying worldview rivaling pagan philosophical systems."[8]

---

7. While Tertullian expresses rejection of pagan Greek philosophy, avoidance of philosophy is ultimately impossible.

8. Scott MacDonald, "Augustine, *Confessions* (ca. 400): Real-life Philosophy," in *The Classics of Western Philosophy: A Reader's Guide*, ed. Jorge J. E. Gracia et al. (Oxford: Blackwell, 2003), 103.

Life and Work of Augustine

Augustine was born in Thagaste in North Africa in 354. His mother, Monica, was a devout Christian, and his father a pagan. Monica raised him as a Christian, but he lost his faith when he went to Carthage to study rhetoric in 370. He took a mistress, with whom he would live for a decade and father a son. Augustine was a precocious and very able student of rhetoric. When he was nineteen he read Cicero's *Hortensius* and it inflamed in him a love for philosophy and wisdom. He turned to Manichaeism, in which he found a more satisfactory explanation for evil than the Christianity he had been taught as a youth. Manicheans believed that there were two coeternal ultimate principles: Light, which is good, and Darkness, which is evil. Our souls are fragmented particles of Light that have become entrapped in bodies in the material world. An ascetic life could free the soul to rejoin the Light. Augustine's embrace of Manichaeism made his break with Christianity complete.

After a brief return to his hometown, Augustine began to teach rhetoric in Carthage in 374. He left to teach rhetoric, first in Rome and then in Milan in 384. By then he had drifted from his Manichaean position to one of academic skepticism. In Milan he became attracted to Platonism by reading some Platonic treatises—almost certainly Neoplatonic works by Plotinus and Porphyry[9]—which enabled him to see the importance of spiritual reality.[10] He also listened to the sermons of Ambrose, the Neoplatonic bishop of Milan.

Augustine's conversion came in the summer of 386, when he was in a state of turmoil and despair. In a garden he heard a child's voice cry continually *"Tolle lege! Tolle lege!"* (take up and read), whereupon he took the New Testament, randomly read Romans 13:13–14, and was converted. Augustine's understanding of Christianity was deeply Platonic at this early point in his life when he wrote *Against the Academics* (386), in which he spells out his philosophical program. In 387 Augustine was baptized by Ambrose, and he returned to North Africa in 388.

Augustine remained in North Africa the rest of his life as a priest and then bishop in Hippo. He published an enormous number of books during his busy life—five million words survive—so much so that "it has been said that Augustine's output is equal in volume to the entire surviving corpus of previous Latin literature"![11] The most famous works are his *Confessions* (397–400),

---

9. There is debate about which texts by Plotinus or Porphyry were read by and influenced Augustine. See Lewis Ayres, *Augustine and the Trinity* (Cambridge: Cambridge University Press, 2010), 14.

10. Lewis Ayres notes that recent scholarship has been virtually unanimous in rejecting the idea that Augustine first converted to Platonism before converting to Christianity (ibid.).

11. Anthony Kenny, *An Illustrated Brief History of Western Philosophy* (Oxford: Blackwell, 2006), 115.

On the Trinity (417), and *The City of God* (426). *Confessions* and *The City of God* were widely read throughout the medieval period and exercised enormous influence not only on that period but later ones as well. Augustine died in 430 as the Vandals laid siege to Hippo.

Augustine's work covers many subjects and shows clear development: Augustine matured as a Christian thinker, and his later philosophy is much more in harmony with Scripture. Augustine did not see philosophy as a distinct discipline. His philosophy is interwoven with his devotional and theological writing, and so the best we can do is to extract the philosophical thread from its broader literary cloth.

Philosophy as the Pursuit of Wisdom

A good place to start is with Augustine's own words from *Against the Academics*, which we must remember comes shortly after his conversion.

> Let me tell you my whole program briefly. . . . I have turned away from all the things that mortal men consider to be good, and I have set myself the goal of serving the pursuit of this wisdom. . . . Everyone agrees that we are impelled to learning by the double urge of authority and reason. From this moment forward it is my resolve never to depart from the authority of Christ, for I find none that is stronger. However, I must follow after this with the greatest subtlety of reason. For I am disposed now that I have an unbounded desire to apprehend truth not only by believing it, but also by understanding it. In the meantime, I am confident that among the Platonists I shall find what is not opposed to the teaching of our religion.[12]

The goal of Augustine's philosophy is *wisdom*, the knowledge of the truth that culminates in the knowledge of God and brings the happiness that humans long for. In the early chapters of the *Confessions* we see this expressed in categories that mingle Neoplatonism and the gospel. *Confessions* is a remarkable extended prayer to God and offers a spiritual autobiography of Augustine's life up to his conversion. While his desire to know God is deeply biblical, the expression in this work is Neoplatonic. Augustine is immersed in the physical world and has sought his satisfaction in sensible things. He longs to be extricated from the material world so that he might know God. This longing can have the more biblical sense of not attaching one's heart to the creation, but for Augustine it is more than that; it is the material nature of the creation and its desires that hinder him from finding wisdom. Furthermore, Augustine's journey is inward: he scrupulously explores his inner being,

12. *Contra Academicos* III, 20, 43; quoted in Armand A. Maurer, *Medieval Philosophy*, rev. ed. (Toronto: Pontifical Institute of Mediaeval Studies, 1982), 4.

where he believes truth to be found. It is also individual: it is permeated by the first-person singular.

Yet, unlike the Manicheans especially but also Plotinus, Augustine does not see the materiality of the creation as evil.[13] He recognizes that God created the world freely out of nothing and that it is good. The problem is that it is temporal and changing; it cannot satisfy and points to God, who is eternal and immutable. Philosophy is the pursuit of truth that is eternal, unchanging, and immaterial.

The contrast between an inferior material world that is temporal and changing and a superior world that is eternal and immutable affects Augustine's understanding of God. In this early stage it is sometimes the God of the philosophers rather than the God of Abraham, Isaac, and Jacob that is the goal of wisdom. This can be seen, for example, in the way Augustine interprets Exodus 3:14. The name YHWH designates God better than any other because it reveals God as unchangeable, immutable, and eternal. Augustine interprets the name to mean "I am who I am." Some current Old Testament scholars see the meaning of this name as "I will be who I will be," stressing that God is known in his historical acts. But to Augustine's mind it is precisely God's unchangeable nature standing above the flux of history that makes him true being. The knowledge of God comes by way of philosophy and contemplation rather than by active participation in God's mission (contra, for example, Jer. 22:16). For this reason the contemplative life is superior to the active life.

Yet Augustine does not simply take over a Neoplatonic view of God as Being and as One. Unlike Plotinus, he conceives of God in deeply personal terms, as God's character is rendered in Scripture. While he uses similar words for God, like *Truth* and *Goodness*, these terms are filled with biblical content. Thus Augustine's view of God is a synthesis of Neoplatonism and the Scriptures "wherein the divine attributes most prized in the Greek tradition (e.g., necessity, immutability, and atemporal eternity) must somehow be combined with the personal attributes (e.g., will, justice, and historical purpose) of the God of Abraham, Isaac, and Jacob."[14]

Ontology, Epistemology, and Anthropology

Augustine appropriates not the dualism of Plato but the unified hierarchy of Plotinus. But for Augustine the living God of the Bible has replaced the abstract One of Plotinus's thought. Augustine did not see reality as ever-diminishing emanations of God's being but held fast to a fundamental Creator/creature

---

13. Augustine wrestled again and again with Genesis and its doctrine of creation.

14. Michael Mendelson, "Saint Augustine," in *The Stanford Encyclopedia of Philosophy*, Winter 2010 edition, ed. Edward N. Zalta, http://plato.stanford.edu/archives/win2012/entries /augustine/.

distinction between the being of God and the creation. For Augustine the Platonic forms have now found a home in the mind of God. Unlike in Plotinus, for whom the world is a necessary emanation from the divine, God fashions the creation freely out of nothing according to these ideas, which function as a kind of blueprint. The changing creation thus finds its stable ground in the eternal and transcendent God. Some things God created in perfect and complete form. Other things were created in embryo or with "seminal principles," which, like seeds, gradually grow to full development. This explains change in the world that yet conforms to stable ideas in God's mind.

Augustine's long-standing struggle with the nature of evil finds an answer in this unified hierarchy. In Augustine's reading of Scripture, evil is found in the will's idolatrous attachment to aspects of creation that forgets that the chief end of human life is to know God the Creator.

All things that exist and live have a soul that enlivens them, but only human beings have the added rational capacity of the soul that animates the body. It is this cognitive capacity that enables humanity to disentangle itself from an immersion in the material world. The rational soul is the true center of the human being, the essence that defines the human person. Augustine defines the soul as a "certain substance, sharing in reason and suited to the task of ruling the body."[15] It is important to note that Augustine identifies two types of rational faculty in the soul—namely, *scientia* and *sapientia*. The former enables us to understand the world around us; the latter enables us to grasp transcendent ideas and ultimately to see God. As a person begins to use reason (*sapientia*) to discover the truth, he or she is able to transcend matter, and so the soul knows itself to be immaterial. As reason (*sapientia*) grasps truth, which is eternal and immutable, it also knows itself to be immortal. And so the soul is rational, immaterial, and immortal.

Yet humans are more than a soul: they are composite creatures made up of body and soul. "Anyone who wishes to separate the body from human nature is foolish," says Augustine.[16] The soul rules and uses the mortal and earthly body as its instrument to accomplish its purposes. The body is as a weight on the soul, but it is not evil as Plotinus said, for the creation is very good. Rather, the body can become engrossed and absorbed in the sensible world and be sidetracked from its ultimate destiny of rising to eternal truth and knowing God.

Augustine likewise articulates an understanding of knowledge not for its own sake but to provide a path to know the truth and find true happiness in God. The question is, how can we, as temporal and changing creatures living

---

15. Maurer, *Medieval Philosophy*, 8.
16. Quoted in ibid., 9.

in a temporal and changing world, attain certain knowledge of eternal and unchanging truth? The lowest level of knowing comes through the senses. But true knowledge (*sapientia*) must move beyond the senses to make a judgment of truth. It is the role of reason (*sapientia*) to apprehend eternal truths. Thus reason is the apex of the human soul because it is able to give us eternal and unchanging truth. As Ronald Nash puts it, because "man possesses reason and brutes do not, man can have a rational knowledge of sensible things: he can make rational judgments about them and regard them as exemplifications of the eternal forms."[17]

The question is how reason is able to grasp enduring truth of eternal ideas out of the sensory data. Here Augustine employs the notion of *illumination*. By grace, the light of God illumines to reason (*sapientia*) unchanging truths, enabling the mind to grasp them. These truths and ideas are in the mind of God and were used to fashion the universe. As God illumines the mind, enabling us to make true judgments regarding "straightness" or "justice" or whatever, our mind is in real contact with eternal and unchanging truths in God's mind. There is a harmony between the rationality of human beings and the rational structure of the world that conforms to the ideas in the mind of God.

HISTORY AND THE CITY OF GOD

The City of God was composed to defend Christianity against the pagan charge that the fall of Rome was the result of Christian influence in the empire. Indeed, Curtis Chang rightly argues that *The City of God* is an attempt to "out-narrate" the Roman narrative of Rome's fall. Chang shows that the Roman narrative had three intertwined threads: religious, philosophical, historical. Religiously, Roman intellectuals argued that Rome had forsaken the gods. Historically, Rome had forsaken its founding myth of Romulus/Remus, as told by Virgil and others. Philosophically, it had forsaken the Platonic tradition. Augustine refutes all three of these by tracing the biblical storyline.[18]

The City of God is a story of two invisible societies, the City of God (Jerusalem) and the city of the world (Babylon), battling through history until the last judgment. The first is bound together by love for God and the second by love for self. These cities are not to be identified with the church and the political state. Rather, they are more like spiritual forces at work in the world. It is true that the City of God is primarily found in the church, and the worldly city in various historical states including Rome, but there can be no strict identification.

17. Ronald H. Nash, *The Light of the Mind: St. Augustine's Theory of Knowledge* (Lima, OH: Academic Renewal Press, 2003), 9.
18. Curtis Chang, *Engaging Unbelief: A Captivating Strategy from Augustine and Aquinas* (Eugene, OR: Wipf and Stock, 2000).

In this book Augustine moves away from the static and spiritualistic Christianity of Neoplatonism toward a more dynamic, historical vision of God's
purpose in history. It is a narrative of universal history that is given its meaning by God's providential rule, not ideas that stand above history. As Michael
Mendelson puts it, "Augustine is acutely aware that scripture has an historical
dimension, and he is sensitive as well to the tensions between the scriptural
tradition and the Neoplatonic framework upon which he is relying. . . . Augustine's increasing familiarity with the contents of scripture leads him to focus
more and more upon the historical dimension of this tradition, a dimension
alien to the intellectualism of the books of the Platonists."[19] Thus, for example,
the struggle of evil and good is not between the material and spiritual aspects
of reality but is now articulated as spiritual forces at work in the context of
an unfolding story.

Nevertheless, Augustine's attention to history does not leave behind Neoplatonic elements. While God's providence oversees all of history, including the
cultural unfolding of Babylon, in the end this city will be destroyed. It is not
just evil but the city itself that will be destroyed. The significance of cultural
development and life in this world is diminished. The end of history is not the
restoration of creation but the establishment of the City of God, an intriguing
mix between the new creation and Platonic heaven, in which the elect finally
escape the vagaries of this temporal world in the eternal one of the next.

Evaluation

Augustine is a philosophical colossus whose influence has been and continues
to be profound. His *Confessions* has profoundly influenced autobiography; his
doctrine of inwardness deeply influenced René Descartes[20] and Edmund Husserl; his *The City of God* has never been out of print and has been formative
for philosophy of history and political thought. And so we could continue.
The contemporary Catholic philosopher Alasdair MacIntyre identifies the
Enlightenment, the Aristotelian-Thomistic, and the Augustinian traditions
as the three great streams available to us today. And indeed, in terms of these
traditions we would position ourselves as Augustinian.

To evaluate Augustine from a Christian standpoint necessarily involves,
however, a judgment on the degree to which his philosophy was compromised
by pagan Neoplatonism. There are varying views, which range almost from
complete faithfulness to complete corruption. We conclude with three sum-
marizing comments.

19. Mendelson, "Saint Augustine."
20. With his statement "Because I doubt myself, I am," Augustine anticipates Descartes's
"Cogito ergo sum." On the relationship between Augustine and Descartes, see Stephen Menn,
Descartes and Augustine (Cambridge: Cambridge University Press, 1998).

First, it is clear that Augustine does not simply adopt Neoplatonism un-critically. Indeed, much of Neoplatonism is transformed and the idolatrous categories filled with biblical content, as noted above.

Yet, second, many biblical accents are muted, if not corrupted and even eclipsed, in Augustine's synthesis of the Christian faith and Platonic phi-losophy. Ultimately the verticalization, individualization, and interiorization of Augustine's philosophy devalues the significance of history as a story of God's restoration of creation. Moreover, in this context *sapientia* becomes an ability that is used only to know God and the soul and not to examine the world, which is reserved for the lower faculty of *scientia*.

Finally, we must recognize that in Augustine there is a journey toward in-creasing biblical faithfulness. Even though a Neoplatonic structure remains central to his thought until the end of his life, there is a growing recognition, from his work *Against the Academics* in 386 (3.20.43) to *Confessions* in 397–400 (7.20.26) to *The City of God* in 426 (book 8), that the gospel is not entirely compatible with Platonic philosophy.

Early Medieval Philosophy (Fifth through Eleventh Centuries)

Introduction

As Augustine lay dying in 430, the Germanic peoples were laying siege to Hippo. An amalgamation of three worldviews—Germanic-pagan, pagan-classical, and Christian—throughout the Middle Ages eventually formed European culture.

In a context of cultural poverty, some philosophers functioned as media-tors between the older pagan-classical era and the dawning era of Christian Europe. These philosophers salvaged, translated, and transmitted pagan-classical philosophy to the generations that followed. The most important of these was Boethius (480–524) and the anonymous author known as Pseudo-Dionysius (ca. 500).

From Boethius to Abélard

Boethius had one foot in the old Greco-Roman world and the other in the world now settled by the victorious invaders. He was a Roman who was trained in Athens; there he mastered the ancient philosophical tradition and the Greek and Latin languages. He was an orthodox Christian of a Neoplatonic stripe who was given a high position in the court of the Gothic ruler Theodoric. Unfortunately, he ran afoul of Theodoric, was charged with treason, and was executed in 524.

Boethius had set out for himself the ambitious program to translate and comment on all the works of Plato and Aristotle, and to show that the philosophies of these two giants were really in harmony. He had to settle for a more modest agenda. During his lengthy imprisonment, he wrote his most influential work, *The Consolation of Philosophy*, a Neoplatonic piece that sought to make sense of his bad fortune. His foremost legacy is as the primary conduit by which the Greek philosophical tradition was passed along in Latin to later scholars in the Middle Ages.

Boethius was a Neoplatonist. Much of his thought is similar to Augustine's; however, Boethius was not as careful to transform the pagan Platonism by the gospel. In both his epistemology and his ontology, the primary issue Boethius struggled with was the problem of universals. He passed along this problem to future philosophers in the medieval period right down to Aquinas. True knowledge and morality depends on knowing universal truth that transcends the particulars of any historical context. Were these universals only conceptions in the mind (nominalism), or did they have real existence apart from particular things (realism)? Boethius believed that universals were not simply concepts but had real incorporeal existence in particular things as they reflected the ideas in the mind of God. His lengthy discussion produced various battles throughout the medieval period between the realists and later nominalists, to which Aquinas would finally offer a resolution.

Like Augustine before him, Boethius articulated in a letter to the pope an important Scholastic dictum: "As far as possible, join faith to reason." Gilson comments that "this is precisely the reason why he is rightly considered as one of the founders of scholasticism."[21] In Boethius's works on the Trinity we get a glimpse into the way reason and faith are to be joined. Reason is employed to rationally examine the dogma that is accepted in faith on the authority of scriptural revelation. Reason is thus pressed into the service of theology. But interestingly, when Boethius writes on the Trinity, "not a single Bible quotation is to be found in these tractates, even though they deal with virtually exclusively theological subjects. Logic and analysis is all."[22] On the basis of faith one accepts the content of revelation, and then autonomous reason is employed to examine that content independent of any reference to Scripture. Thus, in this way, faith is joined to reason. Here we see the Scholastic principle: "Philosophy could stand on its own virtues apart from, and yet complementary to, theology."[23]

21. Gilson, *History of Christian Philosophy*, 106.
22. Josef Pieper, *Scholasticism: Personalities and Problems of Medieval Philosophy*, trans. Richard Winston and Clara Winston (New York: McGraw-Hill, 1964), 38.
23. Richard Tarnas, *The Passion of the Western Mind: Understanding the Ideas That Have Shaped Our World View* (New York: Ballantine, 1991), 181.

Another set of writings that has exercised extraordinary influence on the history of philosophy is a Neoplatonic work written under the pseudonym Dionysius the Areopagite. Dionysius was a member of the Areopagus in Athens and was one of the people who heard the gospel from Paul during Paul's visit to the city and believed, becoming a follower of Jesus (Acts 17:34). An unknown person wrote a work in about AD 500 claiming to be Dionysius. He sought to harmonize the Christian faith with Neoplatonic philosophy. Remarkably, by the beginning of the seventh century this work was considered to have almost canonical authority because Dionysius was a disciple of Paul. It exercised enormous influence; its importance can be seen in the way that Harnack often refers to the whole early medieval tradition as the "Areopagitic-Augustinian view."[24]

In this work the lines between the gospel and Neoplatonism are blurred. A Christian understanding of creation is synthesized with the Neoplatonic notion of emanation. A hierarchy similar to Neoplatonism is articulated, with God at the top and a series of spiritual beings in between him and human beings. The spiritual ascent of the soul to union with God is accomplished through the threefold process of "purification-illumination-union," terms that later mystics employed to describe mystical ascent.

Neoplatonic influence is also present in Dionysius's *apophatic* philosophy of religious language: we cannot say positively what God is like; we can only say what he is not. Once again we see philosophy in the service of knowing God conceived as an unstable synthesis of Scripture and pagan philosophy.

After Boethius there is a period of stagnation in terms of philosophy until the eleventh century. One philosopher, however, appears during this time who is worthy of note. John Scotus Eriugena (815–77) was another significant Neoplatonist Christian who exercised formative influence on the medieval period. He was an Irish monk who went to teach in the court of the emperor of the Franks, Charles the Bald. He translated all of Pseudo-Dionysius's works into Latin and developed an intricate ontology to elaborate his Neoplatonic-Christian vision.

Eriugena's ontological hierarchy, like Augustine's, has the goal of knowing God through the Holy Scriptures. Philosophy explains true religion, which consists of humbly worshiping and rationally investigating God. Thus Eriugena can write: "No one can enter heaven except by philosophy."[25] Coming to know, worship, and understand God means one must understand the way God has structured the world so that humanity might climb that ladder back to God. Like so many of these early philosophers, Eriugena sees a religious goal to philosophy and utilizes Neoplatonic categories to realize that goal.

24. Adolf von Harnack, *History of Dogma*, trans. from the 3rd German edition by Neil Buchanan, 7 vols. (Boston: Little, Brown, 1907), e.g., 6:156, 160.
25. Maurer, *Medieval Philosophy*, 37.

Like Pseudo-Dionysius, Eriugena combines creation with emanation and offers a hierarchy that flows from God. In his book *The Division of Nature* he attempts to offer an account of the structure of the world. "Nature" for Eriugena means everything that exists, even God; so it is a synonym for reality. We might paraphrase the title as "the structure of reality." Eriugena divides the world into four basic categories: God as source (Nature that creates and is not created), ideas (Nature that is created and creates), world of things (Nature that is created and does not create), and God as goal (Nature that neither creates nor is created). In this hierarchy there is an ontological movement downward from God, through universal ideas, to the world of things, and then back to God. Not only is God the source of creation and human life; God is also the goal. The purpose of human life is finally to return to God and recover the unity that was lost.

During the tenth century, France descended into a time of decadence, political disorder, war, and violence. A glimmer of intellectual life remained in the Benedictine monasteries, as it had for three or four centuries. And yet, says Gilson, "when it is all said and done, there is for historians of philosophy little to reap on the desolate grounds which extends from the death of Eriugena up to the early eleventh-century theological controversies between 'dialecticians' and 'anti-dialecticians.'"[26] The controversy to which Gilson refers was a battle about the use of reason to explore the faith. Some manifested supreme confidence in the use of dialectical reason, while others were suspicious of or even denounced its use. Anselm (1033–1109) and his teacher Lanfranc occupied a middle position that recognized the value of reason but sought to keep it within bounds. That said, it remains that "Saint Anselm's confidence in reason's power of interpretation is unlimited,"[27] so much so that Anselm has more than once been referred to as a Christian rationalist. Josef Pieper speaks of the "peril of deductive rationalism which Anselm of Canterbury conjured up, and which thereafter lingered in Western Christianity."[28]

Anselm entered the Benedictine order and moved to become a prior and then abbot at Bec. He was physically forced to become Archbishop of Canterbury in 1093, a post he held until his death in 1109. Anselm was a devoted disciple of Augustine, and his work breathes the Neoplatonic spirit and categories of his master. But his theological and philosophical work manifests a more dialectical form that became more common in later Scholastic thought, and so Anselm has been called the father of Scholasticism.

26. Gilson, *History of Christian Philosophy*, 128.
27. Ibid., 129.
28. Pieper, *Scholasticism*, 61.

For Anselm there are two sources of knowledge—reason and faith. Two phrases capture the way Anselm understood the role of reason in relation to faith: "I believe in order to understand" and "Faith seeking understanding." In the preface of *Monologion* Anselm makes clear his methodology. In response to a request from his fellow monks, Anselm agrees to set out an argument for the existence of God that is based not on the authority of Scripture but solely on the compelling force of rational argumentation. By rational argumentation he sets out to prove the existence of God, the necessity of the Trinity, and the necessity of salvation through the incarnation. For Anselm, it is not that this argumentation will lead to faith; rather, faith is the starting point for the Christian, and one employs dialectical reason to penetrate these dogmas more deeply and to defend them against opposition. Not to do so would be negligence.

Anselm demonstrates in this position tremendous confidence in the power of reason. His argument proceeds in some cases with no reference to Scripture and in most other cases with little deep engagement with Scripture. It is through rational argumentation that the necessity of the Christian faith can be demonstrated.

Anselm is especially known in history for what has been called the ontological proof for God's existence. The argument goes like this: God is a being than which nothing greater can be conceived. Therefore, God must exist. For if God did not exist, we could conceive of a greater being—that is, one that does exist, since a being that exists is always greater than a being that does not exist. While it is difficult to refute this argument, at a naive level one cannot suppress the nagging sense that there is something specious about it. It was subjected to ridicule and refutation immediately in Anselm's day and has been since; the conversation about its validity continues to this day.[29]

The second philosopher at the boundary of the early and later medieval period is Peter Abélard (1079–1142). His was a life full of controversy as he moved from place to place, always drawing students and making new enemies. The most notorious event of his life was the seduction of Héloïse—his sixteen-year-old student—while he was master at Notre Dame school. They had a child together and then were secretly wed. Unfortunately, this romance was not a happily-ever-after affair. When Héloïse's guardian found out, he ordered a gruesome revenge carried out by two thugs, who attacked and castrated Abélard. His life also ended in controversy. He was condemned by a council at Sens in 1140 for nineteen heresies. Yet his place in the history of philosophy is secured by two things: his contribution to logic and to the development of

29. See Alvin Plantinga, ed., *The Ontological Argument from St. Anselm to Contemporary Philosophers* (London: Macmillan, 1968).

the Scholastic method. There are three areas in which Abélard utilized his dialectical powers of logic: the problem of universals, ethics, and theology.

As regards universals, Abélard argued that they are not real things or essences but a name that describes real likenesses or resemblances that certain things really have in common. In ethics, he examined intentionality, or motivation, and concluded that acts are not to be judged by an objective moral order but by intentionality alone. In theology, Abélard established the foundation for the Scholastic method in his work *Sic et Non* (Yes and No). Here he gathered conflicting opinions from biblical and patristic sources on 150 theological topics and placed them beside one another to stimulate reflection. He believed these divergent positions could be reconciled through the proper use of dialectical reason. Later, Peter Lombard (1100–1160) authored a book titled *Sentences* that employed this theological method and became a standard textbook in the universities.

Abélard stands out as by far the most important philosopher of this period and is known for his vigorous exercise of reason in matters of faith. His opponent Bernard of Clairvaux (1090–1153) commented that Abélard "presumes to imagine that he can entirely comprehend God by the use of his reason."[30] Indeed, Abélard did believe that dialectical reason must be enlisted to buttress matters of faith. However, he would be misunderstood if he was seen as an advocate of reason over faith. He wrote to Héloïse near the end of his life: "I do not want to be a philosopher if it is necessary to deny Paul. I do not want to be Aristotle if it is necessary to be separated from Christ. For there is no other name under heaven whereby I must be saved (Acts 4:12)."[31] Reason was employed in the service of faith.

Abélard was the last major philosopher before the seismic changes that shook Europe and transformed philosophy as a discipline. To those changes we turn in the next chapter.

Summary and Conclusion

The appreciation for human reason and the task of rightly relating the human rational capacity to faith are important insights that arise from this period of medieval synthesis. Rationality is a good gift from God, and the Greeks fully explored this creational gift. The attempt by medieval Christian philosophers to embrace and purify their insights was an important struggle. However, too often these Christian philosophers left untouched the autonomy of reason. Thus a dualism between two sources of knowledge—one from revelation and one from reason—plagued the whole discussion.

30. Quoted in Pieper, *Scholasticism*, 83.
31. Quoted in Maurer, *Medieval Philosophy*, 59–60.

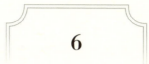

6

The Middle Ages

Aristotle Rediscovered

From: percy@secular.edu
To: abby@longobedience.edu
Subject: The Dark Ages

Hey Abby,
Surprised to hear that you are doing quite a bit of work on Augustine and Aquinas. As you suggested, I have been reading Augustine's *Confessions*; quite fascinating. I also dipped into Thomas Aquinas's *Summa Theologica*—a Catholic friend, Roy, swears by it—but found it hard going. Not a style I am used to. Roy thinks that far from the medieval period being the "dark ages," it was *the golden age* of Christian philosophy. Thoughts?

As ever,

Percy

Late Medieval Scholasticism (Twelfth through Fourteenth Centuries)

Introduction

During the first half of the medieval period, life was oriented upward to another world, and life in this world was diminished. However, when a good aspect of God's creation is suppressed, like a tightly coiled spring it will finally snap back. Indeed, this is what begins to happen after the year 1000. A new interest in this world began to envelop medieval society, and a cultural renewal took place—a renewal that dramatically affected philosophy.

After several centuries of wars and invasions, Europe achieved a measure of stability, and social and cultural activity quickened. As a part of this cultural renaissance there were "three innovating impulses"[1] in the thirteenth century that transformed philosophy in the late Middle Ages: the founding of the university as a new educational institution, which resulted in a dramatic increase in scholarly work and an exponential increase in the number of philosophers; the translations of numerous classical authors; and the establishment of the *mendicant orders* (Franciscans, Dominicans). The five greatest philosophers of the late medieval period all belonged to one of these orders: Albert the Great and Thomas Aquinas were Dominicans, and Bonaventure, John Duns Scotus, and William of Ockham were Franciscans.

In this context of cultural revival, the work of Aristotle was introduced. Exposure to his philosophy—with its fine-tuned reasoning, empiricist spirit, and remarkable encyclopedic breadth—was dazzling and shocking to those trained in an Augustinian Neoplatonic vision. Much of Aristotle's philosophy directly contradicted Christian doctrine—for example, that the world is eternal, that the human soul is not immortal, and that God does not providentially rule the world. Although the church sought to resist the emerging Aristotelianism, by the mid-thirteenth century, teaching his philosophy was commonplace and well established in the curriculum. The process of synthesizing an otherworldly Platonic form of the Christian faith with this new philosophy was the dominant project to which the philosophers of the time devoted themselves.

The basic aspiration remained the same: harmonize faith with reason. But with the introduction of Aristotle, reason took on a new meaning. Reason now included a focus on this creation and a new interest in the senses, in observation and experiment as essential to the knowing process. It was the remarkable achievement of Thomas Aquinas (1225–74) to accomplish this synthesis. But he was led on the way by his teacher Albertus Magnus (1206–80).

Albert the Great

The first philosopher to take up the Aristotelian challenge seriously was Albertus Magnus. His encyclopedic mind mastered all the current knowledge of the day. Despite an active ecclesiastical life, he still managed to be one of the most prolific authors during the entire medieval period.

1. Anthony Kenny, *Medieval Philosophy*, vol. 2 of *A New History of Western Philosophy* (Oxford: Clarendon, 2005), 57.

Albert had two firm commitments. The first was to the Bible and the Christian faith as it had been received and handed down in the church fathers. This meant an embrace of the Neoplatonic form in which the Christian faith had been cast. The second was to the growing volume of knowledge of the natural world that was emerging through Aristotle's work and a new appreciation for human reason. While many during Albert's time would see these two loyalties as antithetical, Albert saw no incompatibility. He set out to master Aristotle and introduce him to the medieval world. Yet "the tremendous abundance of material heaped up in Albert's works was still incommensurate with his powers of assimilation."[2] Aristotelian and Neoplatonic strands lay side by side unharmonized, sometimes shaped by Arabic and other times by Christian sources, and so Albert's work has been variously labeled by his interpreters as Aristotelian or Neoplatonic. "Albert's was a nature given more to conquest than to establishing order. The task of integration was left to his pupil, Thomas Aquinas."[3]

Nevertheless, Albert did introduce a distinction that would form the foundation for Thomas's thought. He distinguished between knowledge that came from revelation (theology) and knowledge derived from the natural world (science). Knowledge of the natural world must begin with an empirical encounter with creation, since God has created the world and has given the various creatures their own particular being. Moreover, since the soul is immersed in the body, the intellect depends on the senses for knowledge. Thus it is only through observation and experiment that the particular nature of these creatures can be known. Empirical reason apart from faith and revelation is capable of a true knowledge of the natural world. Yet reason is insufficient to gain knowledge of theological matters; theological knowledge is dependent on revelation.

The Summit of Scholastic Medieval Philosophy: Thomas Aquinas

Because of his massive bulk and shy nature, fellow students of Thomas Aquinas at Cologne not so kindly dubbed him the "Dumb Ox." Yet the schoolmaster, Albert the Great, perhaps the greatest scholar alive at that moment, saw something more in Thomas during his performance in a Scholastic disputation[4] and prophesied famously: "We call him the Dumb Ox, but the bellowings of that

2. Josef Pieper, *Scholasticism: Personalities and Problems of Medieval Philosophy*, trans. Richard Winston and Clara Winston (New York: McGraw-Hill, 1964), 113.
3. Ibid.
4. A formalized method of debate used during the medieval period for pedagogical purposes.

ox will resound throughout the whole world."[5] Undoubtedly the high point of philosophy in the high medieval period, Thomas's remarkably comprehensive synthesis of the gospel, Augustinian Christianity, and Platonic and Aristotelian philosophy established a tradition that would dominate not only the Christian faith but the whole history of Western civilization.

The Life and Times of Thomas Aquinas

Thomas was born in 1224 or 1225 to the prominent clan of Aquino. His family had high ambitions for him, and he was given to the powerful abbey of Monte Cassino as an "offered child" for his religious and intellectual training. At fifteen he was moved to Naples, where he studied the liberal arts: the trivium and quadrivium.[6] Here he encountered two things that would shape his life: Dominicans and Aristotle's work. In Naples, Aristotle's work had not been banned, as it was in Paris, and it was here that Thomas got his first exposure to the great philosopher. He also encountered the evangelical Dominicans, a freshly organized order committed to voluntary poverty, holiness, serious engagement with Scripture, and the preaching of the gospel. The Dominicans were also committed to academic study and aligned themselves with the newly established universities. All this appealed to Thomas, and so at nineteen he decided to become a Dominican. This decision did not sit well with his family, and he was abducted by his brothers. Thomas was finally released two years later and headed for Paris in 1245. For the next three years in Paris and four more years in Cologne, Thomas had the good fortune of coming under the tutelage of Albert the Great, which set the course of his life.

Thomas returned to Paris in 1252 at the age of twenty-seven. There he would spend the remaining twenty-plus years of his life. During his first four or five years at Paris he lectured on Scripture and theology, specifically on the *Books of Sentences* by Peter Lombard. This well-established theological textbook was a systematic collection of texts from the church fathers, especially Augustine, on the subjects of God, creation, Christ, redemption, sacraments, and eschatology. Thus, Thomas imbibed deeply the Augustinian theological tradition.

In 1256 Thomas was made a magister, or professor, of theology. What faced him in Paris and continued to form the context of his life's work was the turmoil that surrounded the introduction of Aristotle. There were those

5. James A. Weisheipl, *Friar Thomas D'Aquino* (Washington, DC: Catholic University Press of America, 1974), 44–45.

6. The trivium were the three subjects taught first—grammar, logic, and rhetoric. The four subjects of the quadrivium were arithmetic, geometry, astronomy, and music. Together they comprised a curriculum that was considered foundational for the study of philosophy.

like Siger of Brabant—sometimes called "Latin Averroists" because of their commitment to Aristotle as interpreted by Averroës—who had embraced Aristotle uncritically with little concern for the truth of Christian revelation. Among the Averroists, the danger of secularism, naturalism, and rationalism was very real. There were also the highly influential "medieval Augustinians" like Bonaventure and John Peckham who continued to defend the traditional otherworldliness of Augustinian theology against the incursion of Aristotle. Thomas rejected both paths and set for himself the Herculean life task of understanding and incorporating Aristotle into the orthodox Christian theology of the Augustinian tradition. Throughout his writings he refers to Aristotle as "the Philosopher."

Thomas's best-known works are his two *summae*—one against the gentiles (*Summa Contra Gentiles*) and one positively expositing the Christian faith (*Summa Theologica*). Both offer comprehensive accounts of the Christian faith that survey the same field—God, the world, and humanity. Moreover, both employ the Neoplatonic cyclical structure coupled with Aristotle's notion of teleology that the world's purpose is directed to God as the Highest Form. In the first section of both works all things emerge (*exitus*) *from* God (God as origin), while in the second part all things return (*reditus*) *to* God (God as goal). But the works serve two different purposes: *Summa Contra Gentiles* serves an apologetic and missionary purpose in equipping Christians for their missionary encounter with Muslims, Jews, or heretics. Here it is necessary to "have recourse to the natural reason, to which all men are forced to give their assent."[7] *Summa Theologica* has the more positive purpose of systematically surveying Christian doctrine for beginners in theology. Throughout, the truth of the Christian faith and the authority of revelation is assumed and cited.

Thomas was first and foremost a Christian, a disciple of Christ who as a scholar, teacher, and preacher was committed to Scripture and the importance of prayer for scholarship. Thomas's habit of prayer was exemplary. Shortly after his death, one of Aquinas's secretaries, Reginald of Piperno, commented that

> always, before he studied or disputed or lectured or wrote or dictated, he would pray from the heart, begging with tears to be shown the truth about the divine things that he had to investigate. . . . And when any difficulty arose he . . . had recourse to prayer, whereupon the matter would become wonderfully clear to him. Thus, in his soul, intellect and desire somehow contained each other, the two faculties freely serving one another in such a way that each in turn took the lead: his desire, through prayer, gained access to divine realities, which then

7. Thomas Aquinas, *Summa Contra Gentiles*, ed. Joseph Kenny (New York: Hanover House, 1955–57), 1, 2, 3.

---

the intellect, deeply apprehending, drew into a light which kindled to greater intensity the flame of love.[8]

Aidan Nichols notes of Thomas's theological method that "it is worth noting at the outset how comparatively little Thomas has to say about this subject. He did not get lost in methodology, or entangled by an oversophisticated and ultimately obfuscating hermeneutics. He took his Bible, a decent metaphysics, the antecedent theological tradition, and got on with the job."[9] As André Hayen puts it, Thomas "seeks to be faithful to the deeper intention of Saint Augustine, as well as to that of Aristotle; the deeper aim of human reason as well as of divine faith."[10]

As a theologian Thomas employed philosophy to offer a more faithful and comprehensive theological vision of the world in the service of the church. His appropriation of Aristotle was "for the sake of people in the present with a theological and pastoral intent."[11] Owens notes that "Aquinas did all his writing as a theologian, not as a philosopher. Nevertheless, his Aristotelian formation permeates this theological work. To use his own metaphor, the water of philosophy was absorbed into the wine of theology. Yet, it remained philosophy. . . . Philosophy was essential to his theological thinking as water is to wine, even though the water might be separated merely by distillation."[12] Thus, if we are to discern Thomas's philosophy, we must distill his philosophical beliefs from his theological work as one distills water from wine.

Starting Points and the Two-Story Structure

Thomas's foundational allegiance was threefold:

1. to the Augustinian medieval theological tradition,
2. to Aristotelian philosophy with its analytical tools and appreciation of the natural world and its lawfulness, and
3. to the Bible as God's revelation that can correct and critique both Augustine and Aristotle.

8. *The Life of Saint Thomas Aquinas: Biographical Documents*, trans. and ed. Kenelm Foster (London: Longmans, Green, and Company, 1959), 70n44.

9. Aidan Nichols, *Discovering Aquinas: An Introduction to His Life, Work and Influence* (London: DLT, 2002), 167.

10. André Hayen, quoted in Josef Pieper, *Guide to Aquinas*, trans. Richard Winston and Clara Winston (San Francisco: Ignatius, 1962), 21.

11. Hans Küng, *Great Christian Thinkers*, trans. John Bowden (New York: Continuum, 1995), 106.

12. Joseph Owens, "Aristotle and Aquinas," in *The Cambridge Companion to Aquinas*, ed. Norman Kretzmann and Eleonore Stump (Cambridge: Cambridge University Press, 1993), 38.

Whether his ultimate synthesis faithfully and sufficiently in light of Scripture corrected Augustinian Platonism or Aristotle's naturalism and rationalism remains the critical question. As G. K. Chesterton poses the question, did Thomas bring Aristotle to Christ or Christ to Aristotle?[13]

Aquinas's quest was to incorporate the philosophy of Aristotle, with its focus on the earthly realm, into the prevailing Augustinian theological tradition, with its focus on the heavenly realm. "The task presented by the age itself, then, was this: to effect a legitimate union between the two realms that threatened to break apart by their own mutual repulsion."[14]

First, Aquinas sees the biblical insights in Aristotle. According to the Bible, the creation is good. In his commentary on the book of John, Aquinas affirms that there are three different uses of the word *world*, and two are positive: the world as created good and the world as renewed by Christ. The third use is the "creation" as it is twisted by sin.[15] Thus the created world is good: sexuality is good, the body is good, sensuality and passion are good, even anger is good.[16] God created the world with its order, each creature with its own nature, and humanity in God's image with the rational capability of understanding this world. Thomas affirms the natural world on the basis of not only the good creation but also the incarnation and sacraments—both are material in nature. Thus the otherworldly diminishment of the natural world is not Christian, and Aristotle's high evaluation of it must be embraced. Moreover, human rationality and creation's order permit the development of a rational knowledge of the world. As Chesterton notes, intriguingly, both Francis (1181–1226), the venerated monk who founded the Franciscan order, and Thomas were seeking to recover the doctrine of the incarnation with its affirmation of creation.

Yet in all this Aquinas did not lose Augustine's verticalized "Godward orientation": this knowledge would ultimately lead our minds to God. Harnack comments that the whole of Thomas's system leads to this. "Just as the perfect Gothic Cathedral . . . expresses a single architectural thought, and subordinates all to this, even making all practical needs of worship serviceable to it, so this structure of thought . . . still proclaims the *one* thought, that the soul has had its origin in God, and returns to Him through Christ, and even the Augustinian-Areopagite turn given to this thought, that God *is* all in all, is not denied by Thomas."[17]

13. G. K. Chesterton, *St. Thomas Aquinas: "The Dumb Ox"* (New York: Doubleday, 1956), 10.

14. Pieper, *Guide to Aquinas*, 120.

15. Thomas Aquinas, *Commentary on the Gospel of St. John; Part I: Chapters 1–7*, trans. James A. Weisheipl (New York: Magi, 1998), 1, Lecture 5, 128. Commentary on John 1:10.

16. See Pieper, *Guide to Aquinas*, 122, 174, for references in Aquinas.

17. Adolf von Harnack, *History of Dogma*, trans. from the 3rd German edition by Neil Buchanan, 7 vols. (Boston: Little, Brown, 1907), 6:160.

But Thomas does more than affirm creation; he relates the natural realm of Aristotle to the spiritual realm of the Augustinian theological tradition in a hierarchical way. There are two realms, but the upper spiritual realm of grace is needed to make up for the deficiencies of the lower realm of nature. Thomas distinguishes between the natural and the supernatural. His "starting point is to be two spheres, two levels of knowledge, metaphorically *two storeys*, which are clearly distinguished but not simply separated: one of higher certainty, the other fundamental and rationally clearly superior, both of which are in the last resort not contradictory but in fundamental accord."[18] Reason functions in the lower realm to gain knowledge, and faith in the upper realm; natural law gives knowledge in the lower realm, revelation in the upper realm; philosophical knowledge founded on the natural light of reason is proper to the lower realm, and theology is the product of faith in revelation in the upper realm. In this synthesis grace *perfects and completes* nature but does not destroy it. "Revelation does not basically oppose human philosophy (though it will oppose *false*, incorrect philosophy), but rather supplements it and bring it to completion and perfection. Thomas's system is like a two-story house: Aristotelian philosophy provides the foundation and the first story; Catholic theology perfects and completes it by adding the second story and the roof (with the assistance of philosophy)."[19] Philosophy thus can stand on its own; it has its own value apart from its service to theology.

Upper Story	Grace	Faith	Revelation	Augustinian Theology
Lower Story	Nature	Reason	Natural Laws	Aristotelian Philosophy

Grace completes, supplements, perfects, fulfills nature. All these words indicate that the lower story is not twisted and corrupted but simply incomplete. Reason will take you so far (reliably), but it is insufficient. Faith and revelation must add more and complete it. Philosophy can take you so far up the ladder of truth, but theology takes you the rest of the way.

The question is whether or not this way of relating grace to nature is sufficiently radical. Does it sufficiently subvert and challenge the naturalism and rationalism of Aristotle? Does it have a strong enough view of sin and what sin has done to the "natural realm" and reason? Does it have a strong enough view of grace and how grace transforms (not simply completes) the natural realm and human reason? Has the autonomy of reason been sufficiently challenged—do we see how it is vitiated by sin and the need for grace to redirect it? Put another way, is Thomas as radical in dealing with pagan philosophy

18. Küng, *Great Christian Thinkers*, 111.
19. Tony Lane, *The Lion Concise Book of Christian Thought* (Herts, UK: Lion, 1984), 94–95.

as the New Testament? Is a Christian appropriation only fulfillment, or is it also subversive or contradictive fulfillment?[20] There is no doubt that Aquinas has transformed and given new meaning to Aristotle's philosophy. One cannot question that he reconciled Aristotle to Christ. But is that transformation sufficiently radical, or is there still much in the structure of his thought where he has brought Christ to Aristotle?

We see how this synthetic structure works, for example, in the doctrine of God—a theological rather than a philosophical doctrine, to be sure. Reason can enable us to see *that* God exists, but revelation tells us *who* he is. Thomas employs five proofs or *ways* for the existence of God:

if there is motion in the creation, there must be a Mover;

if there are various effects in creation, there must be an Efficient Cause;

if there is possible existence in the creation, there must be Necessary Existence;

if there are degrees of perfection in the world, there must be Perfection; and

if there is order in the creation, there must be an Intelligent Being that orders it.

All of these arguments are based on sense experience of the creation and employ causality to move to God's existence. However, these proofs can at best prove only that God exists, not who he is—the personal triune God. Revelation must supplement natural theology to provide this extra information.

Thomas Aquinas's Anthropology, Epistemology, and Ontology

In his anthropology, Thomas maintains the Greek and Christian medieval dualism of body and soul, with an emphasis on the freedom and rationality of the soul. However, the influence of Aristotle leads Aquinas to value the body and its senses much more highly. But it isn't only Aristotle: it is also the biblical hope of the resurrection of the body. The body is necessary for human existence. Indeed, while the soul is immortal in the sense that it can exist apart from the body, such a state is unnatural and points forward to the resurrection of the body. And so Thomas believes that there is a very close union between body and soul. He employs Aristotelian terminology of form and matter: the rational soul is the substantial form of the body. Over against the prevailing theological assumption that the invisible soul is most like God precisely in its

20. This is the language of Hendrik Kraemer, "Continuity and Discontinuity," in *The Authority of the Faith*, by the International Missionary Council, Tambaram Series 1 (London: Oxford University Press, 1939), 4.

invisibility, Thomas contends that the whole person—body and soul—is in God's image. "The soul united with the body is more like God than the soul separated from the body because it (the soul in the body) possesses its nature in more complete fashion."[21] This affirmation has important implications, such as that bodily life, including sexuality, is good and that the senses are important for knowledge.

Nevertheless, the valuation of the spiritual over the material remains. Thomas distinguishes even in prefall Adam a distinction between the higher (spiritual) and lower (material) parts of his nature. A prizing of the spiritual over material is especially evident in Thomas's hierarchy of perfection. In the human person, there is a hierarchy of powers from the purely physical (e.g., heart beating), to the senses, to the highest power, which is intellectual.

Thomas's attention to Aristotle also deeply impacts his ontology. Since God has created all creatures after their own kind, there is order in the world. Drawing on Aristotle, Thomas speaks of the various forms or types in matter that make creatures what they are. These ideas or forms were in the mind of God and functioned as a blueprint does for a builder when God created the world. But these forms also make a substance what it is. We must remember also that with Aristotle these forms not only made a thing what it was but also were the principle of dynamic change. The creation was not a static order but a dynamic one.

An important distinction in Aquinas's thought protects his theology from the naturalism of Aristotle—the distinction between existence (that something exists) and essence (what it is). There is human (essence) being (existence), or angelic (essence) being (existence), or animal (essence) being (existence). Only in God are existence and essence one. Yet God in an act of free love communicates his being to his creation. Thus the creation and all its creatures exist because they participate or share in his being. Here Aquinas affirms the Platonic notion of participation; however, the participation is not of individual entities participating in an ideal form. Rather, each creature, indeed the whole creation, participates in the being of God. In this way the creation is deeply dependent on God. "For the being of every creature depends on God, so that not for a moment could it subsist, but would fall into nothingness were it not kept in being by the operation of the Divine power."[22]

In this emphasis on creation in the way of Aristotelian terminology, we must ask about sin and evil in the world. Aquinas's dependence on Aristotle seems to offer an inadequate answer to the power, scope, and gravity of sin.

21. Quoted in Pieper, *Guide to Aquinas*, 122.
22. Thomas Aquinas, *Summa Theologica*, in 5 vols. (Notre Dame, IN: Ave Maria, 1948), 1a, 104, 1.

The finite character of created being also accounts for the deficiencies and physical evils we find in it. Evil is not a being: every being as such is good, for it is a reflection of the divine being, which is supremely good. Evil is the absence in a being of what it should naturally possess. . . . God is not the cause of such evils. . . . But he may be said to cause evil *per accidens*, inasmuch as he has willed to create a finite universe in which the interplay of secondary causes can introduce deficiencies and physical defects into creatures. Moral evil results from the free will of man, and it is but another sign of the limitation found in anything created.[23]

Aquinas's epistemology flows from both his anthropology and his ontology. The tight unity of body and soul means that all knowledge must flow first through the senses. "Now it is natural to man to attain to intellectual truths through sensible objects, because all our knowledge originates from sense."[24] Knowledge moves from the concrete, which is observed by the senses, to the universal, which is perceived by the intellect. It is the function of the intellect to "abstract intelligible natures from these likenesses by disengaging the universal from the particular; for example, the nature of man from the particular characteristics of individual men."[25] For Augustine, divine illumination enables humanity to know the universal, but for Aquinas, the natural light of reason is capable of coming to true knowledge.

Following Albert the Great, Aquinas offers resolution to the ongoing problem of universals in medieval philosophy. For the realist, the universal "really exists" either in a spiritual world or in the entity itself. Much of the medieval theological tradition followed Augustine in the belief that these ideals really exist in God's mind. However, the nominalist reaction believed that these ideas exist just in the mind; universals are mere names (*nomina*). Thomas sees these universals existing in three ways: as patterns in the mind of God, as essential forms in the actual creature, and as concepts in the mind. Thus in the threefold elaboration of the universal there is a foundation for true knowledge. An identity of thought (concept in the mind) and being (form in the creature) is rooted in the transcendent God and his creational blueprint. Thus true knowledge takes place when the intellect conforms to the thing itself and finds its being and nature in God's creation.

Again it must be noted that Aquinas never lost the Augustinian sense of God as the ultimate goal of the creation. All knowledge ultimately finds its final goal in God, beginning now in faith and culminating in the beatific vision

23. Quoted in Armand A. Maurer, *Medieval Philosophy*, rev. ed. (Toronto: Pontifical Institute of Medieval Studies, 1982), 184.

24. Aquinas, *Summa Theologica*, 1a, 1, 9.

25. Maurer, *Medieval Philosophy*, 184.

of God. Following Augustine, Aquinas believed that God alone will satisfy human longing. "Now the object of the will, *i.e.*, of man's appetite, is the universal good; just as the object of the intellect is the universal true. Hence it is evident that naught can lull man's will, save the universal good. This is to be found, not in any creature, but in God alone; because every creature has goodness by participation."[26]

Evaluation

Albertus Magnus was surely right: the bellowing of the dumb ox has been heard throughout the world. Thomas "exercised . . . an enduring influence on the period that followed, and his influence is still at work at the present day."[27] From the standpoint of later Western history, Richard Tarnas correctly pinpoints perhaps Aquinas's greatest contribution when he says that the "extraordinary impact Aquinas had on Western thought lay especially in his conviction that the judicious exercise of man's empirical and rational intelligence, which had been developed and empowered by the Greeks, could now marvelously serve the Christian cause." But what makes it difficult to evaluate this extraordinary impact is what Tarnas says on the next page: "Thus Aquinas gave to Aristotelian thought a new religious significance—or, as it has been said, Aquinas converted Aristotle to Christianity and baptized him. Yet it is equally true that in the long run Aquinas converted medieval Christianity to Aristotle and to the values Aristotle represented."[28] There lies the crux of the matter: was Aristotle converted to Christianity or was Christianity converted to Aristotle? The answer is both, of course. But how various components of this matter are weighted and elaborated makes quite a difference.

There is a strong Protestant critique that sees the synthesis that Aquinas constructed as dualistic. Herman Dooyeweerd believed that Aquinas constructed an "artificial synthesis between the Christian and Greek world of Ideas"[29] that combined two different religious spirits—that of creation-fall-redemption and that of nature/grace. Aquinas split the world into the natural and supernatural and restricted the scope of the fall and redemption to the supernatural. Thus sin does not corrupt the deepest religious root of humanity; humanity is only weakened by the fall and so maintains "an autonomy—a relative independence

26. Thomas Aquinas, *Summa Theologica*, 1a, 2ae, 2, 8.

27. Harnack, *History of Dogma*, 6:155.

28. Richard Tarnas, *The Passion of the Western Mind: Understanding the Ideas That Have Shaped Our World View* (New York: Ballantine, 1991), 188–89.

29. Herman Dooyeweerd, *A New Critique of Theoretical Thought*, trans. David H. Freeman and William S. Young, 4 vols. (Jordan Station, ON: Paideia, 1984), 1:183.

and self-determination" in the realm of nature. So, too, is nature "independent, losing every point of contact with grace."[30]

Those who offer such a critique see the secularism that results in Western
culture as the fault of this synthesis. Hans Küng summarizes the result.

> Modernity was to draw conclusions from this: a belief in God apart from the
> world and a worldliness without faith, an unreal God and a godless reality. That
> was of course the last thing that Thomas himself intended. But was his grandiose
> and balanced synthesis between reason and faith, nature and grace, philosophy
> and theology, secular and spiritual power sufficiently protected against this
> split? . . . In connection with the history of his influence the fact cannot be
> overlooked that the Christian medieval synthesis presented by Thomas is one
> of extreme tension, and in the dynamic of historical development had effects
> which were to prove self-destructive: there was to be an unprecedented and all-
> embracing *movement of secularization and emancipation* "at the lower level."[31]

Others, including Josef Pieper and Étienne Gilson, offer high praise of
Thomas Aquinas. They see his comprehensive and unified synthesis as a pin-
nacle in the history of philosophy. Pieper believes that "the very special status
accorded to St. Thomas . . . cannot very well mean anything but this: that
in his works he succeeded in stating the whole truth in a unique, exemplary
fashion."[32]

We are not as enamored with the great synthesis of Thomas as are Gilson
and Pieper. There is to our minds an inherent structural instability to the
whole framework. On the other hand, it is likely that Dooyeweerd's critique,
like many others, is more indebted to the then-contemporary Thomists' interpretation of Aquinas.[33]

There is much in the great Thomas to be commended. But in terms of his
overall system the question is, what does "perfect" entail in relation to grace
perfecting nature? It seems that the problem with the language of perfecting
the imperfect, completing the incomplete, fulfilling what is lacking, is that
grace adds something to nature. To be sure, there is in Thomas also correction.

30. Herman Dooyeweerd, *Roots of Western Culture: Pagan, Secular, and Christian Options*,
trans. John Kraay (Toronto: Wedge, 1979), 117–18.

31. Hans Küng, *Christianity: Essence, History, and Future* (New York: Continuum, 1995),
425–26 (italics in the original); cf. 685–86.

32. Pieper, *Guide to Aquinas*, 20.

33. Cf. Arvin Vos, *Aquinas, Calvin, and Contemporary Protestant Thought: A Critique of
Protestant Views on the Thought of Thomas Aquinas* (Washington, DC: Christian University
Press; Grand Rapids: Eerdmans, 1985), 152–58. He notes that "later Thomists departed significantly from Aquinas's original teaching sometime during the sixteenth and seventeenth centuries,
and that in fact the later Thomist tradition resembles closely the position that Protestants have
long attributed to Aquinas himself" (152–53).

But there is not the needed emphasis on a fundamental correction, renewal, and transformation of what has been distorted and mangled. Human life and reason is not just incomplete but mutilated and corrupted by sin. So a question remains for us as to whether sin in its radical depth, comprehensive scope, and distorting nature finds a sufficient place in this system. Hendrik Kraemer uses language we find more congenial to the Bible: he speaks of "contradictive and subversive fulfillment" in the way that the New Testament authors dealt with non-Christian thought and practice.[34] That is, grace didn't just fulfill; it also radically subverted non-Christian thought. Grace is a transforming power that renews, restores, and reconciles all of human life, including reason.

Aquinas carefully knit two "realms" together. However, fusing two realms was not radical enough, and it is not surprising that lesser thinkers in the centuries that followed "did not always follow the careful distinctions made by Thomas."[35] Indeed, already in the next century the carefully constructed two-story structure would "increasingly . . . fall to pieces,"[36] and the realm of nature, including reason and philosophy, would be set on its autonomous way. Thus, as Pieper says, "On the distant horizon could be discerned the opposition between on the one hand a theology which distrusted *ratio*, and on the other hand that attitude of mind which Dilthey has characterized as the 'atheism of scientific thinking.'"[37]

Closely related is the question of Thomas's understanding of revelation. In spite of his fine interpretive work on Scripture, he integrated biblical insight "into the strict system of apparently timeless doctrinal principles."[38] His view of truth is fundamentally Greek—ideas that stand above history. Thus we have a tension between faith and reason: faith offers certain timeless truth about the world, and reason gains truth about the world through empirical and rational processes. How do we relate these two sources of and methods for attaining truth? Rather, we believe Lesslie Newbigin is on the right track when he says that the "dogma, the thing given for our acceptance in faith, is not a set of timeless propositions: it is a story." The Christian faith is not "a system of timeless metaphysical truths about God, nature, and man" but a story within which reason operates to make sense of the world.[39]

34. Kraemer, "Continuity and Discontinuity," 4.

35. Lesslie Newbigin, *Proper Confidence: Faith, Doubt, and Certainty in Christian Discipleship* (Grand Rapids: Eerdmans, 1995), 18.

36. F. C. Bauer, quoted in Harnack, *History of Dogma*, 6:161n1.

37. Pieper, *Scholasticism*, 135.

38. Küng, *Christianity*, 426.

39. Lesslie Newbigin, *The Gospel in a Pluralist Society* (Grand Rapids: Eerdmans, 1989), 12–13.

In the Wake of Thomas Aquinas: John Duns Scotus, William of Ockham, and the End of the Middle Ages

In response to the inexorable advance of Aristotelian philosophy, the church stated in 1277 (with a nod to Job 38:11), "This far you may come and no farther; here is where your proud reason halts." In official ecclesiastical decrees released in the cities of the two leading universities—Paris and Oxford—the heresies of the Averroists, including even some from Thomas, were condemned. Gilson sees this date as a "landmark in the history of medieval philosophy" that became a "dividing line . . . that after it the attitude of many theologians toward philosophy underwent a perceptible change whose effects are visible in their work."[40] Two contradictory streams emerged in the fourteenth century: on the one hand, a paralyzing suspicion of Aristotelian philosophy and reason, and on the other, a burgeoning empiricist spirit that continued to extend the scope of Aristotelian reason into new territory. Various historical factors combined to lead to a "complete divorce between the supernatural theology of the theologians and the natural theology of the philosophers."[41] The synthesis between faith and reason that Thomas had so carefully constructed was coming apart. This, Pieper tells us, was "the end of the Middle Ages," since that period was defined by the devotion of almost a thousand years of energy to their conjunction.[42] The most important philosophers of this period that engineered this divorce, albeit unwittingly, are John Duns Scotus (1266–1308) and William of Ockham (1288–1347).

The separation of faith and reason in both Scotus and Ockham had as its impulse the desire to protect the Christian faith from encroaching rationalism, and especially the view derived from Greek philosophy that God acts under necessity.[43] To protect the Christian faith, a corrective was required, and it came to be seen as essential to limit reason to the natural world and acknowledge only the authority of faith in theological matters. There are two kinds of truth: revelational truth available only to faith, and truth about the natural world available to reason. If these two truths are kept in their own compartments, then reason will be confined to the natural world and pose no danger. So in the fourteenth century a double-truth universe gradually emerged to keep reason in its place.

John Duns Scotus was born in Duns, Scotland, to the Duns family around 1266. He studied at Oxford, which at this time was permeated by a mathematical

---

40. Étienne Gilson, *The Spirit of Medieval Philosophy* (Notre Dame, IN: University of Notre Dame Press, 1991), 408, 385.

41. Ibid., 465.

42. Pieper, *Scholasticism*, 150–51.

43. Ibid., 137–39.

and scientific spirit that formed his subtle and tight reasoning. As a Franciscan priest, he lectured in the University of Paris until he was transferred to the Franciscan stadium at Cologne, where he died shortly thereafter at the young age of forty-two.

Scotus offers two philosophical innovations that take the first step out of the Middle Ages. The first is advocating the freedom of God; the second is a new look at the problem of universals. The battle cry of Scotus is "freedom"—especially the freedom of God. It is a reaction against what Gilson calls "Greek necessitarianism."[44] The appropriation of Aristotle's philosophy had led to a theology that articulated a view of God who *must* act in rational ways. To Scotus this is unacceptable: it threatens the very freedom of God. Rather, he believes that in creation God's will comes into play. God may have many ideas of creatures, but he can freely choose which of those creatures he desires to bring into existence. He is free to create what he wants and how he wants. It is clear that this strengthens an empiricist approach to the world. Only by observation and experiment can one grasp the creation God actually has created.

Closely tied to this is the vexing question of universals, which had dominated epistemological reflection during the medieval period. Instead of starting with the universal and seeing all particulars as parts of that whole, Scotus starts with the particular. He stresses the particularity and the individuality of specific creatures. He uses a technical Latin word, *haeccitas*, which means "thisness"—each particular and discrete particular thing has its own individuality that makes it unique. What makes this creature distinct is its very unique particularity. So, for example, Scotus emphasizes what makes Socrates unique and not that he is a particular instance of the universal "humanity," or what makes up this particular act of justice rather than its being a particular instance of universal justice. Nevertheless, he couples this notion of "thisness" with the idea of a "common nature." While each creature possesses unique individual existence, all these discrete individuals also possess characteristics in common with other individuals of the same class, genus, or species. Socrates was a specific individual, different from all others, but at the same time possessed a common nature shared with other human beings.

So the proper object of our knowledge is not the individual only, but the common natures that exist in them. For Scotus, knowledge comes through our cognitive powers of sensation and abstraction. Our senses observe the various particular individuals, but it is our intellect that has the power of abstraction. Abstraction means that we draw out of our observation what is common to the various individuals. The common nature of an object of knowledge "must

44. Étienne Gilson, *History of Christian Philosophy in the Middle Ages* (New York: Random House, 1955), 409.

be released, so to speak, from its bondage to individuals by the abstractive power of the intellect before it fulfills completely the conditions of a universal. In short, universals exist only in the intellect."[45]

Both of these modifications would encourage the empiricist spirit. Human beings must examine the world through observation and experiment if they are to understand it. The nature of God and redemption, however, can only be known by revelation. As Pieper rightly notes, "Duns Scotus's theological starting point has made the conjunction of the believed with the known every bit as difficult a matter as Siger of Brabant's secularistic-philosophical point of view. 'Double truth' comes to the fore again as a danger threatening from *both* sides."[46] Nevertheless, Scotus remained within the earlier medieval tradition. It would be left to Ockham to take the final step, but "in order to do this, he first had to eliminate those elements in Scotism that introduce some necessity into God and the universe; namely, the divine Ideas and common natures."[47]

William of Ockham was born around 1288 close to London in Ockham. Early in his life he was given to the Franciscan order, and he received his education in the prestigious school of London Greyfriars. He spent time at Oxford University studying theology and returned to the stimulating intellectual environment of Greyfriars. There he wrote most of his theological and philosophical work, which raised questions about his orthodoxy. In 1328, when he was charged with heresy, he fled Avignon and found safe haven with the Holy Roman Emperor, who was engaged in a dispute with the pope. William spent the rest of his days in Munich, writing mostly on political issues relating to a controversy with the pope about Franciscan poverty and the ownership of property. He died in 1347 at the age of sixty.

Like Scotus, Ockham set out to buttress the truth of revelation by limiting the competency of reason. Central to his whole philosophical project is his advocacy of *nominalism*: universals do not have real existence either in the mind of God or as forms in particular things. True and valid knowledge is of particulars that come through our sense experience. Marilyn McCord Adams, who has written what is widely regarded as the definitive recent treatment of Ockham, notes that

> Ockham dismissed not only Platonism, but also "modern realist" doctrines according to which natures enjoy a double mode of existence and are universal in the intellect but numerically multiplied in particulars. He argues that everything real is individual and particular, while universality is a property pertaining only to names and that by virtue of their signification relations. Because Ockham

45. Maurer, *Medieval Philosophy*, 235.
46. Pieper, *Scholasticism*, 146.
47. Maurer, *Medieval Philosophy*, 241.

understands the primary names to be mental (i.e., naturally significant concepts), his own theory of universals is best classified as a form of *conceptualism*.[48]

A second aspect of Ockham's nominalism was his program of "ontological reduction," in particular his reduction of Aristotle's list of categories from ten to two: substance and quality. This relates to one of the primary ways that people hear of Ockham—namely, in reference to "Ockham's razor." This is the principle that entities are not to be multiplied beyond necessity, so that the simpler the theory, the better. However, as Eleonore Stump perceptively comments in her comparison of Aquinas and Ockham on cognition, "A simpler theory is to be preferred to a more complicated one only if the simpler theory can explain as well what the more complicated theory can explain."[49] Ockham's nominalism required that he account for how language and thought work in relation to the world. His work in this area is complex. Claude Panaccio sums up his view of semantics and mental language as follows: "The foundation of Ockham's whole semantical system is ontological: only singular beings are accepted as real; only they can be referred to in any way, whether by natural internal concepts or by conventional words. Through a wide variety of analytical devices, Ockham consistently strives to highlight that only singular beings are needed for true knowledge and language."[50]

Ockham's consistent nominalism privileged understanding the world through empirical examination and observation. This stimulus to empiricism was strengthened by his rigorous advocacy of the omnipotency and freedom of God. God is not constrained by any rational necessity to create the world as he did. God's freedom means he could create the world any way he wanted; it also means he could redeem the world any way he wanted. It is not necessary for God to do anything that conforms to our reason. This consistent and ardent defense of God's freedom did two things: it fostered a growing empiricism, since this was the only way to know how God in fact did make the world, and it chastened reason in its reach for theological truth.[51]

It is obvious that Ockham would deny any kind of natural theology.[52] Thomas had great confidence that by the use of his senses and reason he

---

48. Marilyn McCord Adams, "Ockham, William," in *The Cambridge Dictionary of Philosophy*, 2nd ed., ed. Robert Audi (Cambridge: Cambridge University Press, 1999), 627.

49. Eleonore Stump, "The Mechanics of Cognition: Ockham on Mediating Species," in *The Cambridge Companion to Ockham*, ed. Paul Vincent Spade (Cambridge: Cambridge University Press, 1999), 194.

50. Claude Panaccio, "Semantics and Mental Language," in Spade, *Cambridge Companion to Ockham*, 71–72.

51. See Pieper, *Scholasticism*, 147–51.

52. See Alfred J. Freddoso, "Ockham on Faith and Reason," in Spade, *Cambridge Companion to Ockham*, 326–49. Freddoso describes Ockham's view as an "irenic separatism" that

could form five arguments proving the existence of God. According to Ock-ham, human reason has no such competence. The only way to know how God redeemed the world is by believing his revelation. The only way to know the natural world was by examining it, observing it, and experimenting on it, to know how God made it. Reason is confined to understanding this world; faith is able to understand revelational truth.

Thus Ockham opened up a potential double-truth universe: religious or theological truth can be known only by faith, and natural or philosophical truth can be known only by empirical reason. Ockham thereby fatally weak-ened the unity that was so carefully constructed by Aquinas. There are two truths—theological and philosophical, knowledge of revelation by faith and knowledge of the natural world by empirical reason. As Pieper notes, "In the realm of the mind . . . a progressive divergence between faith and reason was taking place. Inexorably, and justified by reasons on both sides, divorce was taking place between *fides* and *ratio*—to whose conjunction the energies of almost a thousand years had been devoted. What was taking place, in short, was the end of the Middle Ages."[53]

For Pieper the way out of the Middle Ages was thus taken by Ockham. The way of Thomas Aquinas, and indeed the whole of the medieval period, to join faith to reason was called the *via antiqua* (the old way), while the joining of nominalism to empiricism to sever this connection became known as the *via moderna* (the modern way).

With the *via moderna*, the creeping encroachment of reason had been checked. But at what cost? The basic ontological and epistemological as-sumptions that enabled Thomas to construct his synthesis were eroded. No comprehensive system was now possible. What was ultimately catastrophic was the emancipation of reason from faith. Human rationality was increas-ingly set free to operate autonomously. And since reason never functions neutrally or in a vacuum but always in service of some faith commitment, reason was now freed to serve another god. All philosophy will serve some god, some faith commitment. The task of the Christian is to see that it is the God revealed in the gospel, the faith nurtured by Scripture. The philosophy of Ockham cut off that very possibility. He set out to protect revelation from reason, but little did he know that his work would serve exactly the opposite end. In the centuries that followed, the naturalism, rationalism, and secularism first articulated by Aristotle became the dominant spirits of Western culture.

"stops short of disdaining the light of natural reason in the manner of radical intellectual separatism" (346).

53. Pieper, *Scholasticism*, 150–51.

From: abby@longobedience.edu
To: percy@secular.edu
Subject: RE: The Dark Ages

Dear Perc,

Apologies for taking a while to reply. This medieval stuff has stretched my brain something awful!! It has taken several coffees with my prof and many more with fellow students to begin to get my head around all of this. Here are my key thoughts:

a. It helps me to think—despite the gross oversimplification—of Plato = Augustine and Aristotle = Aquinas.

b. Christian philosophy is *missional* through and through. This is the enormity of Augustine's and Aquinas's achievements. They facilitated a missionary encounter of the gospel with the philosophy of their day and sought to bring every thought captive to Christ.

c. The evaluative question comes in terms of how successful they actually were in transforming Platonism and Aristotelianism. At this stage I would say "partially." Insofar as I understand them, the upward focus of Augustine and the nature/grace dichotomy in Aquinas seem problematic to me. The one detracts from the good creation, and the other has too high a view of *unaided* human reason.

So, Dark Ages or Golden Age? I would say neither but something in between.

Yours as ever,
Abby

7

The Renaissance and Reformation

From: percy@secular.edu
To: abby@longobedience.edu
Subject: Reason a whore!!

Hey Abby,
You won't believe what I discovered today. Martin Luther apparently said of reason that she is a whore; she will sleep with whoever pays the highest price! This view would NOT go down well in our philosophy course, where reason is a god. Do you think Luther held the same view of philosophy as Tertullian?

Yours,
Perc

NB: Better you don't forward this email, especially not to family members!

The Renaissance

In the figures of Scotus and Ockham we witnessed the unraveling of Aquinas's two-story house. However, it would be several centuries before that unraveling came to fruition in the Enlightenment. In between the Middle Ages and the Enlightenment lie the Renaissance and the Reformation. The Renaissance was a threshold period in which new ideas and inventions were interwoven with medieval tradition.[1] *Renaissance* means "rebirth" in French and points to a fresh discovery of the world and the changing views of what it means to be human.

---

1. It was only in the nineteenth century that the term *Renaissance* was used by Jules Michelet in his *History of France*.

The Renaissance was a period of extraordinary vitality, and even during this period people were aware that it was a new era. In 1550 the painter Vassari published his famous *Lives of the Artists*, in which he coined the phrase "the middle ages" to refer to what he saw as the degenerate period between antiquity and his time. The emergence of the universities in the twelfth century and the rediscovery of Aristotle set the context for the burst of energy in all areas of life in the Renaissance. The wealth of the later Middle Ages, the invention of intermediate technology such as the wheelbarrow, the breeding of the cart horse, and the development and spread of printing provided the catalyst for this time of renewal. "Hence," Paul Johnson notes, "the background to what we call the Renaissance was a cumulative growth and spread of wealth never before experienced in world history, and the rise of a society in which intermediate technology was becoming the norm, producing in due course a startling revolution in the way words were published and distributed."[2]

Although the Renaissance originated largely in Italy, printing was a German invention. The first best seller in this new world was Thomas à Kempis's *The Imitation of Christ*, which went through ninety-nine editions from 1471 to 1500. Apart from the Bible, it remains the most influential writing in Christian spirituality.[3] The Renaissance witnessed a remarkable flowering of culture: literature, sculpture, painting, architecture, building, science, and so on. Florence was the most influential city in the Italian Renaissance, and Dante Alighieri (1265–1321) one of its most celebrated writers. The embrace of the vernacular was central to the Renaissance throughout Europe, and Dante led this by publishing works in Italian rather than Latin, most notably his *Divine Comedy*. "Dante not only launched the Italian language as a vehicle for high art; in a sense he launched the Renaissance itself, as a new era of creative endeavor by individuals of unprecedented gifts."[4]

In their quest for renewal, Renaissance individuals looked back to antiquity and to the insights of other cultures as journeys were made and new countries discovered. Monasteries were scoured for ancient manuscripts; every attempt was made to recover the literature and art of the ancient world, and this was abetted by imports from Constantinople. A renewed interest in the study of Greek and Hebrew emerged, with major consequences for biblical studies, leading, inter alia, to Erasmus's new version of the Greek New Testament. In 1497 the Englishman John Colet, who had spent four years in Italy studying how to interpret ancient texts, gave a sensational series of lectures at Oxford on Paul's Letter to the Romans, in which he abandoned the Scholastic approach and read Romans against its historical background.

2. Paul Johnson, *The Renaissance* (London: Phoenix, 2000), 17.
3. Thomas à Kempis's *The Imitation of Christ* is shaped from the start by a Platonic *contemptus mundi* (contempt or scorn for the world) reading of Ecclesiastes inherited from Jerome.
4. Johnson, *Renaissance*, 24.

The arts exploded. Characteristic of the art of the Renaissance was its realism; the human form was realistically portrayed and celebrated. In this respect we witness a recovery of what philosopher Charles Taylor calls "the ordinary."[5] Thus Nicola Pisano (ca. 1220–84), in the marble reliefs of his Pisan pulpit, depicted real human beings with careworn faces, miles apart from the saints and angels characteristic of medieval art.

In its quest for renewal, the Renaissance inevitably became innovative as well. With the innovative side of the Renaissance emerged a doctrine of progress, which became central to modernity. The idea gained ground, not least in the arts, that modern men—which was how they saw themselves—should not only recover the glories of antiquity but build on them and surpass them. One of the Renaissance's greatest artists, Leonardo da Vinci, commented that "he is a wretched pupil who does not surpass his master."[6]

The humanists were fascinated by the world and made major advances in science. The discovery of gunpowder in Europe and the invention of the firearm facilitated new forms of the state. The invention of the compass made possible the geographical discoveries of explorers such as Columbus and Vasco da Gama. Writing in 1620, Francis Bacon asserted that "printing, gunpowder and the nautical compass . . . have changed the face and condition of things all over the globe; innumerable changes have followed; so that no empire or sect or star seems to have exercised a greater power and influence on human affairs than those mechanical things."[7]

The latter half of the twentieth century witnessed an explosion of fresh work on Renaissance philosophy, which has rightly alerted us to the complexity, dynamism, and diversity of Renaissance philosophy. Traditional views of Renaissance philosophy have been revised, deepened, and challenged, with the debate in many areas ongoing.[8] In terms of philosophy, three major traditions characterized the Renaissance.[9]

Humanism

Humanism emerged in Italy at the end of the thirteenth century. Its distinctive emphasis was the study of the classical Greek and Latin writers. The humanists

5. Charles Taylor, *Sources of the Self: The Making of the Modern Identity* (Cambridge: Cambridge University Press, 1989).

6. Johnson, *Renaissance*, 107.

7. Francis Bacon, *The New Organon*, ed. Lisa Jardine and Michael Silverthorne, Cambridge Texts in the History of Philosophy (Cambridge: Cambridge University Press, 2000), I, cxxix.

8. See James Hankins, ed., *The Cambridge Companion to Renaissance Philosophy* (Cambridge: Cambridge University Press, 2007).

9. This is a generalization; there was a serious attempt to recover *all* the ancient Greek philosophies.

devised rules for interpreting these texts and promoted imitation of the Roman authors for rhetoric and writing. They coined the phrase *studia humanitas* (study of humanity) for their focus on rhetoric, poetry, history, and ethics, and thus they called themselves "humanists." They professed disdain for the study of logic and natural philosophy, so much the concern of the Scholastics. But they were by no means antireligious. The humanists sought a type of education that formed a desirable human being, and philosophically they found—especially through Augustine—resources in Neoplatonism adequate to ethics and the religious imagination. "The Neo-Platonism of the Florentine Academy or the 'philosophy of Christ' of an Erasmus or a Lefèvre d'Étaples is a turning-away from scientific questions to the problems of the moral life and the religious imagination."[10] With its wide-ranging concerns, humanism enriched the study of philosophy in the Renaissance but did not itself produce great philosophers.

Francesco Petrarca (1304–74), known as Petrarch, is considered the father of humanism and became its great symbol. In fact, he was the major figure in the *third* generation of Italian humanists.[11] He was deeply influenced by Roman authors such as Seneca and his beloved Cicero, whose style he assimilated and embodied. Reading Augustine's *Confessions* profoundly impressed him, so that "from the moment he devoured Augustine's spiritual autobiography he was under the Father's guidance and became as much an Augustinian as was possible for a man of the fourteenth century."[12] In Petrarch's *The Secret*, Augustine appears as his confessor, to whom he pours out his inner life and sorrows. Petrarch sought to detach theology from what he saw as its dangerous link with Aristotelian naturalism and to connect it with his own style of learning. His life revolved around the struggle to reconcile the celebration of this world inspired by ancient humanism and medieval religiosity, a struggle he never resolved. "Petrarch's inner world is divided between Cicero and Augustine. . . . From the religious viewpoint he belittles what he otherwise considers to be the intellectual content and the intellectual value of life."[13]

Platonism

The rediscovered Plato was like a magnet in this context. Petrarch's program led to the translation of some of Plato's dialogues by the early humanists, and this

10. Paul O. Kristeller and John H. Randall, general introduction to *The Renaissance Philosophy of Man*, ed. Ernst Cassirer, Paul O. Kristeller, and John H. Randall (Chicago and London: Phoenix, 1948), 6.

11. James Hankins, "Humanism, Scholasticism, and Renaissance Philosophy," in Hankins, *Cambridge Companion to Renaissance Philosophy*, 39.

12. Hans Nachod, introduction to Cassirer et al., *Renaissance Philosophy of Man*, 27.

13. Ernst Cassirer, *The Individual and the Cosmos in Renaissance Philosophy* (New York: Harper & Row, 1963), 37.

was strengthened when infused with Byzantine (Neo)Platonism. Nicholas of Cusa (1401–64) was the first Western Platonist of the Renaissance. In his *On Learned Ignorance* (1440), he takes the incomprehensibility of God as his starting point and investigates epistemology in this light, thereby emphasizing the constructive dimension of our knowing. Intriguingly, Cusa's emphasis on the (platonically inspired) radical distinction between the finite and the infinite (God) led him to regard all knowledge as relative and incomplete but still attainable, since the particular is infused with the infinite. For Ernst Cassirer, "this position towards the problem of knowledge makes of Cusanus the first modern thinker."[14] More recent scholarship has been more cautious in making such a direct connection.[15] Like Petrarch, Nicholas struggled with the relationship between his faith and his public activity and search for knowledge. His solution was to deepen his understanding of Christianity. Christ, he argues, is the "bracket of the world" who embraces the finite and the infinite in one.[16] In contrast to Platonism and much medieval thought, this leads to a positive view of the world: "If man as a microcosm includes the natures of all things within himself, then *his* redemption, his rising up to the divinity, must include the ascension of all things. Nothing is isolated, cut off, or in any way rejected; nothing falls outside this fundamental religious process of redemption. Not only man rises up to God through Christ; the universe is redeemed within man and through him."[17]

Marsilio Ficino (1433–99), who led the newly established Platonist Academy of Florence, translated Plotinus as well as Plato, and even the strange natural philosophy of Francesco Patrizi embodies the framework of the Neoplatonic emanations. However, it is significant that in Ficino, "the dualistic elements of Neo-Platonism are entirely stripped off, and the monistic tendency brought out more purely and fully. On this account the Neo-Platonist of the renaissance places in the foreground *the beauty of the universe*. . . . Even the deity . . . is for him a sublime world-unity."[18]

Among the Platonists, mention should also be made of Pico della Mirandola (1463–94). In his *Oration on the Dignity of Man* (1486), he reflects on the dignity, uniqueness, and glory of humankind, an important theme in the Renaissance. In paragraph 3 God is imagined as speaking to humanity at the creation:

> We have given to thee, Adam, no fixed seat, no form of thy very own, no gift peculiarly thine, that thou mayest feel as thine own, have as thine own, possess

---

14. Ibid., 10.
15. For a moderate view see Dermot Moran, "Nicholas of Cusa and Modern Philosophy," in Hankins, *Cambridge Companion to Renaissance Philosophy*, 173–92.
16. Cassirer, *Individual and the Cosmos*, 39.
17. Ibid., 40 (italics in the original).
18. Wilhelm Windelband, *A History of Philosophy* (New York: Macmillan, 1901), 358.

as thine own the seat, the forms, the gifts which thou thyself shalt desire. . . .
Thou art confined by no bounds; and thou wilt fix laws of nature for thyself. . . .
Thou, like a judge appointed for being honorable, art the molder and maker of
thyself, thou mayest sculpt thyself into whatever shape thou prefer. Thou canst
grow downwards into the lower natures which are brutes. Thou canst again
grow upwards from thy soul's reason into the higher natures which are divine.[19]

Recent studies have rightly stressed the importance of reading this quote
in its historical context and not as an anachronistic modern assertion of the
autonomy of the human person. Nevertheless, as a Christian, in stressing
the freedom and relative autonomy of man, Pico betrayed an unbiblical sense
of human creatureliness. This emphasis on human freedom and autonomy
emerged front and center in the Enlightenment.

Philosophical Exclusivism: Aristotelianism

Aristotelianism, albeit in diverse forms, remained a, if not the, dominant
philosophy in the Renaissance and beyond. In this section our focus is on varia-
tions of Aristotelianism that stressed the autonomy of philosophy. Dominick
Iorio notes that the claim of philosophy to be an autonomous source of truth
was dealt with in four ways by the believer in the Middle Ages:[20]

1. Theological exclusivism: this is the sort of view Tertullian held, which
   privileges the gospel and theology and sees little or no value in philosophy. Bernard of Clairvaux is the outstanding example.
2. Theological reductionism: this view grants primacy to revealed truth
   but finds a place for reason in elaborating and developing theology.
   Examples are Bonaventure and Anselm.
3. Theological rationalism: faith and reason are two paths to truth, each
   with their own methods and rules of evidence. Conflicts between faith
   and reason must be resolved by appeal to faith, but reason still plays
   a significant role as handmaiden to theology and through its analysis of the natural world. Examples are Peter Lombard and Thomas
   Aquinas.
4. Philosophical reductionism (exclusivism): for this approach the adven-
   ture of philosophy has its own integrity and must be carried out on its
   own terms even if that leads it into conflict with theology and faith.
   Examples are Siger of Brabant and John of Jandun.

19. Pico della Mirandola, *On the Dignity of Man*, trans. Charles G. Wallis et al. (Indianapolis: Hackett, 1965), 4–5.
20. Dominick A. Iorio, *The Aristotelians of Renaissance Italy: A Philosophical Exploration*, Studies in the History of Philosophy 24 (Lewiston: Edwin Mellen Press, 1991), 14–18.

The third major strain of Renaissance philosophy was the humanistic Aristotelianism of thinkers like Pietro Pomponazzi of Mantua (1465–1525) and Jacopo Zabarella (1533–89), which fits into the category of philosophical exclusivism. Significantly, whereas in Paris Aristotelianism was closely bound up (positively or negatively) with theology, there were no such constraints in Italian universities. "But where Ficino and the Platonists went back to the Hellenistic world and the religious philosophies of Alexandria, the naturalistic humanism, initiated by Pomponazzi and culminating in Zabarella, built on the long tradition of Italian Aristotelianism an original philosophy in accord with the spirit of the emerging natural science and strikingly anticipatory of Spinoza."[21] This version of Aristotelianism is known as Averroism, after its chief inspiration Averroës (1126–98), a prolific Muslim commentator on the entire Aristotelian corpus.

Unlike Thomas, this approach as it developed did not hesitate to follow Aristotle where he disagreed with the Christian faith. John of Jandun, who taught in Paris during the first twenty years of the fourteenth century, acknowledged in his philosophy no authority apart from reason and experience, and as an open rationalist he mocked faith and labeled Thomas a compromising theologian. Pomponazzi's work indicated a growing intent to sever relations between philosophy and theology.[22]

One has to beware of being anachronistic in one's judgment of these Aristotelians. In making strong connections with later, modern developments in philosophy, scholars have been divided. James Hankins evocatively discerns two approaches, that of the "lumpers" and that of the "splitters."[23] The lumpers make the connections strongly with later developments in philosophy, whereas the splitters stress the differences. Of course the two approaches are not mutually exclusive and, as Hankins notes, "Any project to understand the genealogy and nature of modernity cannot fail to give Renaissance philosophy a central place."[24] Kristeller, a major "splitter," himself says of Pomponazzi that "he belongs to the long line of thinkers who have attempted to draw a clear line of distinction between reason and faith, philosophy and theology, and to establish the autonomy of reason and philosophy within their own domain, unassailable by the demands of faith, or of any claim not based on reason. . . . All those who have a stake in reason . . . should be grateful for this attitude, and embrace it for ourselves."[25] It is precisely this dichotomy

21. Kristeller and Randall, general introduction, 9.
22. See Iorio, *Aristotelians of Renaissance Italy*, 114–40.
23. James Hankins, *Humanism*, vol. 1 of *Humanism and Platonism in the Italian Renaissance* (Rome: Edizione di Storia e Letteratura, 2003), 573–90.
24. Ibid., 3.
25. Paul Oskar Kristeller, *Eight Philosophers of the Italian Renaissance* (Stanford: Stanford University Press, 1964), 90.

that leads to modernity, and it is one that we do not wish to embrace or recommend.

The increasingly naturalistic and scientific philosophy of some Aristotelians was strongly opposed by the humanists: "Thus the two great philosophic rivals in early sixteenth-century Italy are a naturalistic and an imaginative and religious humanism, with the former widespread and rapidly increasing in strength."[26] The former turned out to be very influential: the rationalists of the sixteenth century inspired the free thinkers of the seventeenth, especially in France. Galileo owes little to Platonism but much to the critical Aristotelianism of the Italian universities. Baruch Spinoza and Gottfried Leibniz demonstrate the continuing influence of Italian Aristotelianism in the mid-seventeenth century.

The Renaissance, as we noted at the outset, was a threshold period of enormous vitality. Positively, it involved a renewed fascination with *this* world. John Dewey speaks of a shift in focus "from another world to this, from the supernaturalism characteristic of the Middle Ages to delight in natural science, natural activity, and natural intercourse."[27] Many Christians were deeply involved in the Renaissance, and it is impossible to imagine the Reformation without them. Indeed, at the time it must have been hard to know what legacy the Renaissance would yield. Christianity remained prevalent, and yet the seeds of secular humanism were already present, particularly in the humanistic Aristotelianism. Ronald Wells is thus correct: "In another context, shorn of its religious casing, a new pattern of human assertiveness *will* (necessarily) issue in a secular worldview. But in the Renaissance we do not have that final break. Though the potential for it is definitely there, and will come in time, it does not happen in the fourteenth to sixteenth centuries."[28]

Thus the humanism "born again" in the fourteenth century was not to claim the status of "the light of the world" until the Enlightenment of the eighteenth century. Aquinas's two storys were coming apart: the natural world—the *saeculum*—was becoming separated from the realm of grace and also becoming the principle focus of scholarly interest. In itself, this renewed delight in God's good creation was undoubtedly a healthy development, but increasingly it would come at the cost of diminishing or even denying God's involvement and authority in this world. Thus Windelband argues that

> the *new birth of the purely theoretical spirit* is the true meaning of the scientific "Renaissance," and in this consists also its kinship *of spirit with Greek thought*, which was of decisive importance for its development. . . . Knowledge of reality

26. Kristeller and Randall, general introduction; 11.
27. John Dewey, *Reconstruction in Philosophy* (1920; repr., Boston: Beacon Press, 1957), 47–48.
28. Ronald A. Wells, *History through the Eyes of Faith* (New York: Harper Collins, 1989), 75.

appeared again as the absolute end of scientific research. . . . Its first independent intellectual activity was the return to a disinterested conception of Nature.
The whole philosophy of the Renaissance pressed toward this end, and in this
direction it achieved its greatest results.[29]

The Reformation

Ironically, Ignatius Loyola (1491–1556)—founder of the Jesuits, who led the
Counter-Reformation—and the early Reformers were contemporaries. Both
Ignatius and John Calvin, as well as Desiderius Erasmus, studied at the Collège
de Montaigu in Paris under the principalship of the influential Jan Standonck,
who had received his early education with the Brethren of the Common Life at
Gouda. Erasmus became the great symbol of the Christian humanism of the
Renaissance, and the Greek text he published of the New Testament provided
the basis for the vernacular translations of the sixteenth century, beginning
with Luther's German version in 1522. As we noted above, humanists reacted
against the Scholasticism of the previous centuries and were not uncritical of
the church. The critical question was how far their criticism would go. Erasmus
backed off from Luther's stand against the medieval church and took umbrage
at Luther over the question of the freedom of the will. Calvin followed on
from Luther and used the resources of humanism to shape the Reformation
in a major way, not least with his monumental *Institutes*. Ignatius provided
the troops for the Counter-Reformation.

We must acknowledge the Reformation to have been a thoroughly Christian
renewal, recovering many dimensions of the gospel that had become obscured.
The Reformers reaffirmed the goodness of creation. Reacting against the
dualism that had placed monks and priests on a higher, "sacred" plane, the
Reformers Martin Luther (1483–1546) and John Calvin (1509–64) insisted
that in *all* cultural callings we serve God by serving our neighbors. Thus
Luther imagines that Mary, immediately after her visit by the angel Gabriel
(Luke 1:26–38), simply returns to her household duties—milking, cooking,
washing, and sweeping. For Luther *every* human responsibility is a sacred
vocation—and equally sacred whether one is called to bear the Christ child
or to put supper on the table. The Reformers also insisted on the scope and
depth of sin, a concept they believed had been neglected in the euphoric
reemergence of humanism. Furthermore, the Reformers taught (though not
always consistently) that salvation was the renewal of human creational life.

The Reformers concentrated on theology, and their immediate legacy
philosophically is limited. With his view of sin, Luther railed against not

---

29. Windelband, *History of Philosophy*, 350 (italics in the original).

just Scholasticism but also the unaided view of reason that dominated philosophy. Notoriously, he declared that philosophy is a whore; she will sleep
with whoever pays the highest price. Calvin was more moderate in his critique of philosophy, and in practice Lutherans and Calvinists made use of
Aristotle in the educational programs they set up, as well as in their own
scholarship.

It is thus important to distinguish between the Reformers' rhetoric and
practice when it comes to philosophy. Like many of the Renaissance thinkers, the Reformers reacted strongly against medieval Scholasticism and thus
against Aristotle. Luther and Calvin argued against the use of philosophical
concepts in theology and ruled out any explicit use of models such as the
Christian Aristotelian worldview. They were wary of metaphysical discussions of the divine essence and attributes but did not deny the truth of the
traditional attributes of God of simplicity, infinity, eternity, omnipresence,
omniscience, and so on.

Some scholarship discerns a firm break between the Reformers and the
Reformed orthodoxy that followed them, not least with respect to philosophy. With other scholars, Richard Muller has demonstrated that this is not
as pronounced as is sometimes stated, particularly once one attends to the
universities and academies of the sixteenth and seventeenth centuries. In a
reform between 1520 and 1523 in the Lutheran world, courses on Aristotle's
Physics, *Metaphysics*, and *Ethics* were discontinued, but courses on his *Logic*,
Rhetoric, and *Poetics* were retained.[30] The tools of logic and rhetoric were
seen as necessary for the teaching of theology and preaching. The *Praeceptor Germaniae* (Teacher of Germany), as Philipp Melanchthon was called,
published a commentary on Aristotle's *Ethics* in 1529 and soon thereafter
introduced the study of physics and natural theology into the curriculum. As
Windelband notes,

> Little as the theoretico-aesthetical and religiously indifferent nature of the Hu
> manists might accord with the mighty power of Luther's soul with his profound
> faith, he was nevertheless, obliged, when he would give his work scientific form,
> to accommodate himself to the necessity of borrowing from philosophy the
> conceptions with which to lay his foundations. Here, however, Melanchthon's
> harmonizing nature came in, and while Luther had passionately rejected scholas
> tic Aristotelianism, his learned associate introduced *humanistic Aristotelianism*
> as the *philosophy of Protestantism*, here, too, opposing the older tradition to
> the remodeled tradition. . . . The Peripatetic system was in this instance treated

30. Richard Muller, *Post-Reformation Reformed Dogmatics: The Rise and Development
of Reformed Orthodoxy, ca. 1520–ca. 1575*, 2nd ed., 4 vols. (Grand Rapids: Baker Academic,
2003), 1:363–64.

as but a supplement to theology in the department of profane science . . . and as such was taught at the Protestant universities for two centuries.[31]

Colossians 2:8 was central to Tertullian's rejection of philosophy as incompatible with the gospel. The Reformer's exegesis of this verse manifests no such rejection of philosophy.[32] Calvin rightly notes the relationship of 2:8 to its context, which exhorts the reader to be rooted and built up in Christ. According to Calvin, "As many have *mistakenly* imagined that Paul here condemns philosophy, we must define what he means by that word. In my opinion, he means everything that men contrive of themselves when wishing to be wise in their own understanding—and that not without the specious pretext of reason and apparent probability."[33] Christ has been appointed by the Father as our sole teacher, and Calvin is concerned to maintain the simplicity of the gospel. Colossians 2:9 alerts us to why certain philosophy is to be rejected; it seeks to supply a deficiency. "But in Christ is a perfection to which nothing can be added."[34]

Calvin declares Plato to be the most religious of the ancients and lauds him for his understanding of the immortality of the soul. He criticizes Aristotle because of his association with Scholasticism, but in his view of the world order and causality, Calvin clearly reveals his dependence on Aristotle. Calvin's view of philosophy is thus complex, and his precise view of philosophy is contested, and this not least in the different Reformed traditions that lay claim to his ancestry.

Abraham Kuyper and the different strands of neocalvinism that have come to emphasize the importance of distinctively Christian philosophy trace their roots back to Calvin. Herman Dooyeweerd, for example, stresses that a "radical Christian philosophy can only develop in the line of Calvin's religious starting point."[35] This is because Calvin stresses the corruption of reason by the fall. However, Calvin's theology is by no means so clear as such a statement suggests. After a detailed examination of Calvin's view of our knowledge of God, Dewey Hoitenga concludes that

31. Windelband, *A History of Philosophy*, 364 (italics in the original). Cf. Muller, *Post-Reformation Reformed Dogmatics*, 1:364–65. Peripatetic system refers to the Aristotelian school of philosophy, so named because Aristotle walked around when he lectured.

32. The French Huguenot minister Jean Daillé (1594–1670) wrote an important and massive commentary on Colossians. For his view of 2:8, see Muller, *Post-Reformation Reformed Dogmatics*, 1:367.

33. Jean Calvin, *Paul's Epistles to the Galatians, Ephesians, Philippians and Colossians*, trans. T. H. L. Parker, ed. David W. Torrance and Thomas F. Torrance (Grand Rapids: Eerdmans, 1965), 329 (italics added).

34. Ibid., 230.

35. Herman Dooyeweerd, *A New Critique of Theoretical Thought*, trans. David H. Freeman and William S. Young, 4 vols. (Jordan Station, ON: Paideia, 1984), 1:515.

Calvin does not, however, incorporate into his position or into his thinking the Augustinian formula, faith seeks understanding. This is because *he fails to spell out the noetic effects of grace on human reason* and because he tends to cast doubt on the possibility of pious philosophical inquiry in the midst of his vigorous rejection of "idle speculation." . . . The heart of Calvin's religious epistemology is the immediacy and vitality of human knowledge of God, in believer and unbeliever alike.[36]

Calvin teaches that humans are created with a *sensus divinitatis*: by our nature we know that there is a God, that he is our Maker, and that he is majestic. This knowledge is immediate and vital, or, as we might say today, existential. One source of this knowledge is the universe, which bears all the marks of God's craftsmanship. As John Baillie notes, "Nature is not an argument for God, but it is a sacrament of Him."[37] Human beings are thus *always responding* to God, but the nature of this response is determined by the presence or absence of Christian faith. Apart from such faith, humans fly off into empty speculations and idolatry. Christian faith, however, restores our fallen natural knowledge of God into the properly worship-full knowledge of God that characterized humans prior to the fall. From the outset of the *Institutes* Calvin holds our knowledge of God and self-knowledge inseparably together. And he is clear that the fall corrupts such good gifts in us as reason, but for Calvin this corruption manifests itself primarily in relation to "heavenly things."[38] For "earthly things" like the liberal arts, government, household management, and mechanical skills, "no man is without the light of reason."[39]

On one reading of Calvin, therefore, he can be construed as embracing an epistemological dualism whereby the corruption of reason affects spiritual knowledge, whereas unaided human reason is perceived to function perfectly well in nonspiritual areas. Not surprisingly, therefore, a writer such as Arvin Vos argues that Calvin and Thomas Aquinas are much closer philosophically than is often recognized.[40] Similarly Benjamin B. Warfield and much Princeton Reformed theology has assumed it is working in Calvin's line by arguing that science done properly and objectively will agree with God's written revelation.

36. Dewey J. Hoitenga Jr., *Faith and Reason from Plato to Plantinga: An Introduction to Reformed Epistemology* (Albany: SUNY, 1991), 174 (italics added).

37. John Baillie, *Our Knowledge of God* (New York: Charles Scribner's Sons, 1939), 178. On this issue, see Hoitenga, *Faith and Reason*, 156–57.

38. Hoitenga, *Faith and Reason*, 163–64.

39. John Calvin, *Institutes of the Christian Religion*, ed. John T. McNeill, trans. Ford Lewis Battles (Philadelphia: Westminster Press, 1960), II, ii, 13.

40. Arvin Vos, *Aquinas, Calvin, and Contemporary Protestant Thought: A Critique of Protestant Views on the Thought of Thomas Aquinas* (Washington, DC: Christian University Press; Grand Rapids: Eerdmans, 1985).

A softer, more "generous" reading of Calvin might argue, as does Hoitenga, that Calvin fails to develop his view of how grace affects reason. And there is certainly something to be said for this view. As Europe split into Protestant and Catholic nations, political philosophy emerged into prominence, and the importance of Calvin's thought in this respect has recently been acknowledged. Calvin's political, social, and economic thought is deeply affected by his faith and is certainly not "objective," neutral scholarship. In sum, there is a degree of ambiguity in Calvin's view of philosophy, and both the Princeton approach and that of neocalvinism can find resources in Calvin to support their views of philosophy.

Certainly neither Calvin nor Luther argued for, let alone developed, a distinctively Christian philosophy. It is really only in the twentieth century that Calvinism, especially through Dutch Calvinism, has come to fruition philosophically. However, the potential for this development in Calvin's thought should be noted. Calvin's idea of the creation as the theater of God's glory and his insistence, with Luther, that reason, too, is affected by sin are foundational elements for the rationale of a distinctively Christian philosophy.

The Reformed orthodoxy that followed the Reformers tended to have a more positive view of philosophy, as witnessed, for example, in Pietro Martire Vermigli (1499–1562), who played a major role in the Swiss and English Reformations. Vermigli asserts that true philosophy is a gift of God by which rational creatures discern justice, goodness, and other truths implanted in the mind by God. True philosophy "nourishes and instructs the soul itself."[41] Thus philosophy is only to be rejected when it becomes corrupt.

As Muller points out, if Aristotelianism is defined more loosely as affirming a primary and secondary causality—assuming the working of first and final causality through instrumental, formal, and material causes, and thereby able to explain levels of necessary and contingent existence—then it is rightly understood as a stable philosophical background to seventeenth-century Reformed theology.[42] The locus of the forms was debated throughout the seventeenth century, but Christian Aristotelianism located them in the mind of God. This Christian Aristotelianism was fluid and flexible, not least in relation to seventeenth-century philosophical developments. Some Reformed thinkers, for example, accepted Cartesian premises, but this was not without controversy.[43]

In the late sixteenth and seventeenth centuries the medieval debate about double truth was revived.[44] Within the Reformed tradition, theologians like

41. Quoted in Muller, *Post-Reformation Reformed Dogmatics*, 1:366.
42. Ibid., 371–73.
43. Ibid., 381.
44. Ibid., 382–405.

Bartholomaus Keckermann (1572–1609) opened the way forward by affirming the unity of truth: "Therefore truth is not contrary to itself whether presented in theology or philosophy."[45] This led to some very interesting debates among Reformed thinkers that are worth excavating for philosophy today. In different ways, Nicolas Taurellus (1547–1606) and Theophilus Gale (1628–78) sought to develop a distinctively Christian philosophy not least on the basis of the effect of sin on reason.[46]

In response to the Socinians and Cartesians, Reformed thinkers developed an *instrumental* view of reason: as a critical instrument reason is a limited but God-given tool that assists in formulating, defending, and drawing conclusions from Christian doctrine. However, reason must always remain subordinate to the truth of Scripture. As Muller therefore notes, "In sum, if we cannot speak of a mere recrudescence of Aristotelianism in the late sixteenth century but must instead examine a series of traditions and modifications that identify the course of a living, changing philosophical tradition, so also must we be prepared to modify greatly the thesis of the loss of Aristotelianism at the close of the era of orthodoxy."[47]

Catholicism responded to the Reformation with the Counter-Reformation, and the Council of Trent (1563) declared Thomism to be authoritative in its essentials for philosophy. Indeed, the sixteenth and seventeenth centuries are sometimes referred to as the period of Second Thomism. This revival of interest in Thomas drew its impetus from John Capreolus's (1380–1444) *Defense of Thomas's Theology*.

Conclusion

Philosophically, the Renaissance, Reformation, and Counter-Reformation were not times of great innovation and development. Looking back, we can see the impetus toward the secular philosophies of the Enlightenment, especially in the Aristotelianism of the Renaissance, but for the time being philosophy and religion remained entangled. From the perspective of Christian philosophy, the split of the Western church into Roman Catholic and Protestant wings was highly significant and with time would open the door for the development of distinctively Reformed philosophy. The seeds may have been present in Calvin's thought, but it would take centuries for these to be worked out.

45. Quoted in ibid., 385.
46. See ibid., 390–94.
47. Ibid., 381–82.

From: abby@longobedience.edu
To: percy@secular.edu
Subject: RE: Reason a whore!!

Hey Perc,

I gather that Luther was well known for his earthy rhetoric! I guess he was under-standably reacting against an overemphasis on reason in the Middle Ages. However, the Reformers continued to lean on Aristotle in their writings and in education. So alas, no, I don't think Luther can be lumped with Tertullian. I love the Reform-ers' emphasis on the Word and the sovereignty of God and Calvin's notion of the creation as the theater of God's glory. But I guess they were busy enough with all they did without focusing adequately on the Christianity-philosophy relationship. Work remains to be done!

Abby

NB: My mom really enjoyed your email about Luther! Only kidding!!

8

Early Modern Philosophy

Bacon to Leibniz

From: abby@longobedience.edu
To: percy@secular.edu
Subject: Epistemology

Hey Perc,

In our last lecture, as a lead-in to modern philosophy, our prof emphasized that the BIG shift in modern philosophy is from starting with God and the created world (*ontology*) to starting with *epistemology*—that is, how *we* know the world truly. This seismic shift—his words—inevitably involves a focus on humans as knowers, so *anthropology* is something to watch out for too. In the process, irresolvable tensions emerge in modern philosophy, as too much is expected of the human. Did you find this so in your study of the moderns?

Abby

God's central position and commanding role are gradually displaced by an increasing preoccupation with human subjectivity, crystallized in the Cartesian *cogito* in ways that we now associate with an emergent modernity. Biblical patterning of human experience gives way to disenchantment, and the divine will is set in competition with—if not altogether eclipsed by—an autonomous human subject.[1]

---

1. Gordon E. Michalson Jr., *Fallen Freedom: Kant on Radical Evil and Moral Regeneration* (Cambridge: Cambridge University Press, 1990), 2.

The rise of modern philosophy is generally described as framed by two giants, René Descartes and Immanuel Kant, with David Hume between them. Descartes and Hume represent the opposing traditions of *rationalism* and *empiricism*, whose tensions Kant sought to resolve with his *idealism*. This way of telling the story goes back to Kant and Hegel but is far from neutral. Christian philosophers such as Blaise Pascal, Thomas Reid, Johann Georg Hamann, Friedrich Heinrich Jacobi, and others were giants in their own way, and the way we tell the story of the rise of modern philosophy will depend significantly on our own philosophical views.

Many of the major philosophers in this period were mathematicians and scientists and sought to develop methods for acquiring knowledge that were objective and certain, just like that of mathematics. Modern philosophy, as it emerged, aimed at objective, scientific knowledge in all areas of life. However, especially with the steady marginalization and then elimination of God from the picture, this emphasis on scientific knowledge of *all* of nature raised in acute form the problem of human freedom. As part of nature, are humans not also subject to the same scientific laws and analysis? But if so, how then can we account for human freedom? In this way, an irresolvable tension emerges between the two poles of nature and freedom in modern philosophy. As Dooyeweerd perceptively notes,

> "Nature" and "freedom," science ideal and personality ideal turned out to oppose each other as declared enemies. A genuinely inner reconciliation between these antagonistic motives was impossible, since both were religious and thus absolute. Although the freedom motive had evoked the new motive of nature, each motive excluded the other. Humanism had no choice but to assign religious priority to one or the other.[2]

Francis Bacon

The emphasis on scientific knowledge of nature surfaces clearly in Francis Bacon's work. His reputation rests largely on his work on scientific method in his *New Organon*, an ambitious attempt to replace Aristotle's *Organon*. Bacon (1561–1626) is clear that progress in knowledge requires a new method.[3] Indeed, we need to begin anew from the very foundations.[4] Everyday perception offers

---

2. Herman Dooyeweerd, *Roots of Western Culture: Pagan, Secular, and Christian Options*, trans. John Kraay (Lewiston: Edwin Mellen, 2003), 153–54.

3. Francis Bacon, *The New Organon*, ed. Lisa Jardine and Michael Silverthorne, Cambridge Texts in the History of Philosophy (Cambridge: Cambridge University Press, 2000), I, xviii; I, xxxi.

4. Ibid., I, xcvii; I, c.

no sure basis for our knowledge of nature.[5] Reason is the key to knowledge, and two ways are open to us in this respect: deductive and inductive.[6] Bacon analyzes the weaknesses of deductive reasoning and argues for an inductive method if true, useful knowledge is to be acquired; he urges his readers to attend to the particulars, to the facts.[7] Bacon is unapologetic about his focus on this world; it is through attention to the particulars of this world that we attend to "the true marks of the Creator on his creatures."[8]

According to Bacon, we should not underestimate the obstacles to such a novel approach. Four major types of idols stand in the way of progress.[9] *Idols of the Tribe* are our projections of our view on the world, thereby distorting it so that human understanding operates like a false mirror. *Idols of the Cave*—an allusion to the allegory of the cave in Plato's *Republic*—are our individual prejudices. *Idols of the Market Place* are views we acquire through social intercourse and association. *Idols of the Theater* are "all the philosophies that men have learned or devised [and] are, in our opinion, so many plays produced and performed which have created false and fictitious worlds."[10] So serious are these idols that understanding needs to be freed and cleansed "so that there will be only one entrance into the kingdom of man, which is based on the sciences, as there is into the kingdom of heaven, 'into which, except as an infant, there is no way to enter.'"[11] Only thus will humans be able to make progress in knowledge. For Bacon such knowledge and progress are not disinterested; the true goal of the sciences is that humans may make new discoveries and have new powers. "Science would be the guide of the human mind in its victorious journey through Nature. By her inventions, human life should be completely transformed."[12] Bacon is not opposed to religion but is critical of types of Christianity that impede scientific exploration of the world: "But truly, if one thinks about it, natural philosophy, after the word of God, is the strongest remedy for superstition and the most proven food of faith. Therefore it has deservedly been granted to religion as its most faithful handmaid; for one manifests the will of God, the other his power."[13]

Bacon's inductive method involves an ascent from particulars to axioms.[14] Yet the execution of his method is Scholastic: "All the beginnings of modern

5. Wilhelm Windelband, *A History of Philosophy* (New York: Macmillan, 1901), 383.
6. Bacon, *New Organon*, I, xix.
7. Ibid., I, xxxvi.
8. Ibid., I, cxxiv.
9. Ibid., I, xxix–lxviii.
10. Ibid., I, xliv.
11. Ibid., lxviii.
12. Windelband, *History of Philosophy*, 387.
13. Bacon, *New Organon*, I, lxxxix.
14. Ibid., civ.

philosophy have in common an impulsive opposition against 'Scholasticism,' and at the same time a naïve lack of understanding for the common attitude of dependence upon some one of its traditions, which they nevertheless all occupy."[15] Knowledge of nature involves understanding the *causes* of things, of which there are four, according to Aristotle. However, in Bacon's work only the "formal" cause comes into consideration. For example, when Bacon searches for the form of heat, *form* is understood in the sense of Scotism as the abiding essence or nature of the phenomena. "What Bacon presents accordingly as Induction is certainly no simple enumeration, but an involved process of abstraction, which rests upon the metaphysical assumptions of the scholastic Formalism."[16]

Bacon's importance lies in his insistence that the new science must turn to the things themselves. There is, however, an incipient *naturalism* in his philosophy. With Bacon we see the turn to reality and the inherent order of creation that was indispensable for the development of science. Already many of the emphases that would later come to full expression in the Enlightenment are present. Among these are the mistrust of perception and lived experience, the consequent understanding of scientific method as the royal road to truth about nature, the focus on epistemological foundations and the perceived need to start afresh, the optimism about progress, and a stress on the domination of nature. Bacon remains a believer, but it is notable that unbelief is not identified as an idol; the gap between faith and sure knowledge is widening and will soon become an unbridgeable gulf.

Copernicus and Galileo

Science has played a central role in the development of the Western worldview. It was Renaissance Neoplatonism, and especially the Pythagorean conviction that nature was understandable in simple mathematical terms of a transcendent nature, that motivated Nicolaus Copernicus (1473–1543) toward his new view. In 1543 his astronomical theses, according to which the sun is the center of the planetary system and the planets move in epicycle paths around the sun, were published. His insight symbolized and catalyzed the break from the ancient and medieval worldviews to that of the modern era. Protestants were the first to react negatively toward Copernicus's theory since it appeared to contradict Scripture. By Galileo's time the Catholic Church had also come to see it as a grave danger. "Ever since the Scholastics and Dante had embraced Greek science and endowed it with religious meaning, the Christian world view

15. Windelband, *History of Philosophy*, 384.
16. Ibid., 385.

had become inextricably embedded in an Aristotelian-Ptolemaic geocentric universe."[17] Not surprisingly, therefore, Copernicus's revolution seemed to threaten the very heart of Christian faith.

Copernicus made the first break from the old cosmology, but it fell to Johannes Kepler (1571–1630), Galileo Galilei (1564–1662), and Isaac Newton (1642–1727) to solve the remaining problems and present a comprehensive scientific theory. Kepler, under the influence of Neoplatonism, believed passionately in the transcendent power of numbers and geometrical forms. Writing to Galileo, he exclaimed, "Plato and Pythagoras, our true preceptors."[18] After a decade of slow work, Kepler concluded that the planets' orbits were elliptical and thus precisely related to each other by mathematical proportions. Significantly, his mathematical formulae matched the most rigorous observations.

What did Aristotle's heaven look like? It was a large yet finite ball. Its outer layer and boundary contained the sphere of the stars, which surrounded a series of other concentric spheres of crystalline, liquid, or airy substance whose sole visible elements were the planets, and their circular motions followed the outer sphere but were unchanging. The earthly region was at the center and stable but subject to change and decay. Through his telescope Galileo saw craters on the moon and marks on the sun—evidence that the heavenly bodies were not made out of a uniform crystalline substance but of materials similar to the earth. Galileo published these discoveries in *A Messenger from the Stars* in 1610. This shook the Aristotelian consensus to its foundations.

Galileo's observations of Venus further indicated that Copernicus was right about the planets moving around the sun. Galileo eventually published his *Dialogue on the Two Chief World Systems* in 1632; in it, one character, Salvati, presents the Copernican system, and another, Simplicius, the traditional Aristotelian one. Simplicius was the name of one of the greatest of Aristotle's Greek commentators, but it could also mean "simpleton." The pope concluded that Galileo had shown his hand in favor of Copernicus. Tragically, Galileo was condemned to life imprisonment, an injustice publicly acknowledged by Pope John Paul II in 1992.

Philosophically, Galileo is most significant in terms of his insistence that philosophy must be scientific and mathematical. The new element in Galileo's philosophy was his concern to prove the mathematical significance of the cosmos by facts. With Pythagorean emphasis, Galileo asserted that "philosophy is written in the great book that lies open before the eyes of all of us, the universe. But we can only read it if we know its letters and have learnt its language. It is written in the language of mathematics and its letters are triangles, circles

17. Ibid., 253.
18. Quoted in ibid., 255–56.

and other geometric figures. Without these means, it is impossible for Man to understand a single word."[19]

In terms of Galileo's approach, induction in natural sciences involves finding the mathematical relation that remains constant in the series of phenomena as that relation is determined by measurement. He maintained that, to make accurate judgments concerning nature, scientists should focus only on measurable "objective" qualities (size, shape, number, weight, and motion) while ignoring those qualities that are only perceptible and "subjective" (color, sound, taste, touch, and smell). "Only by means of an exclusively quantitative analysis could science attain certain knowledge of the world."[20]

A materialist dimension was added to Galileo's theory through the revival of the atomism of Leucippus and Democritus, which posited a universe consisting of small, indivisible particles moving freely in an infinite void and, through their collisions, creating all phenomena. "*Galileo* created *mechanics as the mathematical theory of motion.*"[21] The new principle of mechanics excluded all tracing of corporeal phenomena back to spiritual forces: "Nature was despiritualised; science would see in it nothing but the movements of smallest bodies, of which one is the cause of the other. . . . No room remained for the operation of supernatural powers."[22] Leonardo da Vinci had already argued that the world should be explained by natural factors; now teleology was also obliged to give way. Here we have a clear example of the "nature" pole of modernity being privileged, and it is important to note that nature is here no longer conceived in terms of the astonishing richness of creation but is reduced to mathematics and motion. As Johann Hamann would later perceptively comment, "All the colors of this most beautiful world grow pale once you extinguish its light, the firstborn of creation."[23]

René Descartes

René Descartes (1596–1650) has been called the father of modernity because of his commitment to autonomous scientific reason as the final arbiter of truth. Like Bacon, Descartes believed that by science humans could capture the laws of nature, and by technology they could apply those laws, to make humans

19. Quoted in Christoph Delius et al., *The Story of Philosophy: From Antiquity to the Present* (New York: Konemann, 2000), 39–40.
20. Richard Tarnas, *The Passion of the Western Mind: Understanding the Ideas That Shaped Our World View* (New York: Ballantine, 1991), 263.
21. Windelband, *History of Philosophy*, 388 (italics in the original).
22. Ibid., 401.
23. Johann G. Hamann, *Writings on Philosophy and Language*, Cambridge Texts in the History of Philosophy (Cambridge: Cambridge University Press, 2007), 78.

the "masters and possessors of nature"[24] and the authors of progress itself. To realize this vision, he too offered a method to render knowledge rigorously objective and to purify the mind from all subjective prejudices—of the senses, imagination, emotions, tradition, authority, and opinion.[25]

Amid the religious wars of Europe, in which he participated, Descartes sought a method that would secure certain knowledge—knowledge of the sort provided by mathematics,[26] in which he was trained. His first publication was a slim, intellectual autobiography titled *Discourse on the Method of Rightly Conducting Reason*. Descartes explains that he arrived at his method in Germany after spending a day in seclusion in a room heated by a stove. He sought a new beginning and wanted, in his words, to "build on land that belongs entirely to me." His Archimedean point is that of systematic doubt; in order to find a secure starting point for knowledge, he decided to doubt everything he could until he found that which he could not doubt. Through this process he arrived at his famous *cogito, ergo sum*: I think, therefore I am. "But I soon noticed that while I thus wished to think everything false, it was necessarily true that I who thought so was something. Since this truth, *I think, therefore I am*, was so firm and assured that all the most extravagant suppositions of the skeptics were unable to shake it, I judged that I could safely accept it as the first principle of the philosophy I was seeking."[27] His point is that once all existence independent of thought is separated off, there remains a sphere of pure consciousness that cannot be doubted.

Descartes's solution is expressed in an architectural metaphor: *methodological doubt* is the solid foundation on which to build a structure of knowledge; therefore begin by doubting everything you think you know. On such a foundation you may build a solid edifice of knowledge by following a rational method, subjecting every truth claim to judgment by reason alone, and embracing as true only that which can be analyzed and measured in quantitative terms.

Descartes immediately moves to prove the existence of God from this starting point, but ironically he uses the resources of Scholasticism.[28] For Descartes the fact that he doubted meant he was not perfect, but from where had he obtained this idea of perfection? "The only hypothesis left was that this idea was put in my mind by a nature that was really more perfect than I was . . .

24. René Descartes, *Discourse on Method and Meditations*, trans. Laurence J. Lafleur (New York: Liberal Arts Press, 1960), 45.

25. Descartes notes that "we are much more greatly influenced by custom and example than by any certain knowledge" (ibid., 13–14).

26. He argues, for example, that a geometrically planned town is far better than ancient cities that have evolved organically (ibid., 12).

27. Ibid., 24.

28. See Windelband, *History of Philosophy*, 393.

in a word, God."[29] There was of necessity another, more perfect Being upon whom he depended and from whom he received all he possessed. Fundamental to Descartes's philosophy is the distinction between body and mind (corporeal and incorporeal), and since a mixture of both is a sign of dependency, God must, as perfect, be incorporeal. Descartes compares his certainty of God's existence to the way in which he knows that the sum of the angles of a triangle add up to 180 degrees: it is evident in *the idea* of a triangle, and "consequently, it is at least as certain that God, who is this Perfect Being, exists, as any theorem of geometry could possibly be."[30]

There is a circularity to Descartes's starting point and his belief in God. He notes that even his principle that all the things that we clearly and distinctly perceive are true—an extension of his cogito, ergo sum—is only certain because God exists. Similarly, because our clear and distinct ideas flow from God, they must be true. Nevertheless, Descartes is quite clear that we should only ever take something to be true on the basis of reason.

Alasdair MacIntyre, in his *Whose Justice? Which Rationality?*, alerts us to the fact that there is more than one tradition of rationality. It is thus worth paying close attention to what Descartes means by reason. In his *Discourse* Descartes sets out the four principles according to which he conducted his search:

1. One must accept ideas that are presented to the mind so clearly and distinctly as to preclude doubt. The cogito is in this respect the first basic rational truth whose evidence is that of immediate intuitive certainty.[31] As with Galileo, Descartes seeks out the basic, self-intelligible elements from which everything else is to be explained. Ideas are true that are as *clear* and *distinct* as self-consciousness. For Descartes an idea is "clear" when it is intuitively present to the mind; an idea is "distinct" when it is clear in itself and precise in its determination. *Innate ideas* are those that are clear and distinct and whose evidence is not deduced from any others.

2. In any difficulty under examination, one must divide the problem into as many parts as possible and as necessary for its solution.

3. One must start with objects that are the easiest and simplest to know and then gradually ascend to knowing the more complex.

4. One must be so comprehensive as to ensure nothing is omitted. Indeed, Descartes argues that since the truth on any point is univocal, whoever apprehends the truth knows all that can be known on that point.

29. Descartes, *Discourse*, 26.
30. Ibid., 28.
31. Windelband, *History of Philosophy*, 392.

It follows from these principles that in relation to finite things, as much can be known as can be clearly and distinctly perceived. Here the mathematical dimension of Descartes's philosophy comes to the fore as he distinguishes between quantitative determinations and sensuous-qualitative ones, which are unclear and confused. Genuinely scientific insight rests on intellectual knowledge and not on imagination, related to the sensuous. Such intellectual knowledge yields a dualism of substances that is central to Descartes's philosophy: all that can be known scientifically is either of a spatial species or of conscious Being. Spatiality and consciousness (extension and thought) are the ultimate simple, original attributes of reality. The one is not the other. Bodies are real insofar as they are spatial-extension and motion. Bodies are parts of space, and empty space is thus impossible. All things are bodies or minds; these are finite, but God is infinite Being.

Although Descartes was a Christian and has been seen in many ways as "profoundly Augustinian,"[32] his philosophy is revolutionary and in many ways unchristian. Indeed, William Temple described the day Descartes spent in an "oven" as the most disastrous day in the history of Europe.[33] Michael Buckley analyzes the shift brought about by Cartesianism in the rationality of our conception of God: "In their search for proof of the divine existence, the theologians had shifted from the god defined and disclosed in Christ and religious experience to the god disclosed in impersonal nature."[34]

Despite Descartes's move to prove God's existence after establishing the cogito, from a Christian perspective the damage was done. Now, knowledge of God depended on first establishing valid human knowledge. In time to come, Descartes's Scholastic proof of God's existence was abandoned, but his positioning of the autonomous self at the starting point and center of valid knowledge remained, as it does today. As Michael Buckley argues, it is this type of epistemology that is "at the origins of modern atheism"; it is one that Christians adopt at their peril.

Charles Taylor refers to Descartes's anthropology as one of the "disengaged self," and Dooyeweerd asserts that "in conformity with the dualistic motive of nature and freedom, Descartes split human existence into two rigorously separated parts: the material body and the thinking soul. The ultimate ground of scientific certitude and, for that matter, of moral freedom, lay in consciousness, in the 'I think.'"[35]

---

32. Charles Taylor, *Sources of the Self: The Making of the Modern Identity* (Cambridge: Cambridge University Press, 1989), 143.

33. William Temple, *Nature, Man and God* (Edinburgh: T&T Clark, 1934), 57.

34. Michael J. Buckley, *At the Origins of Modern Atheism* (New Haven: Yale University Press, 1987), 350.

35. Dooyeweerd, *Roots of Western Culture*, 154.

Taylor rightly notes that with the idea of disengagement Descartes articulated one of the central ideas of modernity. The universe has to be understood mechanistically with the order of ideas embodied in knowledge being *built* rather than *found* or *discovered*. This construction of a representation of reality is intrinsically related to Descartes's view of the human person:

> Coming to a full realization of one's being as immaterial involves perceiving distinctly the ontological cleft between the two, and this involves grasping the material world as mere extension. The material world here includes the body, and coming to see the real distinction requires that we disengage from our usual embodied perspective, within which the ordinary person tends to see the objects around him as really qualified by colour or sweetness or heat, tends to think of pain or tickle as in his tooth or foot. We have to objectify the world, including our own bodies, and that means to come to see them mechanistically and functionally, in the same way that an uninvolved external observer would.[36]

Here we see a major tenet of modernity emerging: lived experience is not to be trusted, but disengaged reason and science will tell us the truth about the world. As Taylor rightly notes, this "does violence to our ordinary, embodied way of experiencing."[37] The result is a damaging reductionism, in which major elements of the rich creation are filtered out as unimportant or confused. As Taylor notes, "Of course, Augustine's theism remains. . . . But on the human, natural level, a great shift has taken place. If rational control is a matter of mind dominating a disenchanted world of nature, then the sense of the superiority of the good life, and the inspiration to attain it, must come from the agent's sense of his own dignity as a rational being."[38]

Thomas Hobbes

The founder of British empiricism, Thomas Hobbes (1588–1679) was the son of the vicar of Westport, near Malmesbury in England. After he had graduated from Magdalen College, Oxford, he traveled to the Continent, where he became acquainted with Francis Bacon, who confirmed in him his dislike of Scholastic and Aristotelian philosophy. On his second visit to the Continent in 1629 he discovered and fell in love with geometry; he came to believe that true knowledge in every sphere of life is to be gained by the method of the geometer: "For REASON, in this sense, is nothing but *Reckoning* (that is, Adding and Subtracting) of the Consequences of generall names agreed upon,

36. Taylor, *Sources of the Self*, 145.
37. Ibid., 146.
38. Ibid., 151–52.

for the *marking* and *signifying* of our thoughts."[39] On his third visit to the Continent he became converted to materialism and became a close friend of Pierre Gassendi, the French exponent of materialism.

Hobbes was one of several eminent academics invited to comment on Descartes's *Meditations* in 1641. Both Hobbes and Descartes were fired by a passion for mathematics and shared a contempt for Aristotle. They agreed that the material world was to be explained solely in terms of motion: "The cause of Sense, is the Externall Body, or Object, which presseth the organ proper to each Sense. . . . Neither in us that are pressed, are they any thing else, but divers motions; (for motion, produceth nothing but motion)."[40] Indeed Hobbes denied the objective reality of all accidents. Where Hobbes disagreed with Descartes was over philosophy of mind; in his view there was no such thing, at least according to Descartes's definition. According to Hobbes's materialism, sense impressions give the only elements of consciousness, and by their combination and transformation memory and thought come about. The origin of all thought is *sense*, so that single thoughts are a representation or appearance of some quality or accident of an object. A train of thoughts may be unguided or regulated; the latter either seeks the causes that produced an effect or the possible effects that can be produced by it. "For besides Sense, and Thoughts, and the Trayne of thoughts, the mind of man has no other motion; though by the help of Speech, and Method, the same Facultyes may be improved to such a height, as to distinguish men from all other living Creatures."[41] Like Descartes and Locke, Hobbes wanted to start from scratch; one must start from first definitions and then move from one consequence to another, and then to general rules, theorems, or aphorisms.[42]

In terms of the nature/freedom dialectic of modern philosophy, Hobbes clearly comes down on the side of nature: his materialism was "a modern and humanistic materialism, one driven by the religious force of a humanistic freedom motive that had dissolved itself into the nature motive."[43]

Hobbes attached great importance to his philosophy of language; he was a nominalist and argued that universal names name many individuals. For Hobbes, "*truth* consisteth in the right ordering of names in our affirmations,"[44] so that attention to careful definition is central to gaining true knowledge.

The interiorization that Charles Taylor finds so central to modernity is clearly present in Hobbes's introduction to his *Leviathan*, as expressed in

39. Thomas Hobbes, *Leviathan*, ed. C. P. MacPherson (London: Penguin, 1968), 111.
40. Ibid., 85–86.
41. Ibid., 99.
42. Ibid., 115.
43. Dooyeweerd, *Roots of Western Culture*, 155–56.
44. Hobbes, *Leviathan*, 105.

his imperative, "Read thy self."[45] According to Hobbes, whoever does this will thereby know what are the thoughts and passions of all other men on similar occasions. Especially in his political philosophy, Hobbes goes out of his way to reconcile his view with Scripture. In this he is not altogether successful, and indeed there is a tension between his naturalism and his Christianity. On the one hand, he is quite clear that "a man can have no thought, representing any thing, not subject to sense,"[46] and yet, on the other hand, he wants to take the Christian faith and revelation seriously. In the process he articulates not only a nature/freedom dualism, as noted above, but a dualism between Scripture and natural reason: "The Scripture was written to shew unto men the kingdome of God; and to prepare their mindes to become his obedient subjects; leaving the world, and the Philosophy thereof, to the disputation of men, for the exercising of their naturall Reason."[47] Natural reason does, however, lead one to the First Mover, an Eternal Cause of all things, which in Hobbes's view is what is meant by "God."[48]

John Locke

Henceforth, man's sphere of exploration was the mind of man and its unfathomable riches.[49]

Born in Somerset, it was while he took refuge in Holland for political reasons that John Locke (1632–1704) worked on his famous *Essay Concerning Human Understanding*, which went through four editions in his lifetime. In opposition to the English Neoplatonists,[50] Locke argued that there are no innate ideas in the human mind—all our ideas are derived, whether directly or through their combination, from experience. In response to the notion of innate ideas Locke argued that there simply are no principles to which humans give universal consent.

Knowledge is acquired through the senses, which let into the mind particular ideas and furnish the yet-empty cabinet. This is Locke's empiricism.

45. Ibid., 82.
46. Ibid., 99.
47. Ibid., 145.
48. Ibid., 401.
49. Paul Hazard, *The European Mind: 1680–1715*, trans. J. Lewis May (Cleveland and New York: Meridian, 1963), 244.
50. The Cambridge Platonists were a group of about six philosophers who were at odds with both Hobbes and Descartes. They were anti-Puritan and anti-Calvinist but strongly opposed to Hobbes's materialism. Their maxim was "No Spirit, no God."

The senses convey into the mind distinct perceptions of things, and we thereby gain ideas of yellow, white, cold, soft, and so on. The mind grows familiar with these; they become lodged in the memory and are named. Ideas are *simple* and *complex*: they enter the mind simple and unmixed, but the understanding has the power to repeat, compare, unite, and develop complex ideas. The mind abstracts from the ideas given through the senses and thereby derives general names. In this way a vast store of ideas is developed in the mind. All ideas thus come from *sensation* or *reflection*. *Reflection* refers to the operations of our own mind within us, and it cannot be had from things without. Perception, thinking, doubting, believing, knowing, willing—this source "every man has wholly within himself."[51] Locke writes, "These two, I say, namely external material things, as the objects of sensation, and the operations of our own minds within, as the objects of reflection, are to me the only origin from where all our ideas take their beginnings."[52] Locke leaves the relation of the intellectual activities to their original sensuous content in a popular indefiniteness, which gives rise to the most various reshapings.[53]

Nicholas Wolterstorff argues that Locke's view of the self is best categorized as that of the *claustrophobic* self.[54] For Locke, one apprehends by reason one's mind and its modifications, including ideas. The irony of this outcome should be noted. With his empiricism, Locke seeks to establish the scientific knowledge of nature but ends up being restricted to contemplating his mind. Dooyeweerd notes that in Locke we can discern the seed of critical reflection on the science ideal of knowing nature, a seed that would bear fruit in an emphasis on the opposing pole of freedom and the ideal of personality.[55] This shift is evident, for example, in the work of Berkeley, as we will see below.

In terms of political philosophy, Locke's *Of Civil Government* provided the philosophical basis for classical liberalism with its argument for limited, representative government. His political ideas served as the justification of the English "Glorious Revolution" of 1688 and influenced the eighteenth-century revolutions in America and France. He based government on the natural rights of the individual and on the social contract. The origin of government is secular and based on individualism.

51. John Locke, *An Essay Concerning Human Understanding*, 27th ed. (London: T. Tegg and Son, 1836), 51.

52. Ibid., 52.

53. Windelband, *History of Philosophy*, 451.

54. Nicholas Wolterstorff, *John Locke and the Ethics of Belief*, Cambridge Studies in Religion and Ethical Thought (Cambridge: Cambridge University Press, 1996), 240.

55. Herman Dooyeweerd, *A New Critique of Theoretical Thought*, trans. David H. Freeman and William S. Young, 4 vols. (Jordan Station, ON: Paideia, 1984), 1:271; on Locke, see 1:262–71.

Blaise Pascal

A former child prodigy, in 1654 Blaise Pascal (1632–62) experienced a conversion that transformed his life. He became associated with a group known as the Jansenists, centered at the convent of Port Royal. This group stressed the corruption of human nature by sin and the notion of irresistible grace. When Pascal died, a paper was found stitched into his coat with the words "God of Abraham, God of Isaac, God of Jacob, not of the philosophers and scholars." His most famous work, the *Pensées*, was published posthumously in 1670. Stylistically, it is largely made up of aphorisms, many of which remain well known.

Pascal stresses the limits of human reason: "Reason's last step is the recognition that there are an infinite number of things which are beyond it. It is merely feeble if it does not go as far as to realize that. If natural things are beyond it, what are we to say about supernatural things?"[56] Again, "Let us then concede to the sceptics what they have so often proclaimed, that truth lies beyond our scope and is an unattainable quarry, that it is no earthly denizen, but at home in heaven, lying in the lap of God, to be known only in so far as it pleases him to reveal it. Let us learn our true nature from the uncreated and incarnate truth."[57]

For Pascal, reason is limited because of its creaturely nature and only functions properly in the context of Christian faith. It is only "through Jesus [that] we know God. . . . In him and through him, therefore, we know God."[58] Thus the proofs for the existence of God are of little value.[59] However, this is not for a moment to deny the value of reason but to position it appropriately: "Two excesses: to exclude reason, to admit nothing but reason."[60] "Submission and use of reason; that is what makes true Christianity."[61] "If we submit everything to reason our religion will be left with nothing mysterious or supernatural. If we offend the principles of reason our religion will be absurd and ridiculous."[62]

Pascal roots reason in the "heart," a term that crops up repeatedly in his *Pensées*. He asserts that "the heart has its reasons of which reason knows nothing: we know this in countless ways."[63] "It is the heart which experiences God, and not the reason. This, then, is faith: God felt by the heart, not by

56. Blaise Pascal, *Pensées*, trans. A. J. Krailsheimer (London: Penguin, 1966), 188.
57. Ibid., 131.
58. Ibid., 189.
59. Ibid., 190.
60. Ibid., 183.
61. Ibid., 167.
62. Ibid., 173.
63. Ibid., 423.

the reason."[64] Pascal was immersed in Scripture, and his notion of the heart comes from Old Testament wisdom literature in particular, in which the heart is the religious center of the human person. This emphasis on the heart sets Pascal far apart from Descartes.

Pascal developed an Augustinian view of rationality that has great potential as a philosophical resource today. It is Augustinian in two senses: first, Pascal rejected attempts to reach God apart from faith rooted in love; second, although belief in God cannot be proved, it can still be defended as rational.[65]

George Berkeley

George Berkeley (1685–1753) was born in Ireland and became bishop of Cloyne. Philosophically, he "brought the ascendancy of inner experience to complete dominance."[66] Galileo, Locke, and others distinguished secondary qualities (e.g., colors and temperatures), which are characteristics *we* attribute to things by virtue of subjective sense impressions, from primary qualities (e.g., space and motion), which are expressed in geometric and mathematical quantities and are regarded as objective data of the material world. For Berkeley, however, all qualities are "secondary." In this way he put an end to Locke's wavering over our knowledge of actual bodies, and he did this with extreme nominalism and through returning to the ideas of Hobbes.

Berkeley demolished the concept of *corporeal substance*, according to which part of the complex of ideas that perception presents us in a body should be separated out and another part retained as real. The mathematical qualities of bodies are as truly ideas within us as the sense qualities. Thus body is nothing but a complex of ideas. "The *idealism* which sees in a body nothing farther than a bundle of ideas is the view of the common man; it should be that of philosophers also. Bodies possess no other reality than that of *being perceived*."[67] Berkeley's philosophy is captured in the expression *Esse est percipi*; being is being perceived or perceiving. For Berkeley, there can be no existence outside perceptual relationships.

Berkeley combined this strong idealism with a spiritualistic metaphysics by means of which he accounted for the multiplicity of minds whose perceptions and worlds nevertheless correspond with each other. The danger with Berkeley's approach is that of solipsism: each individual mind has certain,

64. Ibid., 110.

65. See James R. Peters, *The Logic of the Heart: Augustine, Pascal, and the Rationality of Faith* (Grand Rapids: Baker Academic, 2009).

66. Windelband, *History of Philosophy*, 469.

67. Ibid., 470 (italics in the original).

intuitive knowledge only of itself and of its states; the reality of all else cannot be demonstrated. For Berkeley, however, ideas spring from God, who harmonizes the ideas in every mind, and the ideas of bodies are communicated by God to finite spirits. The order of succession in which God does this we call *laws of nature*.

Baruch Spinoza

Baruch Spinoza (1632–77) lived in Holland and was from a Jewish background, although he was excommunicated from the Jewish community once his views became public. In 1605 he published his *Tractatus* as a means of justifying his departure from Judaism. Philosophically, he invented his own system out of Cartesian resources. Spinoza's *Ethics* sets out his system:

1. His theory of substance: by comparison with Descartes, for Spinoza there is only a single substance—namely, God or Nature—that possesses thought and extension. God is the general essence of finite things; he does not exist other than in them and with them.[68] "This is Spinoza's complete and unreserved *pantheism*."[69] In relation to Descartes, Windelband describes this as Spinoza's monistic adjustment.[70]
2. The mind is man considered as a mode of *thought*; the body is man as a mode of *extension*. Spinoza's theory of cognition consists of three stages: imagination, reason, and intuition, which is the immediate apprehension of the eternal logic resulting from God as knowledge *sub specie aeternitatis*.[71] According to Spinoza, the world is understandable by reason, and falsity is the result of privation of knowledge resulting from inadequate ideas. Adequate ideas are universal ideas that are logically connected with other ideas. The key to successful human life, according to Spinoza, is the development of adequate ideas. Democratic society, which protects freedom of inquiry, is the best political context for such ideas to develop, and Spinoza is concerned to undermine anything that subverts adequate ideas and tolerance.

Because of his background in Judaism, Spinoza gave sustained attention to the Bible. Spinoza was well aware that the concepts of reason, religion, and scriptural interpretation have immense implications for society. Spinoza's scriptural hermeneutic is shaped by his philosophy, although he does insist that

68. Cf. ibid., 409.
69. Ibid.
70. Ibid., 410.
71. Latin for "under the aspect of eternity," which means what is universally true.

"the Bible must not be accommodated to reason, nor reason to the Bible."[72] Spinoza aims to read Scripture in a fresh and impartial manner and argues for a literal reading by means of natural reason. A major element of such an approach is the historical dimension of scriptural texts: "The universal rule, then, in interpreting Scripture is to accept nothing as an authoritative Scriptural statement which we do not perceive very clearly when we examine it in the light of its history."[73] Meaning and truth must be clearly distinguished, and scriptural meaning must be judged by reason.

There is a tension here. On the one hand, Spinoza acknowledges that Scripture regularly contains what can be known only by revelation; on the other hand, he is opposed to submitting reason to Scripture. Much of this tension is defused by his distinction between the Word of God and Scripture[74] and by his categorization of much of the Old Testament historical and prophetic material as imaginary and adjusted to the masses. Furthermore, Spinoza distinguishes between theology and philosophy by arguing that although Scripture contains a small core of ideas, "the sphere of theology is piety and obedience," whereas "the sphere of reason is . . . truth and wisdom."[75] "Philosophy has no end in view save truth: faith, as we have abundantly proved, looks for nothing but obedience and piety."[76] The practical limits of theology are made quite clear in Spinoza's statement that "theology tells us nothing else, enjoins on us no command save obedience, and has neither the will nor the power to oppose reason: she defines the dogmas of faith . . . only in so far as they may be necessary for obedience, and leaves reason to determine their precise truth: for reason is the light of the mind, and without her all things are dreams and phantoms."[77]

Although Spinoza thus maintains that "the Bible leaves reason absolutely free"[78] and argues that reason should not be submitted to Scripture nor vice versa, in practice his philosophy determines the understanding of scriptural ideas.

Gottfried Leibniz

Gottfried Leibniz (1646–1716) straddles the seventeenth and eighteenth centuries. His major and most well-known work is his *Theodicy* (1710), in which he argues that this is the best of all possible worlds: "The more we are enlightened

72. Baruch Spinoza, *A Theologico-Political Treatise*, trans. R. H. M. Elwes (New York: Dover, 1951), 195.

73. Ibid., 101.

74. Ibid., 169–70.

75. Ibid., 194.

76. Ibid., 189.

77. Ibid., 194, 195.

78. Ibid., 9.

and informed about the works of God, the more we shall be disposed to find that they are excellent and satisfactory in every way we could hope."[79] By the best possible world, Leibniz means the simplest in hypotheses and the richest in phenomena.[80] Voltaire satirized this view ruthlessly in his *Candide* (1759).

Leibniz was a Lutheran philosopher, and his faith is central to his philosophy. Indeed, he embarked on major ecumenical projects to bring Christians together. God, according to Leibniz, is an absolutely perfect being who possesses the perfections we find in nature to the highest degree. Leibniz concludes his *Discourse on Metaphysics* by reminding his readers of the difference the gospel makes.

> The ancient philosophers knew very little of these important truths. Jesus Christ alone has expressed them divinely well and in a manner so clear and familiar that the coarsest of minds have grasped them. Thus his gospel has entirely changed the course of human affairs: he has brought us to know the kingdom of heaven or that perfect republic of minds which deserves the title of City of God, whose admirable laws he has disclosed.[81]

While we need to take the Christian dimension of Leibniz's philosophy seriously, we should note his dangerous equation of the kingdom of God with a "republic of minds." This alerts us to the rationalistic component of his philosophy.

Leibniz rejects the view that extension—size, shape, motion—is a substance (Descartes) or an attribute of a substance (Spinoza). For Leibniz, the basic substance is a monad or a unit of psychic force. Monads are without parts and have no causal interaction with each other, although they do accommodate each other and harmonize; they are not spatially located. Monads have an internal law-like principle of "appetition" (desire or striving) that causes them to change. They appear to influence each other, but this is merely a reflection of the preestablished harmony by which God created them to mirror each other. A monad's entire past and present is contained within it, so that whatever a monad does, it does by a kind of necessity. Every monad is unique; all differ qualitatively and occupy different points of view so that each mirrors the world differently and with different degrees of clarity.

Every monad has a degree of psychic life[82] by which it represents external things. Monads whose perceptions are more distinct and accompanied by mem-

79. Gottfried Leibniz, *Discourse on Metaphysics and Other Essays*, trans. Daniel Garber and Roger Ariew (Indianapolis: Hackett, 1991), 1.

80. Ibid., 6.

81. Ibid., sec. 37, pp. 40–41.

82. Central to Leibniz's philosophy is the attempt to reconcile the mechanical and the teleological view of the world. He wished to do justice to the mechanical understanding of nature

ory occupy a higher level. Thus, for example, the dominant monad of a dog has perceptions and memory of those perceptions. Leibniz calls this monad the "soul" to distinguish it from lower or "naked" monads. In a person the dominant monad is a "spirit," because it is capable of reflective acts. Spirits are able to know the universe and to enter into relationship with the chief monad—namely, God.

Epistemologically, Leibniz came under the influence of Spinoza with the latter's stress on the geometrical nature of truth. Leibniz sought for those truths from which all knowledge was to be deduced. Like Galileo, he sought those truths that are immediately and intuitively certain and that force themselves upon the mind as self-evident. For Leibniz there are two types of intuitive knowledge: universal truths self-evident to reason and facts of experience. The former are timeless, the latter particular. To these two types of basic truth Leibniz attached the Cartesian marks of intuitive self-evidence: clearness and distinctness. He emphasizes the importance of distinct, as opposed to confused, ideas, and real from nominal definitions. Knowledge from experience remains confused; it is only when I can prove a priori that something is possible that my knowledge is distinct.[83] We can still doubt whether a nominal definition is possible, but we cannot doubt the possibility of a real idea. Leibniz relates real ideas to his strong, Platonic doctrine of innate ideas: "We have all these forms in our minds: we even have forms from all time."[84] This knowledge results from God continually acting on us and communicating himself directly to us.

> That idea is clear which is surely distinguished from all others and so is adequate for the recognition of its object; that idea is distinct which is clear even to its particular constituent parts and to the knowledge of their combination. According to this, the *a priori*, "geometrical" or "metaphysical" eternal truths are clear and distinct; while on the other hand the *a posteriori*, or the truths relating to facts, are clear, indeed, but not distinct. . . . In the case of the former the intuitive certainty rests upon the *Principle of Contradiction*; in the case of the latter the possibility guaranteed by the actual fact needs still an explanation in accordance with the *Principle of Sufficient Reason*.[85]

Leibniz views humans as a composite of monads dominated by the spirit. The image of God is located in our minds—"Minds only are made in his image"[86]—and God is "himself the most accomplished of all Minds."[87] Leibniz

---

while retaining the purposeful, living character of the world. See Windelband, *History of Philosophy*, 420–25.

83. Leibniz, *Discourse on Metaphysics*, sec. 24, pp. 26–27.
84. Ibid., sec. 26, p. 28.
85. Windelband, *History of Philosophy*, 398.
86. Leibniz, *Discourse on Metaphysics*, sec. 36, p. 39.
87. Ibid., 35.

rejects the route of Cartesian doubt: "Cartesian doubt, for Leibniz, is a reckless exercise, on the skeptical cusp of gnostic alienation. If we think at all, he maintained, we are entitled to take ourselves and our world as granted in an act of primal faith, however inadequate and confused our ensuing knowledge is."[88]

Leibniz's philosophy appears to exclude the possibility of freedom: if each monad contains its future within it and unfolds that future by necessity, how can we, as colonies of a spirit monad and lower body monads, be free? Leibniz rejects this critique: we are free in that our actions flow from our wills, and there is no contradiction in our willing other than we do.

In our telling of the story of Western philosophy, a recurring motif is that the way we tell the story is never neutral. A consistent characteristic of too much modern philosophy is a downplaying of the Christian faith of many modern philosophers, Leibniz being a notable example. Paul Hinlicky argues that most contemporary Lutheran theology runs from Luther through Kant to the present, a disastrous direction. "A path that yet can be taken, then, for Christian philosophy is 'Leibniz by way of Luther.'"[89]

Hinlicky notes that Leibniz dedicated his life to the cognitive claim of rational, natural, or philosophical theology, the very approach that Kant dismantled.[90] He argues that Leibniz conceived of Christian philosophy as the reflective extension of revealed theology and *not* as a foundation for it,[91] so that Leibniz is properly thought of as the Lutheran-Thomist of the seventeenth century.[92] "His purpose is not epistemologically to found science but hermeneutically to interpret its discoveries to other minds as works of God—and other minds *as well* as works of God."[93] Leibniz's approach is to see ourselves as embedded in nature under God rather than superior to nature in place of God.[94] His philosophy entails a natural theology that will comport with a revealed theology. It is not, like that of Kant, a turn to the subject, but a critical grounding of both subject and object in the nature of things—ultimately in God's nature. For Hinlicky, it is Leibniz who most radically and helpfully challenges the received (Kantian) theological tradition. Leibniz's theological philosophy is "one of the last great attempts in early modern Europe to found culture on the Christian doctrine of creation as parsed by the classic Lutheran thinkers."[95]

---

88. Paul R. Hinlicky, *Paths Not Taken: Fates of Theology from Luther through Leibniz* (Grand Rapids: Eerdmans, 2009), 252.

89. Ibid., 294.

90. Ibid., 2.

91. Ibid., 4.

92. Ibid., 7.

93. Ibid., 11.

94. Ibid.

95. Ibid., 10.

Hinlicky alerts Christians to the need to take care with how we tell the story of philosophy. Leibniz cannot simply be disposed of as a rationalist. His faith is real and decidedly not of a deist sort. However, in our view, a real tension remains in his thought. Leibniz himself asserted that "I start as a philosopher but I finish as a theologian."[96] He was committed to Luther's doctrine of two kingdoms, and there remains an uneasy tension between faith and reason in his thought, a tension insufficient to hold back the onslaught of Enlightenment philosophy.

Conclusion

With Europe ravaged by religious wars, it is understandable that Descartes would seek solid ground in reason. Understandable but fatal, since reason and human autonomy are never an adequate basis for life and truth. Whereas previously philosophers began with ontology and then asked how we know the world truly in that context, Descartes and his successors turn this model upside down and begin with humanity and how we know. This is a seismic shift and leads directly to the overwhelming emphasis on human autonomy in modern philosophy. In the early modern period, two of the major modern epistemologies emerge—namely, rationalism and empiricism.

The early modern period remains fascinating, not least because Christianity is still very much in the air, and in one way or another all the philosophers of this period have to deal with it. In our view it is in the minority perspective of Pascal that the most potential is found. Clearly, however, reason and faith are well on their way to coming apart, a cleavage that will become pronounced in the modern era, even as philosophers increasingly focused on the human mind in an attempt to find an adequate ground for truth.

96. Quoted in ibid., 241.

9

Modern Philosophy

Hume to Schleiermacher

From: percy@secular.edu
To: abby@longobedience.edu
Subject: RE: Epistemology

Hi Abby,
In our course we have done a fair bit of work on Kant, and I think it is in his philosophy that you really see human autonomy at work. What I could not believe is that he thinks *we* generate the moral law that we must obey! Genesis 3 all over again!

Perc

In the 1750s and 1760s seventeen volumes of the *Encyclopédie*, edited by Jean-Baptiste le Rond D'Alembert (1717–83) and Denis Diderot (1713–84), were published. D'Alembert was a gifted mathematician who aimed to bring to all the sciences the clarity of arithmetic and geometry. "The creation motive of the Christian religion gave way to faith in the creative power of scientific thought which seeks its ground of certainty only within itself."[1] The two shared a faith in the inevitability of scientific progress and believed that the Christian religion was a great obstacle to human betterment; they held a *materialist* view of human nature. In terms of Herman Dooyeweerd's nature/freedom dialectic, they emphasized the nature pole. They gathered a group

---

1. Herman Dooyeweerd, *Roots of Western Culture: Pagan, Secular, and Christian Options*, trans. John Kraay (Lewiston: Edwin Mellen, 2003), 151.

of like-minded contributors including Montesquieu and Voltaire. All were anticlerical, but not all were atheists. Voltaire, for example, believed that some notion of the deity was important for the moral law to carry weight, but this was not the Creator God of theism.

David Hume

Born a Scotsman, David Hume (1711–76) published *A Treatise of Human Nature* at the young age of twenty-seven; it received little attention initially but later achieved great fame, and Hume came to exercise greater influence than any philosopher since Descartes. The subtitle explains the aim of Hume's *Treatise*: *Being an Attempt to Introduce the Experimental Method of Reasoning into Moral Subjects*—that is, to do for psychology what Newton did for physics.

Hume rightly recognized the fundamental importance of anthropology for philosophy and determined to march directly to this heartland of science itself. Hume was an empiricist, and in book 1 he classifies the contents of the mind into perceptions of two types: impressions and ideas. Impressions, which include sensations and emotions, are more vivid and forceful than ideas. Ideas are perceptions related to thinking and reasoning. All of our knowledge that extends beyond the immediate input of the senses depends on the concepts of cause and effect, which therefore deserve close attention. In this respect Hume comes to a radical conclusion: our belief in a necessary connection between cause and effect results not from reasoning but custom. "Accordingly we shall find upon examination, that every demonstration, which has been produced for the necessity of a cause, is fallacious and sophistical."[2] Hume extends the same skepticism to time and space and similarly to anthropology: "All the nice and subtle questions concerning personal identity can never possibly be decided, and are to be regarded rather as grammatical than as philosophical difficulties."[3]

Book 2 deals with passions or emotions, a special type of impression. Hume distinguishes between original and secondary impressions: original impressions are sense impressions and physical pains and pleasures; secondary impressions are passions such as pride and humility. For Hume, the conflict between passion and reason is a myth, since all voluntary behavior is motivated by passion; reason is and ought to be the slave of the passions. Book 3 deals with ethics, and Hume argues that not reason but only the passions can lead us to action;

2. David Hume, *An Enquiry Concerning Human Understanding*, 2nd ed., ed. L. A. Selby Bigge and P. H. Nidditch (Oxford: Oxford University Press, 1978), 207.
3. David Hume, *A Treatise of Human Nature*, 3rd ed., ed. L. A. Selby Bigge and P. H. Nidditch (Oxford: Oxford University Press, 1978), 1, 311–12.

reason can neither cause nor judge our passions. *Ought* can never be derived from an *is*; the chief source of moral distinctions is the feeling of sympathy with others.

Hume's empiricism is a strong assertion of the limits of human reason, but this does not mean that he acquiesced to radical skepticism. By the end of his *Treatise* it is clear that our social and individual well-being depends on holding certain nonrational beliefs. In this way Hume seeks to prevent philosophy from becoming alienated from common beliefs and practices. As he notes, "Man is a reasonable being; and as such, receives from science his proper food and nourishment: But so narrow are the bounds of human understanding, that little satisfaction can be hoped for in this particular, either from the extent or security of his acquisitions. . . . Be a philosopher; but, amidst all your philosophy, be still a man."[4] This does not, however, involve an openness to religion.

In 1755 Hume published *The Natural History of Religion*, and his *Dialogues Concerning Natural Religion* were published posthumously in 1779. Both are attacks on natural theology, and in particular radical critiques of Locke's natural theology. For Hume, exceeding the boundaries of our secular, common life equates to a hubris that is inappropriate for our human faculties. Two major arguments are used to support his anti-theism. First, he regards it as unwise to assent to any metaphysical beliefs that cannot be rationally justified by empirical evidence or are not the result of a universal, involuntary mechanism such as those that produce natural beliefs. Second, we should avoid those metaphysical beliefs that create psychic unease and social turmoil.[5] As James R. Peters rightly notes,

> Hume . . . rejects religious faith, including and especially Christian faith, as both psychologically destructive and rationally insupportable. I have argued that Hume's negative diagnosis of Christian faith is defective. Hume fails to understand the inner life of a faith that is animated by love rather than anxiety and ignorance. Furthermore, Hume's powerful criticisms of the Lockean reconciliation of faith and reason simply do not extend far enough to challenge the radically dissimilar outlook on faith and reason characteristic of the Augustinian tradition.[6]

With Hume's skepticism we witness the cracks in the Enlightenment edifice starting to appear. He may have stopped short of radical skepticism, but his

4. Hume, *Enquiry Concerning Human Understanding*, 5.
5. See James R. Peters, *The Logic of the Heart: Augustine, Pascal, and the Rationality of Faith* (Grand Rapids: Baker Academic, 2009), 103–60.
6. Ibid., 160.

rigorous pursuit of rational criticism led precisely in this direction. Ironically, the quest for a sure foundation in human autonomy and reason seemed to lead to doubting everything.

Thomas Reid

From the end of the eighteenth century on through the nineteenth, Thomas Reid (1710–96) was probably the most popular philosopher in the United States and United Kingdom, and he enjoyed considerable popularity in France. Nicholas Wolterstorff says that "I myself judge him to have been one of the two great philosophers of the latter part of the eighteenth century, the other being of course Immanuel Kant."[7] However, Reid has almost disappeared in modern philosophy courses in Western universities, although there is a renewed interest in him nowadays.

A Scotsman, Reid was a contemporary of Hume and was Hume's earliest and fiercest critic. In 1764 he published his *Inquiry into the Human Mind on the Principles of Common Sense*, the same year he was appointed professor of moral philosophy at Glasgow University as Adam Smith's successor. In 1785 he published *Essays on the Intellectual Powers of Man*, and in 1788, the same year that Kant published his *Critique of Practical Reason*, Reid published his *Essays on the Active Powers of Man*. He studied theology for three years in the course of his education and was a licensed Presbyterian preacher.

Unlike Hume, who thought that philosophy's failure to progress resulted from the failure of philosophy to use the experimental method of the new science,[8] and unlike Kant, who thought the problem was philosophy's quest for "pure reason," Reid argues that philosophy's lack of progress should largely be attributed to its failure to take the principles of common sense seriously. *Common sense* refers to those propositions that properly functioning adult human beings implicitly believe or take for granted in their ordinary activities and practices.[9]

For Reid, modern philosophy has flouted common sense because it has embraced "the Cartesian system." The Cartesian system leads inevitably to skepticism: "From the single principle of the existence of our own thoughts, very little, if any thing, can be deduced by just reasoning, especially if we

7. Nicholas Wolterstorff, *Thomas Reid and the Story of Epistemology* (Cambridge: Cambridge University Press, 2001), ix.

8. Reid was far from ignorant of contemporary science; he was probably the most learned in this respect among eighteenth-century philosophers.

9. See Nicholas Wolterstorff, "Reid on Common Sense," in *The Cambridge Companion to Thomas Reid*, ed. Terence Cuneo and René van Woudenberg (Cambridge: Cambridge University Press, 2004), for the ambiguity in Reid's concept of common sense.

suppose that all our other faculties may be fallacious."[10] We should therefore jettison the Cartesian system and embrace a form of foundationalism[11] that is moderate and wide. Moderate, because an idea can be worth belief without being indubitable. Wide, because many of our beliefs are warranted without being inferred from other beliefs. It is a first principle of common sense that the particular deliverances of the faculties of consciousness, perception, memory, the moral sense, and so on are immediately warranted. We should also divest ourselves of the "way of ideas"; this mechanical view does not explain how we apprehend reality, and we should rather stay with our prereflective conviction that we apprehend entities of various kinds.

For Reid, we should start in the thick of human experience by attending to ordinary language use, the principles assumed in human conduct and actions, and the operations of our own minds, or what Reid calls "introspection." "Philosophizing has to start somewhere, and Reid saw no reason that we should leave our commonsensical modes of discourse and convictions at the door when entering into the philosophical workplace."[12] Reid grants priority to introspective consciousness—namely, perception, memory, testimony, deductive reasoning, and inductive reasoning. For Reid, these sources are not reducible to one another, and they are of equal authority.

A moot question is *why* we should trust common sense. In this respect it is important to remember that Reid was a Christian philosopher who saw the world and humans as God's good creation. He placed great emphasis on human free will, but unlike Kant, who positioned free will in the noumenal realm as opposed to the natural realm of necessity, Reid appropriately distinguished between laws of nature and the voluntary actions of humans. In opposition to Kant's doctrine of necessity, Reid stressed contingency. God has created the world in a certain way, but he did not have to.

Reid wrote and taught about a staggering range of topics. "Reid's thought appeared on the world stage as at once amenable to science, Christian beliefs, the rise of a modern public sphere, and democratic politics."[13] Kant, who probably had not read Reid thoroughly, was devastating in his critique of Reid: he thought Reid's philosophy to be an "appeal to the opinion of the multitude, of whose applause the philosopher is ashamed . . . when no

10. Thomas Reid, *The Works of Thomas Reid*, 2 vols., Elibron Classics Series (New York: Adamant Media, 2005), 1:464.

11. Foundationalism is the view that beliefs that are justified are based on certain basic or *foundational* beliefs.

12. Terence Cuneo and René van Woudenberg, introduction to Cuneo and van Woudenberg, *Cambridge Companion to Thomas Reid*, 12.

13. Benjamin W. Redekop, "Reid's Influence in Britain, Germany, France, and America," in Cuneo and van Woudenberg, *Cambridge Companion to Thomas Reid*, 313.

rational justification for one's position can be advanced . . . when insight and science fail."[14]

For our purposes, two of Reid's many influences are particularly significant. He was highly influential among the Princetonian school of theology in America from its earliest days. Charles Hodge's *Systematic Theology*, for example, is deeply influenced by Reid. Hodge's use of Reid reflects the traditional, natural theological side of Reid's philosophy of religion. In contrast, Reformed epistemologists such as Alvin Plantinga have drawn on Reid's opposition to "classic foundationalism" in making the case for belief in God as properly basic.

Jean-Jacques Rousseau

Jean-Jacques Rousseau (1712–78) was a contributor to the *Encyclopédie*. However, he shocked the philosophes when he denied that the arts and sciences had a positive effect on humanity, thereby calling into question the Enlightenment emphasis on science and nature. As Dooyeweerd notes, it was Rousseau who "called humanism to this critical self-examination. . . . For him the root of human personality lay not in exact scientific thought but in the feeling of freedom."[15] Humans are naturally good, but they are corrupted by social institutions. He begins *The Social Contract* with the words "Man is born free, and is everywhere in chains." Rousseau evoked the image of the noble savage and embodied his philosophy in his liaison with a washer-woman. She gave birth to five children by him, each of which he dumped in a foundling hospital.

With his critique of scientific rationalism and his emphasis on freedom, Rousseau is a fundamental source for *Romanticism*, to which we will return at the start of chapter 10. Charles Taylor notes that "Rousseau is at the origin point of a great deal of contemporary culture, of the philosophies of self-exploration, as well as of the creeds which make *self-determining freedom* the key to virtue. He is the starting point of a transformation in modern culture towards a deeper inwardness and a radical autonomy."[16]

Rousseau's insistence on the reality of evil meant that with thinkers like Pascal he affirmed the opacity of human nature. For Pascal what can bring order to the chaos is grace; for Rousseau it is the voice of nature. Nature is good, and our problem is our estrangement from it. The impulses of nature

14. Immanuel Kant, *Prolegomena to Any Future Metaphysics*, ed. Lewis White Beck (Indianapolis: Bobbs Merrill, 1950), 7.
15. Dooyeweerd, *Roots of Western Culture*, 160–61.
16. Charles Taylor, *Sources of the Self: The Making of the Modern Identity* (Cambridge: Cambridge University Press, 1989), 362–63 (italics added).

are always right, and nature speaks to us through conscience. "Conscience is the voice of nature as it emerges in a being who has entered society and is endowed with language and hence reason."[17] In this way Rousseau pushes the emerging modern subjectivism further toward the view that a person's inner voice defines what is the good. Rousseau never finally severs the tie of the inner voice with a notion of providential order, "but he was the crucial hinge figure, because he provided the language, with an eloquence beyond compare, which could articulate this radical view. All that was needed was for the inner voice to cut loose from its yoke fellow and declare its full moral competence. A new ethic of nature arises with Romantic expressivism, which takes this step."[18]

Immanuel Kant

> Without doubt, Kant was one of the harshest critics of the Enlightenment. . . .
> Still, Kant came to save the Enlightenment, not to bury it. His aim was to give a
> lasting foundation to its fundamental article of faith: the authority of reason.[19]

Immanuel Kant (1724–1804) is *the* philosopher of the Enlightenment. "The pre-eminent position of the Königsberg philosopher rests upon the fact that he took up into himself the various motives of thought in the literature of the Enlightenment, and by their reciprocal supplementation matured a completely new conception of the problem and procedure of philosophy."[20]

Kant was born and remained throughout his life in Königsberg. He organized his life so as to attend to his duties. He never married and lived a quiet, disciplined life so that he could act without strain. His parents were simple Pietists; from this tradition he gained a sense of the sovereignty of conscience that he never lost. He received a position at the University of Königsberg in mathematics and logic at age thirty-one; from that point on he devoted himself entirely to philosophy. He was a very popular and influential lecturer. Windelband notes that

> the cheerful, brilliant animation and versatility of his middle years gave place
> with time to an earnest, rigorous conception of life and to the control of a
> strict consciousness of duty, which manifested itself in his unremitting labour
> upon his great philosophical task, in his masterful fulfillment of the duties of
> his academic profession, and in the inflexible rectitude of his life, which was

17. Ibid., 359.
18. Ibid., 362.
19. Frederick C. Beiser, "The Enlightenment and Idealism," in *The Cambridge Companion to German Idealism*, ed. Karl Ameriks (Cambridge: Cambridge University Press, 2000), 22.
20. W. Windelband, *A History of Philosophy* (New York: Harper & Row, 1901), 532.

not without a shade of the pedantic. The uniform course of his solitary and modest scholar's life was not disturbed by the brilliancy of the fame that fell upon his life's evening.[21]

Critique of Pure Reason

Kant's greatest achievement was the publication at age fifty-seven of his *Critique of Pure Reason* (1781), in which he discusses metaphysics and the theory of knowledge. The major works that followed this were his *Critique of Practical Reason* (1788), devoted to ethics, and his *Critique of Judgment* (1790), dealing with aesthetics and design. For our purposes, his controversial *Religion within the Limits of Reason Alone* (1793) is also very important.

Pivotal for Kant's thought was the growing crisis in the very possibility of objective knowledge.[22] By the late eighteenth century, cracks in the Enlightenment edifice were starting to appear. The more the Enlightenment's principles of rational criticism and scientific naturalism were pursued, the more problematic they became. Criticism appeared to end in skepticism, as we saw with Hume, thereby undermining common sense beliefs; and naturalism threatened belief in human freedom and the role of the mind. Kant was profoundly influenced by Leibniz and Hume; the latter he famously described as waking him from his dogmatic slumbers. Hume's skepticism made a huge impression on Kant, who believed that it could be solved only by overthrowing Leibniz's rationalist system. Thus he sought a way to reconcile rationalism and empiricism.[23] To save the Enlightenment Kant sought to achieve two goals: first to secure criticism (reason) without skepticism, and naturalism without materialism, and second to overcome the tension between criticism and naturalism. "A criticism immune from materialism would ensure that reason is an autonomous faculty, a source of universal laws. . . . A naturalism free from skepticism would show that the laws of physics apply to nature itself and do not simply consist in our habit of associating impressions."[24]

In his first *Critique* Kant argues that it is only in the synthesis of reason and experience that genuine, objective knowledge is possible. In articulating this, Kant developed his transcendental critique of reason. Kant distinguishes between the *phenomenal* (how things appear to us) and the *noumenal* (things as they are in themselves). Since all knowledge is a product of reason *and*

21. Ibid., 535.
22. See Beiser, "The Enlightenment and Idealism," 19–22.
23. See ibid., 22–25. Roger Scruton, *Kant: A Very Short Introduction* (Oxford: Oxford University Press, 1982, 2001), 21, notes that "this convenient, though contentious, division of his predecessors into rationalists and empiricists is in fact due to Kant."
24. Beiser, "The Enlightenment and Idealism," 23.

experience, we cannot know things as they are in themselves; this is simply impossible. For Kant the mind plays a formative role, akin to an interpretive grid, in acquiring knowledge, and it is here in particular that he focuses his attention.

Kant calls his argument in this respect the "transcendental deduction" and the theory that results "transcendental idealism." Transcendental deduction is the "name given by Kant to the attempt to show that there is one set of categories basic and ultimate to all human understanding and experiencing."[25] Transcendental deduction must be distinguished from empirical argument; the former leads not so much to knowledge of objects as to how such knowledge is possible a priori. For Kant the forms of thought that govern the understanding are entirely congruent with the a priori nature of reality; there is a harmony between the capacities of the knowing subject and the nature of that which is known. "The world is as we think it, and we think it as it is." "Almost all the major difficulties in the interpretation of Kant depend upon which of these two propositions is emphasized."[26]

Kant is adamant that our knowledge requires both sensibility and understanding. These are the two sources of our knowledge. The first relates to a faculty of intuition, the second to a faculty of concepts. Judgment requires both. For Kant, therefore, the theory of innate ideas is correct; indeed, the premise of self-consciousness is the single starting point of Kant's philosophy. Kant calls the fundamental concepts of the understanding "categories." He identifies twelve in all, examples of which are substance and cause. Intriguingly, he distinguishes these from two forms of intuition—namely, space and time—that he calls a priori intuitions. He denies these the status of categories because concepts are general and allow for a plurality of instances. In Kant's view there is of necessity only one time and one space, and every sensation is imprinted by temporal and, sometimes, spatial organization.

Kant lays great stress on the unity of the individual consciousness. "The essence of Kant's 'transcendental' method lies in its egocentricity. All the questions that I can ask I must ask from the standpoint that is mine; therefore they must bear the marks of my perspective, which is the perspective of 'possible experience.'"[27] Every category corresponds to a principle, and principles are rules for the objective employment of the categories. They tell us how to think if we are to think and how the world must be if it is to be intelligible. The principles lay down synthetic a priori truths concerning everyday life and scientific observation—that is, of things that may be the objects of *possible* experience.

25. Peter A. Angeles, *Dictionary of Philosophy* (New York: Harper & Row, 1981), 55.
26. Scruton, *Kant*, 34.
27. Ibid., 47.

The word *possible* alerts us to the important stress in Kant's philosophy on the limits of knowledge. There is for Kant a logic of illusion: while properly employed, the understanding yields objective knowledge, but it contains a temptation to the illusion that we can acquire *pure* knowledge.[28] Any such attempt transgresses the limits of experience. In this context Kant develops his distinction between noumenal and phenomenal discussed above. This limitation arises from the fact that all attempts to embrace the noumenal world in a rational system will ultimately fail since they always end in irresolvable contradictions or antinomies. An example of such an illusion is the notion of a first cause in cosmology. Kant argues that all the arguments for God's existence reduce to the ontological; existence is thought to belong to the very concept of God. However, says Kant, existence is not a predicate. The idea of a first cause, or God, is not, however, without value; it can function profitably as a *regulative principle*, according to which one acts as if it were true. "The ideal of a supreme being is nothing but a regulative principle of reason, which directs us to look upon all connection in the world as if it originated from an all-sufficient and necessary cause."[29]

If Kant stresses the limitations of reason, he also stresses its autonomy. Rationalism is too ambitious, in his view, and he compares it to the builders of the tower of Babel.[30] However, the desire for autonomy that motivates the project is quite right; what is required is a more modest plan. We need to ask what can be built with the labor and materials available to us. "Kant represents attempts to ground practices of reason as a matter of proceeding with the 'materials' and 'labor power' that our daily practice of defective reasoning has made available to us, and rebuilding these in ways that reduce dangers of collapse or paralysis in thought or action."[31]

Kant proposes that we think of reason as a discipline that rejects external authorities and that is reflexive in that it involves self-discipline and is law-like.[32] In terms of the relationship between reason and faith/religion, the character of reason as negative in the sense of rejecting external authorities is particularly significant. For Kant, autonomy is a fundamental characteristic of reason: "Reason is indeed the basis of enlightenment, but enlightenment is no more than autonomy in thinking and acting—that is, of thought and action that are lawful yet assume no lawgiver."[33]

28. Kant uses *pure* in different ways, both negatively, as we use it here, and positively. See Howard Kaygill, *A Kant Dictionary*, The Blackwell Philosopher Dictionaries (Oxford: Blackwell, 1995), 341–42.

29. Scruton, *Kant*, 69.

30. Onora O'Neill, "Vindicating Reason," in *The Cambridge Companion to Kant*, ed. Paul Guyer (Cambridge: Cambridge University Press, 1992), 289–90.

31. Ibid., 291–92.

32. See Onora O'Neill, "Vindicating Reason," for a useful discussion of Kant's mature view of reason.

33. Ibid., 299.

Critique of Practical Reason

Kant develops his ethics in his *Critique of Practical Reason*. The moral will, unlike the faculty of understanding, aims at duty, not truth. Kant argues that morality is objective and thus rational. His starting point is the concept of freedom: ought implies can.[34]

Our freedom belongs not to the realm of nature but to the transcendental realm to which categories like causality do not apply. We know the practical self *only* through the exercise of freedom. Morality is objective because it issues not in judgments but in imperatives. In practical thought, Kant distinguishes between hypothetical and categorical imperatives. Hypothetical imperatives are conditional—for example, if you want to be accepted, then be quiet—but for Kant their very conditionality means that they can never be objective since they are personal and not universal. Categorical imperatives are unconditional and universal. There is only one principle for the categorical imperative: when deciding on one's action as an end, one will be constrained by reason to "act in accordance with a maxim that can at the same time make itself a universal law."[35] Central to Kant's ethic is the autonomy of the will: "This feeling of human independence is most clearly revealed in the idea of autonomy, in the idea that not God but we ourselves, in so far as we embody pure practical reason, are the legislators of the moral law. We submit to the law not on God's behalf but for our own sake. It is our true will that must be done."[36]

Kant's view of ethics draws attention to his view of the human person[37] (his anthropology), and it is here that the nature/freedom tension is most clear in his philosophy. Richard Kroner discerns ethical voluntarism—the view that the human will is the ultimate ground in discerning moral values and making ethical decisions—at the heart of Kant's worldview.[38] As we noted above, for Kant the freedom involved in our moral acting belongs not to the realm of nature but to the transcendental realm: "The world in which we as moral beings act and pursue our ends obviously cannot be penetrated by mathematical knowledge; therefore this world cannot be grasped in its reality by any theoretical means. The supersensible and eternal world is ac-

34. See Kant, *Critique of Practical Reason*, trans. and ed. Mary Gregor, Cambridge Texts in the History of Philosophy (Cambridge: Cambridge University Press, 1997), 26–28.

35. Immanuel Kant, *Groundwork of the Metaphysics of Morals*, trans. and ed. Mary Gregor, Cambridge Texts in the History of Philosophy (Cambridge: Cambridge University Press, 1998), 44.

36. Richard Kroner, *Kant's Weltanschauung* (Chicago: University of Chicago Press, 1956), 36.

37. See ibid., 32–33. Kant lectured repeatedly on anthropology, but this area of his thought has not received nearly as much attention as his epistemology.

38. Ibid.

cessible only through moral activity; we are in the process of building it by living in accordance with moral laws."[39]

Kroner points out that Kant is a monist in his faith in that he sees an ultimate unity between nature and morality, but a dualist in that he denies the possibility of theoretical knowledge of this unity. As Kroner notes, there is a tension in Kant's thought between his ethical motive and a religious one. Faith in a supersensible unity is a consequence of Kant's system; it is morally necessary to believe in God, and yet Kant tends to absolutize the autonomous moral law. Religion is made subservient to morality, and yet God is higher than even the moral law. As Kroner notes, for Kant "the good will surpasses all understanding; in this way the word of the Gospel is transformed by the Kantian spirit."[40]

Critique of Judgment

Kant's *Critique of Judgment* is one of the most important works on aesthetics in modern times. This *Critique* is also his work in which theology comes to the fore. The aesthetic dimension has its own faculty—beauty, which involves a feeling of pleasure and demands universal agreement. Aesthetic judgment is characterized by the free play of imagination. Kant finds the norm for aesthetic judgment in the contemplation of an object regarded in a disinterested view. Kant further distinguishes between beauty and the sublime: beauty is a sense of the intelligence and purposiveness of what surrounds us; the sublime is a stronger sense, in which, overcome by the greatness of the world, we renounce the attempt to understand and control the world. For Kant, our sense of the sublime presents an inescapable view of the world as created.

Religion is made subservient to morality in Kant's scheme, which defines religion as "the recognition of all our duties as divine commands."[41] Kant was opposed to religious ceremonies and regarded creeds as an imposition on our inner freedom of thought. Morality leads to religion, and we can be justified practically in holding religious propositions, but religious beliefs are necessary only insofar as they support our sense of morality. Religious tutelage is strongly rejected by Kant, and as Roger Scruton puts it, "Kant's writings on religion exhibit one of the first attempts at the systematic demystification of theology."[42] Worship of God is translated into veneration of morality, and faith

39. Ibid., 2–3.
40. Ibid., 21–22.
41. Immanuel Kant, *Religion within the Bounds of Mere Reason and Other Writings*, trans. and ed. Allen Wood and George di Giovanni, Cambridge Texts in the History of Philosophy (Cambridge: Cambridge University Press, 1998), 154.
42. Scruton, *Kant*, 78.

into certainty of practical reason. "The object of esteem is not the Supreme Being, but the supreme attribute of rationality."[43] In this way Kant's philosophy epitomizes the move from providence to progress.

Kant's philosophy is a colossal attempt to secure the autonomy of reason and is far more complex than our brief discussion; however, it provided only a temporary respite in the crisis of the Enlightenment.[44] His philosophy is beset by dualisms, such as those between nature and freedom, the sensory and the suprasensory, and the phenomenal and the noumenal. It is not hard to see how the latter dualism opens up the possibility of a receding world in which we are left with representations in the individual mind. The specter of skepticism and materialism soon returned, as evidenced in Johann Fichte's attempt to rebuild Enlightenment philosophy on the new edifice of his own ethical idealism.

Kant's idealism does take account of human finitude, but his insistence on human autonomy makes it impossible to reconcile his account of reason with a Christian perspective.[45] Kant reinforces the essential Enlightenment belief in the authority and autonomy of reason. The extent to which this is at odds with a view of Christianity as public truth is well captured by the allusive title of Nicholas Wolterstorff's *Reason within the Bounds of Religion.*[46] Plantinga rightly argues that Kant's understanding of reality represents a turning on its head of a Christian perspective, especially if taken to its logical conclusion in what Plantinga calls "creative anti-realism."[47] From a Christian perspective, God's knowledge is creative; from a Kantian perspective, *our* knowledge is creative. Plantinga suggests that it is an easy step from the view that we are responsible for the way the world is to the postmodern view that we do not all live in the same world. Thus Plantinga suggests that the creative anti-realism of postmodernity has its roots in Kantian idealism, and that this tendency is profoundly unchristian.

Johann Georg Hamann

Although well known in Germany, where he was referred to as "the Wizard of the North," Johann Georg Hamann (1730–88) has been widely ignored

---

43. Ibid.

44. See Beiser, "The Enlightenment and Idealism," 25–28.

45. See Immanuel Kant, *An Answer to the Question: What Is Enlightenment?*, trans. H. B. Nisbet (London: Penguin, 1991). Kant argues that "religious immaturity is the most pernicious and dishonorable variety of all" (10).

46. Nicholas Wolterstorff, *Reason within the Bounds of Religion* (Grand Rapids: Eerdmans, 1984).

47. Alvin Plantinga, "Christian Philosophy at the End of the 20th Century," in *Christian Philosophy at the Close of the Twentieth Century*, ed. S. Griffioen and B. M. Balk (Kampen: Kok, 1995), 30–37.

in the Anglo-American world. He provides yet another example of how our worldview affects the way we tell the story of philosophy. The great twentieth-century missiologist Hendrik Kraemer described Hamann as "arguably the most profound Christian thinker of the eighteenth century through his deep sense of the peculiar nature of the historical revelation in Christ."[48] Yet even in Christian circles his work is hardly known.

Hamann was a contemporary and acquaintance of Kant, as well as one of his earliest critics and respondents. Kant and Hamann lived only a few miles apart in Königsberg. Hamann was part of the Enlightenment circle until his radical conversion while on diplomatic service in London. When he returned to Germany from London, now thoroughly converted, he eventually left the house of Berens that he had been working for. However, the Berens's son continued to make every attempt to reconvert Hamann to the view of the Enlightenment, enlisting Kant's help in the process. Hamann wrote a letter to Kant after their first meeting, which marks the start of the *Sturm und Drang* (Storm and Stress) movement. It also, most probably, introduced Kant to Hume. In his correspondence, Hamann stresses faith as providing a special and indispensable kind of knowledge. Negatively, faith alerts us to the limits of reason. Our existence, and the existence of all things external to us, must be believed and cannot be demonstrated. Positively, faith is sensation, a deep sense of the givenness of existence.

Hamann's writings are literary, contextual, performative of his own philosophy, and thus difficult but exhilarating reading.[49] Central to Hamann's philosophy are the following views:

1. Reason is not autonomous but is governed by the subconscious. Reason is inseparable from language, and like language is not universal but relative to a particular culture. As Frederick Beiser notes,

   Although it is not as well known, Hamann's critique of reason was just as influential as Kant's. Its criticism of the purism of reason proved to be especially important for post-Kantian thought. Herder, Schlegel, and Hegel all accepted Hamann's advice to see reason in its embodiment, in its specific social and historical context. Indeed, the emphasis upon the social and historical dimension of reason, which is so important for post-Kantian thought, can trace its origins back to Hamann.[50]

48. Hendrik Kraemer, *The Christian Message in a Non-Christian World* (London: Harper and Brothers, 1938), 117. Cf. James C. O'Flaherty, "Some Major Emphases of Hamann's Theology," *Harvard Theological Review* 51/1 (1958): 39–50.

49. See John R. Betz, "Reading 'Sibylline Leaves': J. G. Hamann in the History of Ideas," *Journal of the History of Ideas* 70/1 (2009): 97–102.

50. Frederick C. Beiser, *The Fate of Reason: German Philosophy from Kant to Fichte* (Cambridge, MA: Harvard University Press, 1987), 18.

2. The "naturalism" of modern science is unsustainable in its attempts to explain everything by mechanical laws without reference to God. Hamann disputes the distinction between natural and supernatural, which is at the heart of modern science's attempt to free itself from theology and metaphysics.

3. The Enlightenment's faith in human autonomy is irrational. "Nature and history are the two great commentaries on the divine word."[51]

4. Self-consciousness is decidedly not self-illuminating. We have no privileged access to ourselves.

5. Reason is not the sovereign royal road to truth: "It is the greatest contradiction and misuse of our reason if it wants to reveal. A philosopher who, to please his reason, puts the divine word out of vision is like those Jews who more stubbornly denied the New Testament the more they hung onto the old."[52]

In 1762 Hamann published his *Aesthetica in nuce*, which became the bible for the aesthetics of *Sturm und Drang* and for the epistemology of the Romantics. His stand against classicism and rationalism was revolutionary. Correct as it is to see the link between Hamann and the *Sturm und Drang* movement, the overtly Christian dimension of Hamann's aesthetics must not be ignored. John Betz notes that "it is now clear that the key to a full-blooded aesthetics is Christ. . . . Whereas without Christ we can neither fully see nor fully feel, with Christ 'the more we are able to see and taste and behold and touch His loving condescension . . . in his creatures.'"[53] As Hamann himself says, "All the colors of this most beautiful world grow pale once you extinguish its light, the firstborn of creation."[54]

Hamann helped to arrange a publisher for Kant's *Critique of Pure Reason*. In the process he obtained the proofs before it was published and wrote the first critical review. The result was Hamann's *Metacritique*, which can be seen as the starting point of post-Kantian philosophy. Indeed, Betz argues that Hamann's critique of Kant's *Critique* "remains to this day perhaps the most incisive critique of the *Critique*."[55]

51. Johann Georg Hamann, *Sämtliche Werke*, 6 vols., ed. Josef Nadler (Vienna: Herder, 1949–1957), 1:303, quoted by Beiser, *Fate of Reason*, 21.

52. Hamann, *Werke*, 1:9, quoted by Beiser, *Fate of Reason*, 22.

53. John R. Betz, *After Enlightenment: The Post-Secular Vision of J. G. Hamann* (Oxford: Wiley-Blackwell, 2012), 133; on Hamann's aesthetics, see 113–40.

54. Johann Georg Hamann, *Writings on Philosophy and Language*, trans. and ed. Kenneth Haynes (Cambridge: Cambridge University Press, 2007), 78.

55. Betz, "Reading 'Sibylline Leaves,'" 103. See also John R. Betz, "Enlightenment Revisited: Hamann as the First and Best Critic of Kant's Philosophy," *Modern Theology* 20 (2004): 291–301; Betz, *After Enlightenment*, 230–57.

It is remarkable, indeed scandalous, that such an influential philosopher as Hamann has largely been ignored in the history of philosophy. No one would tell the story of philosophy without Kant, and yet it is common practice to ignore Hamann. Hamann needs to be recovered as a major figure in the history of philosophy, not least because of his importance for Christian philosophy. He was not an irrationalist, as Isaiah Berlin has argued,[56] but rightly resisted the autonomy of reason and insisted on the formative role of faith in understanding our world. In many respects he is an early exponent of Christian philosophy, and his works contain rich resources that need to be excavated and transfused into the present. Not least is this true of his sustained and creative engagement with Scripture.

Subjective Idealism

Beiser rightly notes that "the net effect of the crisis of the Enlightenment was the return of its old enemies: skepticism and materialism. Now that Jacobi had resurrected Spinoza and the meta-critique of Kant had revived Hume, these monsters seemed stronger than ever. It was the task of the later idealists to slay them, to succeed where Kant had failed."[57]

The first important school to arise out of Kant's thought was the subjective idealism of Fichte, Schelling, and Hegel. Johann Gottlieb Fichte (1762–1814) studied theology at the University of Jena, where he came to admire Gotthold Lessing (1729–81), Spinoza, and Kant. Lessing is most well known for distinguishing between the contingent truths of history and the necessary truths of reason. Between history and the truth determined by reason was a "broad ugly ditch" that Lessing could not cross. Fichte's first book was *Critique of All Revelations* (1792), but his reputation rests on his work *The Science of Knowing* (1804). Fichte shared Kant's concern to combat materialism and skepticism but became convinced that Kant's philosophy ends in a "skepticism worse than Hume's."[58] Fichte, in his attempt to rebuild critical philosophy on a more solid foundation, postulated an absolute ego, of which the ego (subject) and non-ego (the object of experience) are part. This, however, created more problems than it solved. Where, for example, was this absolute ego? And how could it be known, if by definition it transcended experience, which for Fichte was the limit of knowledge? Fichte's response was his concept of "striving"; the absolute ego

56. Isaiah Berlin, *The Magus of the North: J. G. Hamann and the Origins of Modern Irrationalism*, ed. Henry Hardy (New York: Farrar, Strauss & Giroux, 1993).

57. Beiser, "The Enlightenment and Idealism," 29.

58. Quoted in ibid.

is not a reality but an idea. It is the goal after which the finite ego strives. "All that is left for the finite ego is constant striving, the ceaseless struggle to make nature conform to the demands of rational activity."[59] In this way Fichte went beyond Kant by making not only the understanding but also the will the lawgiver of nature.

Friedrich Wilhelm Joseph Schelling (1775–1854) developed a less uncompromising form of idealism known as *absolute idealism*. He argued for a nature philosophy according to which an initial absolute gives rise to two coequal principles existing side by side: a spiritual consciousness and a physical nature. Schelling profoundly influenced Samuel Taylor Coleridge (1772–1834) and is the bridge between Fichte and Hegel. Indeed, Hegel's first book was a comparison of Fichte and Schelling.

Georg Wilhelm Friedrich Hegel (1770–1831) studied theology before turning to philosophy. His first work, titled *Phenomenology of the Spirit*, established his reputation, but his major work was *The Science of Logic*. Hegel's greatest contribution was the central importance he attached to the historical element in philosophy. During his time there were two classic contributions to the philosophy of history, those by Giambattista Vico and Johann Gottfried Herder. "But it was Hegel who gave history a special place in philosophy, and the philosopher a special place in historiography."[60]

For Hegel, only the philosopher really understands that reason is the sovereign of the world and that the history of the world is a rational process. Cosmic history consists of the life story of Spirit (*Geist*). "Everything that from eternity has happened in heaven and earth, the life of God and all the deeds of time are simply the struggles of Spirit to know itself and find itself."[61] Hegel saw history as a manifestation of logic, but logic as historical, as martial. The logic of history is dialectical, unfolding according to thesis, antithesis, and synthesis. Hegel believed the Prussian monarchy was the nearest thing to the realization of an ideal state—that is, the achievement of Spirit in history. However, the most important manifestation of Spirit is in philosophy itself; the history of philosophy brings the absolute (pure thought) face to face with itself. Hegel firmly believed that philosophy makes progress: "The latest, most modern and newest philosophy is the most developed, richest and deepest."[62]

59. Ibid., 30.

60. Anthony Kenny, *The Rise of Modern Philosophy*, vol. 3 of *A New History of Western Philosophy* (Oxford: Oxford University Press, 2006), 112.

61. Georg Wilhelm Hegel, *Lectures on the History of Philosophy*, trans. E. S. Haldane and F. H. Simpson, 3 vols. (Atlanta Highlands, NJ: Humanities Press International, 1966), 1:23.

62. Ibid., 1:41.

Friedrich Schleiermacher

Friedrich Schleiermacher's significance lies in the synthesis he developed between religion and human autonomy in a context that increasingly saw religion as irrelevant. Religious reality is to be understood, according to Schleiermacher (1768–1834), through an analysis of human consciousness focused on feeling and intuition.[63] In this way, Schleiermacher developed a romanticist interpretation of religion that fits with the Enlightenment insistence on human autonomy. As Bernard Reardon points out, "The traditional landmarks are all there: revelation, the Bible, the articles of faith, the church. Yet all show up in a perspective new and somehow altered. . . . The viewpoint has shifted, that is, from a theocentrism to an anthropocentrism, so that what really has happened, one begins to suspect, is that Christian dogmatics has been covertly translated into a philosophy of the religious consciousness, for which a variety of elements have been drawn upon."[64]

Conclusion

With Kant, the high point of Enlightenment philosophy was reached. He entrenched human autonomy in the heart of philosophy, and within this tradition religion could only play a role subservient to such autonomy. From a Christian perspective, this shift in focus to humanity as the center of knowledge should not be underestimated. It represents the antithesis of the fear of the Lord as the beginning of knowledge and is an inadequate basis for truth, as the great diversity of approaches that soon emerged and the looming specter of skepticism demonstrate. Inevitably, the attempt to somehow ground rationality within the creation led to irresolvable tensions that philosopher after philosopher tried to solve. With time, a shift in focus developed from humanity to history, inaugurated by Hegel, a move that led eventually to postmodernism, the theme of chapter 11. In their engagement with the emergence of modern philosophy, Christians should not make the mistake of conceding the epistemological ground and then trying to show that knowledge built on such foundations can be squared with Christianity, as did Schleiermacher. Instead, the very epistemological foundations must be contested.

63. Bernard M. G. Reardon, *Religion in the Age of Romanticism* (Cambridge: Cambridge University Press, 1985), 29–58.

64. Ibid., 57, 58. Reardon notes that the Romantic understanding of religion with its subjectivizing tendency marks the start of "that process of immanentizing religious reality which was characteristic of the nineteenth century in general and which, despite the neo-orthodox reaction, has continued through the present century as well" (10).

As part of our retelling of the narrative of the rise of modern philosophy has shown, modern philosophy itself contains the resources for such a contestation. Philosophers such as Pascal, Hamann, and Reid provide clear places from which to begin to engage critically with modern philosophy without for a moment jettisoning the important insights developed by non-Christian philosophers.

10

Modern Philosophy

Romanticism to Gadamer

At the time that John Locke died and Rousseau was born in the early years of the eighteenth century, it was unimaginable that the authority of Christendom would ever be diminished. . . . Yet in less than a century, traditional Christian authority and the regime it spawned and maintained had either been overturned (as in France) or had been forever weakened.[1]

This chapter brings us squarely into the post-Enlightenment period and on into the twentieth century. Richard Tarnas rightly notes that "it would be the nineteenth century that would bring the Enlightenment's secular progression to its logical conclusion as Comte, Mill, Feuerbach, Marx, Haeckel, Spencer, Huxley, and, in a somewhat different spirit, Nietzsche all sounded the death knell of traditional religion."[2]

Romanticism

Romanticism emerged fully in the late eighteenth and early nineteenth centuries and has not ceased to be a powerful force in Western culture. A common emphasis in Romanticism is that "it is through our feelings that we get to the

---

1. James Davison Hunter, *To Change the World: The Irony, Tragedy, and Possibility of Christianity in the Late Modern World* (Oxford: Oxford University Press, 2010), 75.
2. Richard Tarnas, *The Passion of the Western Mind: Understanding the Ideas That Have Shaped Our World View* (New York: Ballantine, 1991), 310.

deepest moral and, indeed, cosmic truths."[3] Johann Gottfried Herder offered a picture of nature like a great current of sympathy, running through all things: "See the whole of nature, behold the great analogy of creation. Everything feels itself and its like, life reverberates to life."[4] Man is the creature who can become conscious of this and bring it to expression; hence Charles Taylor categorizes the Romantic self as the *expressive* self. Romanticism is a reaction to the rationalism and idealism of the Enlightenment, but it is vital to note that it remains largely within the humanist vision in this respect. It is a reaction within the contours of the Enlightenment vision rather than a move beyond it.

Its reactive element is witnessed in its stress on the following:

- The world as a unitary organism in opposition to the dualism that bedeviled Cartesianism and Kantianism. This central doctrine created as many problems as it appeared to solve. How, for example, do we know that nature exists apart from our consciousness? Furthermore, the idea of nature as an organism is an extrapolation, an analogy of our own nature as organisms, but on what basis?

- Inspiration, both imaginative and spiritual, rather than reason. As Romanticism slipped its moorings from Christian faith, it looked ever more to art to provide the "revelation" required.

- Human life as a drama rather than consisting of abstract truths.

- The complex nature of the human self.

- The multiplicity of realities.

- The will. In contrast to Enlightenment naturalism—with its stress on intellectual enlightenment, that all desire happiness and are similarly motivated—Romanticism followed Rousseau in stressing that "our will needs to be transformed; and the only thing that can do it is the recovery of contact with the impulse of nature within us."[5]

- Classical culture and tradition, which were more positively viewed by the Romantics as a source of meaning and wisdom.

- Religion. While often opposed to institutional religion, Romanticism tended to be more open to the divine, albeit increasingly in a pantheistic sense.

If Romanticism is central to understanding the nineteenth century, so too is the industrial revolution. Starting in Britain, the industrial revolution became

---

3. Charles Taylor, *Sources of the Self: The Making of the Modern Identity* (Cambridge: Cambridge University Press, 1989), 371.

4. Quoted in ibid., 369.

5. Ibid., 370.

the vehicle for science and technology to take hold of Western culture and
dominate it. In the process, nature became irretrievably scarred, and amid
real progress, terrible poverty and oppression developed. In the process, the
Romantic sense of harmony with nature was transformed into one of alienation: "Wordsworth's vision had been displaced by Frost's."[6]

The industrial revolution was the backdrop against which Karl Marx and
Friedrich Engels's radical critique of society was to develop, with catastrophic
consequences. Moreover, the Romantic anthropology of humankind as complex and in need of "redemption" fed into Sigmund Freud's atheistic view
of the human person as governed by psychic depths of a particularly sexual
nature, as well as Carl Jung's emphasis on the unconscious. Jung, however,
was far more positive about the role of religion than was Freud.

Jeremy Bentham and John Stuart Mill

In 1789 Jeremy Bentham (1748–1832) published *An Introduction to the Principles of Morals and Legislation*, which became the charter of utilitarianism.
He argued that the legal system should be reconstructed on sound principles.
The principles he owed to Hume; when he read the *Treatise of Human Nature* the scales fell from his eyes, as it were, and he came to believe that utility
was the test and measure of all virtue and the sole origin of justice. The happiness of the majority of the citizens was the criterion, and thus the goal of
legislation should be the greatest happiness of the greatest number. Bentham
contrasted utilitarianism with the principle of asceticism, which approves of
actions insofar as they diminish happiness. His chief target in this respect
was Christian morality.

John Stuart Mill (1806–73) was tutored by Bentham in the course of his
education. He experienced a breakdown early in life but found help in emerging
from it in the Romantic poet William Wordsworth. He later became a great fan
of Samuel Taylor Coleridge. In 1843 he published his *System of Logic*, in which
he argued that the truths of mathematics are also empirical. Mill venerated his
former tutor Bentham but thought his work needed development. In terms of
his social philosophy, he was influenced by Auguste Comte (1798–1857), a major
figure in the development of positivism who argued that human knowledge and
societies passed through stages: theological, metaphysical, and positive. Positive here means truly scientific. He took from Comte the idea of progress and
looked forward to "a future which shall unite the best qualities of the critical
with the best qualities of the organic periods; unchecked liberty of thought,

6. Ibid., 376.

unbounded freedom of individual action in all modes not hurtful to others; but also, convictions as to what is right and wrong, useful and pernicious, deeply engraven on the feelings by early education and general unanimity of sentiment."[7] Once achieved, no further progress would be necessary because the resulting society would be so grounded in reason and necessity.

Utilitarianism can be summarized with the acronym GGGN—the greatest good for the greatest number. Utilitarianism is alive and well today, but one doesn't have to probe far to see its dangers in a fallen world. While it sounds impressive, who is to decide what is good for humankind? Without a system of ethics, utilitarianism is susceptible to the perpetration of terrible evil in the name of the supposed greater good. Such an approach was used by monsters like Adolf Hitler and Joseph Stalin to validate the genocide of millions.

Arthur Schopenhauer

Although he receives scant attention in university philosophy courses in North America, Arthur Schopenhauer (1788–1850) remains the most widely read philosopher in Germany. Schopenhauer was one of the first philosophers to declare himself an atheist. In a letter he describes the traditional view of God as "having been truly cast forth by Kant. It has been handed down to me as a corpse, and when the smell of it comes back to me, as it did in your letter, I am filled with impatience."[8] In reaction to Leibniz, he declared that we "live in the worst of all possible worlds."[9] Indeed, a central emphasis of his philosophy is the suffering in the world—"We are like lambs playing in the field, while the butcher eyes them and selects first one and then another"[10]—and how to live out one's philosophy.

Schopenhauer's major work is *The World as Will and Idea*. Schopenhauer develops his notion of Idea(s) from Plato, along with whom he ascribes actual being to the Ideas alone.[11] Knowledge of the Ideas is a concrete experience in which one becomes completely absorbed in perceiving nature, with the result that one realizes that one "is the condition, and hence the supporter, of the world and of all objective existence."[12] The world exists only in relation

7. John Stuart Mill, *Autobiography*, ed. J. Stillinger (Oxford: Oxford University Press, 1969), 100.

8. Quoted in Henri de Lubac, *The Drama of Atheist Humanism* (San Francisco: Ignatius, 1995), 48.

9. Quoted in Wolfgang Schirmacher, ed., *The Essential Schopenhauer* (New York: Harper Perennial, 2010), vii.

10. Schirmacher, *The Essential Schopenhauer*, 2.

11. Ibid., 83.

12. Ibid., 82–83.

to consciousness: "The world is my idea." In this respect, Schopenhauer is not very different from Kant, but his presentation of will is highly original. Schopenhauer stressed the limits of science: "The answer to the riddle is given to the subject of knowledge appearing as individual, and the answer is given in the word *Will*. This and this alone gives him the key to his own phenomenon, reveals to him the significance and shows him the inner mechanism of his being, his actions, his movements."[13]

The inner nature of all objects must be will.[14] Willing arises from want and deficiency and thus suffering. There are two ways of escape from the slavery of will: art—especially music—and renunciation. The will to live is renounced not by suicide but asceticism. "We must go beyond virtue to asceticism. I must come to have such a horror of this miserable world that I will no longer think it enough to love others as myself or to give up my own pleasures when they stand in the way of others' good. To reach this ideal I must adopt chastity, poverty, and abstinence, and welcome death when it comes as a deliverance from evil."[15]

Schopenhauer's models of such asceticism were Christian, Hindu, and Buddhist saints, but in his view their religious beliefs are mythical clothing of truths unattainable by the uneducated.

Theodicy and the problem of evil are often regarded as a defeater for Christian theism.[16] There is indeed a mystery to evil, but one thing we learn from Schopenhauer's anthropocentric, individualistic philosophy is that dispensing with God accentuates rather than relieves this problem. Similarly, Gordon Michalson notes of Kant's view of evil that "the problem of evil brings Kant closer and closer to the insight that reason is not fully self-governing, but is subject to forces too murky to specify."[17]

Søren Kierkegaard

Søren Kierkegaard (1813–55) was born and spent most of his life in Copenhagen. His many books were published mainly in print runs of five hundred, which never sold out prior to his premature death at age forty-two. It was only at the beginning of the twentieth century that "he exploded upon the

13. Ibid., 65.

14. See ibid., 59–78.

15. Anthony Kenny, *Philosophy in the Modern World*, vol. 4 of *A New History of Western Philosophy* (Oxford: Oxford University Press, 2007), 15.

16. See Alvin Plantinga, *Warranted Christian Belief* (New York: Oxford University Press, 2000), 357–73, 458–99.

17. Gordon E. Michalson Jr., *Fallen Freedom: Kant on Radical Evil and Moral Regeneration* (Cambridge: Cambridge University Press, 1990), 141.

European intellectual scene like a long-delayed time bomb, and his influence since then has been incalculable."[18]

In his short life, Kierkegaard produced an astonishing corpus of highly creative writings, many under intriguing pseudonyms such as Johannes Climacus and Johannes de Silentio, written from diverse perspectives. We noted in chapter 1 that Christian philosophy is missional, and this was consciously the case with Kierkegaard. The Denmark in which he lived was one of Christendom; it was assumed that because one was a respectable Dane, one must be a Christian. Kierkegaard saw himself as a missionary called to "reintroduce Christianity into Christendom,"[19] hence the style in many of his major works of pseudonymity or indirect communication, in which he was akin to and influenced by Hamann. Kierkegaard aspired to be a modern-day Socrates who pushed his readers to personally appropriate truth. For Kierkegaard, truth involves the whole person—"truth is subjectivity"—and he wrote as he did to prod and push readers into personally engaging with existence and faith.[20]

An effect of Kierkegaard's indirect method of communication is that he has been read in many different ways: as an irrationalist, as a postmodern, as the father of existentialism. It is difficult nowadays for Western intellectuals to take Christian faith seriously, and yet this is at the heart of Kierkegaard's philosophy. He is a profoundly Christian philosopher, and one who is deeply relevant today.

Central to Kierkegaard's philosophy is his concern with human existence as it is lived. In this respect he stresses inwardness and human subjectivity; this is not an irrational move but his way of alerting us to the fact that a self is not just something I am but also something I must become. The unfinished self shapes itself through its choices; every decision I make is also a decision about the type of person I want to be. Kierkegaard affirms human freedom and responsibility but rejects the disengaged, disinterested self that began to emerge in modern philosophy. We make choices because of our desire and passions, and thus any understanding of human existence must extend beyond reason to include our emotional lives. "Subjectivity or inwardness are simply Kierkegaardian terms for this affective dimension of human life that must take center stage if we are to understand human existence."[21] For Kierkegaard the

18. C. Stephen Evans, *Kierkegaard: An Introduction* (Cambridge: Cambridge University Press, 2009), 1.

19. Søren Kierkegaard, *Kierkegaard's Journals and Papers*, trans. and ed. Howard V. Hong and Edna H. Hong, 7 vols. (Bloomington: Indiana University Press, 1978), entry 6271, 6:70–71.

20. See Søren Kierkegaard, *The Point of View of My Work as an Author: A Report to History*, ed. Benjamin Nelson (New York: Harper & Row, 1962); Evans, *Kierkegaard*, 24–45.

21. Evans, *Kierkegaard*, 22.

human self is inherently relational: in regard to itself—it must "relate itself to itself"—in regard to others, and preeminently with respect to God.

For Kierkegaard, human lives can be categorized as aesthetic, ethical, or religious. He describes these as both *stages* and *spheres*. Becoming fully human is not automatic, and humans can become fixed in one stage or sphere. However, the norm is for humans to develop from one stage to the next. It is important to note that such progression does not obliterate the previous stage; it remains but is recontextualized in a larger framework. The stages are not a psychologically watertight theory but a kind of conceptual map that depicts the possibilities of human existence.

The common factor in the aesthetic sphere is concern for "the immediate," for spontaneous sensations central to conscious human existence. The aesthete is concerned with what he or she desires, and lives in and for the moment. Kierkegaard recognizes a continuum of aesthetic life from the immediate aesthete to the highly reflective aesthete. An isolated individualism is characteristic of the latter. Boredom is the great evil to be avoided, and the imagination is to be used to keep boredom at bay. In Kierkegaard's *Either/ Or* the character "A" refers to this as rotation of crops: commitments must be avoided, one's environment and enthusiasms must be carefully controlled, and one must relish the arbitrary in search of the interesting.[22]

The problem for the aesthete is that immediacy is hard to sustain and the ethical insists on inserting itself amid the quest for the interesting. While the aesthetic life reduces to a series of moments, central to the ethical is a quest for a unified self, for identity, for a self that endures over time. The bulk of volume 2 of *Either/Or* is a critique by one "Judge William" of the aesthetic and a plea for the ethical. Against the aesthete, Judge William vigorously defends marriage; it is what enables love to endure. Judge William stresses the conscious becoming of a self as the heart of the difference between the aesthetic and the ethical: "The aesthetic in a person is that by which he immediately is what he is; the ethical is that by which he becomes what he becomes."[23] Choice is central to the ethical, hence the title *Either/Or*.

The sort of morality defended by Judge William is much the same as that of Johannes de Silentio in Kierkegaard's *Fear and Trembling*. It is like Hegel's *Sittlichkeit*, or social morality, according to which one is ethical by fulfilling one's social responsibilities. For Hegel the state is in some sense divine, and not surprisingly Kierkegaard finds this view of the ethical seriously incomplete.

22. Søren Kierkegaard, *Either/Or*, trans. Howard V. Hong and Edna H. Hong (Princeton: Princeton University Press, 1991), 1:281–91.
23. Ibid., 2:178.

In his—very long!—*Concluding Unscientific Postscript* Kierkegaard distinguishes between Religiousness A and Religiousness B. The former is characteristic of a religious attitude in general and is not uniquely Christian. Representative of A, Climacus notes that "I, Johannes Climacus, a native of this city, now thirty years old, an ordinary human being as are the majority of people, assume that a highest good, called an eternal happiness, awaits me just as it awaits a housemaid and a professor. I have heard that Christianity is the condition for acquiring this good: now I ask how I may enter into a relation to this doctrine."[24]

This question is pursued by Climacus for hundreds of pages. It becomes clear that the ethical presupposes the religious; it "is really the God-relationship that makes a human person a human person."[25] There is a universal dimension of human being, but humans are also individuals, each tasked with becoming themselves. The religious person recognizes that he or she is in some way broken and needs to be made whole again. Religion thus involves resignation—a letting go of created goods and a recognition of dependence on God—rather than Hegel's mediation.

Religiousness A is one of immanence; B is one of transcendence. B is Christian faith and involves God's revelation of himself as gift to the individual, thereby transforming the whole person, including the emotions and reason. Kierkegaard is highly critical of a sort of evidentialism that thinks that reason or historical arguments can produce faith. He is not opposed to either but has a strong view of the limits of both when it comes to faith. This is captured in his controversial description of the incarnation as "absolute paradox." That the eternal should become temporal is not, for Kierkegaard, a *logical* contradiction but an event that confronts reason with its boundaries. "It is the boundary or limit of reason, and when reason attempts to comprehend this limit it finds itself enmeshed in apparent contradictions."[26] At the same time, reason finds its fulfillment in the incarnation. For Kierkegaard there is no neutral ground when it comes to the incarnation; we respond with faith or denial.

In reaction to Hegel, Kierkegaard was wary of systems. Hence he rarely sets out his views systematically. We can, however, extrapolate his epistemology from his writings, and it is still surprisingly relevant. Kierkegaard adamantly opposes what has come to be called *classical foundationalism*, an epistemology still dominant today. Classical foundationalism makes two major claims:[27]

24. Søren Kierkegaard, *Concluding Unscientific Postscript to Philosophical Fragments*, trans. Howard V. Hong and Edna H. Hong, 2 vols. (Princeton: Princeton University Press, 1992), 1:15–16.
25. Ibid., 1:244.
26. Evans, *Kierkegaard*, 156.
27. See the more detailed discussion in chapter 13.

1. Genuine, warranted knowledge must be based on a foundation of truths known with a high degree of certainty.
2. Such certainty is only achieved by setting aside emotions and subjective attitudes so that one relies on reason alone.

　　　　　　　　　　　　　　　　・

C. Stephen Evans is right to note of Kierkegaard that "his whole outlook is a challenge to this classical foundationalist picture."[28] We are human, and the sort of absolute certainty sought by classical foundationalism is simply not available to us. "Truth is subjectivity!" Having the truth means being fully caught up in living life as it was intended to be. This is not to deny the importance of propositional truth, but it is to assert that subjective truth is equally important. We know the truth by living it, and the world opens up to us as we pursue that clue which is Christ. Evans notes the affinities between Kierkegaard's epistemology and that of virtue ethicists and externalist epistemology. The former stress the role of the cultivation of certain virtues in the knower, and the latter stresses that knowledge is a matter of being rightly related to the external world.

A distinguishing mark of Kierkegaard's Christian philosophy is his engagement with the Bible, and not only in his more theological works such as *Training in Christianity*, but also in his major philosophical works. *Fear and Trembling* alludes in its title to multiple biblical references, and in its opening section Kierkegaard develops a remarkable reflection on different ways in which the Genesis 22 narrative of Abraham being called to sacrifice Isaac might have worked out. In his *Repetition* Kierkegaard has an evocative reflection on how "he" reads Job:

> If I did not have Job! . . . I do not read him as one reads another book, with the eyes, but I lay the book, as it were, on my heart and read it with the eyes of the heart, in a Clairvoyance interpreting the specific points in most diverse ways. . . . I take the book to bed at night with me. Every word by him is food and clothing and healing for my wretched soul. . . . Have you really read Job? . . . Nowhere in the world has the passion of anguish found such expression. . . . At night I can have all the lights burning, the whole house illuminated. Then I stand up and read in a loud voice, almost shouting, some passage by him. . . . Although I have read the book again and again, each word remains new to me. . . . Like an inebriate, I imbibe all the intoxication of passion little by little, until by this prolonged sipping I become almost unconscious in drunkenness.[29]

28. Evans, *Kierkegaard*, 56.
29. Søren Kierkegaard, *Fear and Trembling/Repetition*, ed. and trans. Howard V. Hong and Edna H. Hong (Princeton: Princeton University Press, 1983), 204.

Even amid the remarkable renaissance of Christian philosophy in North America today, it is rare to find such deep engagement with Scripture. Unsurprisingly, Kierkegaard's reading of Scripture is often "subjective" and engaged, as befits his philosophy. In this regard his work is reminiscent of that of Hamann.

Kierkegaard's achievements were remarkable and his legacy has still to be fully appropriated. His sense of mission to his culture is notable and exemplary in the depth with which he pursued it. One wonders what an equivalent sense of mission might look like philosophically in our late-modern day.

Karl Marx

To a major extent, nineteenth- and twentieth-century philosophy continued to be dominated by the nature/freedom dialectic we identified earlier. Karl Marx (1818–83), Charles Darwin, and Auguste Comte (positivism) privileged the nature/scientific pole.

Marx's was the most violent and influential rejection of Hegel, and he referred to his philosophy as "turning Hegel upside down." He replaced Hegel's dialectical *idealism* with his own dialectical *materialism*. Educated in Germany, Marx learned from Hegel and Bruno Bauer (1809–82) to think of history as a dialectical process, and he found the young Hegelians' stress on alienation attractive. Bauer and Ludwig Feuerbach (1804–72) treated religion as the supreme form of alienation, and Marx agreed, although he thought their remedies inadequate. According to Marx, Hegel viewed man as a mere spectator of a process that he should in fact control, and Feuerbach failed to recognize that men also worship money. Marx was fired with a desire to transform the world: "The philosophers have only interpreted the world in various ways; the point is to change it."[30]

Marx became a political journalist and moved to Paris, where he joined forces with Friedrich Engels (1820–95). In 1848 *The Communist Manifesto* was published and was meant to epitomize the newly founded Communist League. Its message is summed up by Engels in the foreword to a later edition:

> The whole history of mankind (since the dissolution of primitive tribal society, holding land in common ownership) has been a history of class struggles, contests between exploiting and exploited, ruling and oppressed classes; That the history of these class struggles forms a series of evolutions in which, nowadays, a stage has been reached where the exploited and oppressed class—the

30. Karl Marx, *Theses on Feuerbach*, xi, available at http://www.marxists.org/archive/marx/works/1845/theses/theses.htm.

proletariat—cannot attain its emancipation from the sway of the exploiting and ruling class—the bourgeoisie—without, at the same time, and once and · for all, emancipating society at large from all exploitation, oppression, class distinction, and class struggles.[31]

The manifesto's most famous sentences came at the end: "Let the ruling classes tremble at a Communistic revolution. The proletarians have nothing to lose but their chains. They have a world to win. Working men of all countries, unite!"[32]

If ever one needed a reminder that ideas have legs and can march into history with major consequences, Marxism provides it. Marxism became incarnate in the Soviet Union early in the twentieth century and from then onward overshadowed most of the century. For all its lofty ideals—and many aspects of Marx's critique of capitalism remain as pertinent today as they were in his day—its legacy was hugely destructive, as we have seen increasingly since the demise of the Soviet Union.

Charles Darwin

"With Copernicus and Galileo, the medieval Christian cosmology itself had cracked. With Darwin, the Christian world view showed signs of collapsing altogether."[33] Marx and Charles Darwin (1809–82) were the two most influential thinkers of the nineteenth century. By the end of the twentieth century Marx's legacy lay in tatters, but Darwin's continues to influence Western philosophy, as we will see.

During the 1840s and 1850s, Darwin developed his theory of natural selection, which he published in his *On the Origin of Species*. There are three fundamental building blocks to Darwin's theory of evolution. First, organisms manifest great variety in the degree to which they are adapted to their environments. Second, all species are able to reproduce at a rate that would increase their numbers from generation to generation. Thirdly, they do not do this because of "natural selection." Species have to compete to survive, and only the fittest do so; this is the mechanism of evolution.

Darwin distinguished two main types of selection: artificial selection, which was long practiced by breeders, and natural selection, which is not purposive but is enacted by natural pressures on species. Natural selection can easily be

31. Friedrich Engels, preface to the 1888 English edition of *The Communist Manifesto*, available at http://www.marxists.org/archive/marx/works/1848/communist-manifesto/preface.htm.

32. Karl Marx and Friedrich Engels, *Communist Manifesto*, available at http://www.marxists.org/archive/marx/works/1848/communist-manifesto/ch04.htm.

33. Tarnas, *Passion of the Western Mind*, 305.

demonstrated within a single species, but Darwin believed that over a long period of time it could create whole new species of plants and animals.

Newton and Darwin dealt a serious blow to Aristotle's teleology. Teleology explains things in terms of their ends, not of their beginnings, and invokes the notion of goodness. Newton's theory of gravity explains by reference to an end, but without any suggestion that it is good for a body to arrive at such an end. Darwin also explains development in terms of an end but without a pull by the final state or perfected structure; it is the pressures of the system and environment that account for evolution.

In the late nineteenth century, Darwin's theory of evolution was recognized as a great threat to Christianity. However, Darwinism leaves much unexplained, and Darwin himself was cautious about any atheistic conclusions from his theory:

> To my mind it accords better with what we know of the laws impressed on matter by the Creator, that the production and extinction of the past and present inhabitants of the world should have been due to secondary causes, like those determining the birth and death of the individual. When I view all beings not as special creatures, but as the lineal descendants of some few beings which lived long before the first bed of the Silurian system was deposited, they seem to me to become ennobled.[34]

Evolution has been hugely influential, and in recent decades the debate about it has been reignited with the emergence of the intelligent design movement and the so-called New Atheism of Richard Dawkins and company. The intelligent design school may be dated from the publication of the book *Darwin on Trial* (1991) by Phillip Johnson. Probably the most important intelligent design book published is that by Catholic biochemist Michael Behe, *Darwin's Black Box*. Behe argues that there are biological systems so complex that they simply could not have originated by chance. In chapter 14 we will revisit the issue of evolution in the context of Alvin Plantinga's Reformed epistemology.

Friedrich Nietzsche

In comparison with Marx and Darwin, Friedrich Nietzsche (1844–1900) took the freedom pole of modern philosophy to its extreme while executing a devastating attack on any type of realism. Nietzsche was the son of a Lutheran pastor but came to reject Christianity; indeed, his philosophy is virulently

---

34. Charles Darwin, *The Origin of Species and The Voyage of the* Beagle (New York: Alfred A. Knopf, 2003), 912.

anti-Christian. In his first published work, *The Birth of Tragedy* (1872), Nietz-sche contrasts two aspects of the Greek psyche: the wild, irrational passions personified in Dionysius, expressed in music and tragedy, and the disciplined and harmonious beauty personified in Apollo and expressed in epics and the plastic arts. For Nietzsche the great achievement of Greek culture was to synthesize the two. However, in his *Ecce Homo* Nietzsche says of himself, "I am a disciple of the philosopher Dionysos."[35]

In books such as *Daybreak* (1881) and *The Gay Science* (1882) he sought to articulate a worldview that optimistically affirmed life. In the process he denounced Christian self-denial, altruistic ethics, democratic politics,[36] and scientific positivism. From 1883 to 1885 Nietzsche wrote his most famous work, *Thus Spoke Zarathustra*. He says of it that "within my writings my *Zarathustra* stands by itself. I have with this book given mankind the greatest gift that has ever been given it."[37] "*Zarathustra* is the only book that affords entry into Nietzsche's essential thought. It is the explosive core of the work of the philosopher who could say, 'I am dynamite.'"[38] Nietzsche chooses the old Persian prophet Zoroaster as his prophetic persona because he was both the founder of the earliest dualistic Aryan religion we know of and the first thinker to see the battle of good and evil as the wheel at the center of all things. In *Thus Spoke Zarathustra* the prophet returns not to propagate his "earlier" view that time is progress in the moral overcoming of earthly life but to ac-knowledge his terrible mistake and propagate Nietzsche's view. Zarathustra thus becomes through Nietzsche the prophet who proclaims the end of the rule of good and evil.

Thus Spoke Zarathustra contains ideas central to the final period of Nietzsche's life. Humans as they are now will be superseded by a race of superhumans. For Nietzsche humankind has not yet attained full existential self-determination. *Übermensch* refers to a form of humanity still to come, one free from anxiety and guilt and fully reliant on the values it has created *for itself*. With this goes the *transvaluation* of values—a radical overturning of traditional, and especially Christian, morality. Nietzsche is haunted not so much by God's death as by the fact that the full consequences of this death have not yet dawned on civilization. "This 'death' of the Christian God Nietz-sche identifies with the virtual end of the morality of good and evil, and of

35. Friedrich Nietzsche, *Ecce Homo*, trans. R. J. Hollingdale (London: Penguin, 1979), 2.

36. The forms of government that interested Nietzsche were rule through a leader's or oli-garchy's absolute exercise of power.

37. Nietzsche, *Ecce Homo*, "Foreword," 4.

38. Laurence Lampert, *Nietzsche's Teaching: An Interpretation of* Thus Spoke Zarathustra (New Haven: Yale University Press, 1986), 5. The quote from Nietzsche is from *Ecce Homo*, "Why I Am a Destiny," 1.

all forms of idealism. It is for him the cardinal event of modern history and of the contemporary world, the ghost that looms behind his every important thought."[39]

In response to Enlightenment philosophy and metaphysics Nietzsche affirms Heraclitus's view that all is flux and change/becoming: "Everything humankind has clung to in order to assure itself of the universal status of its epistemological and moral preferences, is revealed as prejudice, fiction, untruth, and deception. That which was received or projected as divine assurance is exposed as being no more than a subtle and clever creative inversion—a means of assuaging a terrifying sense of meaninglessness. *Incipit* nihilism."[40]

Nietzsche's analysis of European nihilism has pessimistic and optimistic aspects. The pessimistic side relates to the awareness that continued belief in truth and being and intelligibility will only disappoint. However, we need to see such fictions for what they are so that we can produce a new set of values in the light of reality as it is. This is the task of the Übermensch. Nietzsche also articulates his idea of eternal recurrence in this work: in infinite time there are periodic cycles in which what has happened happens again. When pessimistic, Nietzsche found this idea almost unendurable; nevertheless, he sought to embrace it enthusiastically.

Nietzsche's vitriolic anti-Christian bent is evident in many of his writings. For example, he asserts that "I call Christianity the one great curse, the one great innermost corruption, the one great instinct of revenge, for which no means is poisonous, stealthy, subterranean, *small* enough—I call it the one immortal blemish of mankind."[41]

In his analysis of Nietzsche, Karl Barth discerns behind Nietzsche's antipathy toward Christianity a rejection of the impossibility of "a humanity without the fellow-man" and especially of the fellow suffering neighbor. "The new thing in Nietzsche was the man of 'azure isolation,' six thousand feet above time and man; the man to whom a fellow-creature drinking at the same well is quite dreadful and insufferable; . . . the man beyond good and evil, who can exist only as a consuming fire."[42]

Nietzsche ended his life insane and died in 1900. He belongs with Marx and Freud as one of the three great masters of suspicion. All three were far from disinterested thinkers; they sought concrete change. All three were atheists

39. J. P. Stern, *Nietzsche*, Fontana Modern Masters (London: Fontana, 1978), 92.

40. Nicholas Davey, introduction to *Thus Spake Zarathustra*, by Friedrich Nietzsche, trans. Thomas Common (Ware, Hertfordshire: Wordsworth, 1997), xiv.

41. Friedrich Nietzsche, *The Antichrist*, in *The Portable Nietzsche*, trans. Walter Kauffmann (London: Penguin, 1968), 62.

42. Karl Barth, *Church Dogmatics*, trans. G. W. Bromiley (New York: T&T Clark, 2004), III/2, 240.

who regarded belief in God as symptomatic of man's weakness and subordination. All three directed their thinking toward a single leading idea: motivation through material interest (Marx); sexual motivation (Freud); and the will to power (Nietzsche). All three profoundly influenced the twentieth century.

Nietzsche has been read in a variety of ways, ranging from a mad, evil genius, to an existential thinker, to a major source of Nazism, to a precursor of analytic philosophy, to a timely philosopher for today, to a major source for postmodern philosophy. In Alan Bloom's celebrated *The Closing of the American Mind*, Nietzsche evokes the worst possible scenario of the future of the West. By contrast, Richard Schacht suggests that Nietzsche's "time may at last be arriving; and as we move toward the turn of both his century and the millennium, he may well turn out to have been right as well when . . . he proclaimed his kind of philosophy to be a 'prelude to a philosophy of the future.'"[43]

J. P. Stern's evaluation of Nietzsche is in our opinion correct: "That 'God is dead,' that the world is a product of the will to power, and that true values lie in a morality of strenuousness, are Nietzsche's formulations for convictions on which much of our lives is based. They are not (I believe) true convictions. Yet no man has been more imaginative in trying to see what the world would be like if they were true."[44] The twist in the tale of this astute assessment should not be missed. Nietzsche's convictions are false, but in our late-modern times we are living as though they were true.

Pragmatism

With Charles Sanders Peirce (1839–1914), American philosophy came of age. Peirce is the originator of one of the most influential schools of American philosophy: pragmatism. There are three central claims to Peirce's pragmatism:[45]

1. Scientific method is the most reasonable way of arriving at truth.
2. Scientific method is a self-correcting communal and social process whose goal is "the settlement of opinion."[46] Peirce's pragmatic dimension is evident in his argument that it is only by establishing a consensus of opinion that we can hope to arrive at philosophical truth. He was

---

43. Richard Schacht, *Making Sense of Nietzsche: Reflections Timely and Untimely* (Urbana and Chicago: University of Illinois Press, 1995), 1.

44. Stern, *Nietzsche*, 149.

45. Cornel West, *The American Evasion of Philosophy: A Genealogy of Pragmatism* (Madison: University of Wisconsin Press, 1989), 43.

46. *Collected Papers of Charles Sanders Peirce*, ed. Charles Hartshorne, Paul Weiss, and Arthur Burks (Cambridge, MA: Harvard University Press, 1933–58), 5:376.

strongly critical of Cartesianism and the epistemological focus of idealism, empiricism, and commonsense realism.
3. The scientific quest is linked to the ultimate good of furthering evolutionary love.

Peirce articulated a view called *fallibilism*: our knowledge involves ever-
improving approximation, and in terms of an epistemological criterion, we
need only consider what conceivable effects of a practical kind the object
may involve.

Peirce is clearly committed to scientific method, but he demystifies it into
a human affair, enabling him to defend religion: "Many a scientific man and
student of philosophy recognizes that it is the Christian church which has made
him a man among men. . . . The law of love which, however little it be obeyed,
he holds to be the soul of civilization, came to Europe through Christianity."[47]

William James (1842–1910) was born in New York, the son of a Sweden-
borgian[48] theologian. James was deeply concerned with religious issues and
anxious to reconcile a scientific worldview with belief in God, freedom, and
immortality. In 1901 and 1902 he gave the Gifford lectures, published as *Vari-
eties of Religious Experience*. He subjected religious experience to empirical
investigation, hoping to validate it. The publication of his *Pragmatism* in 1907
established him as the doyen of American philosophy.

James was indebted to Peirce but argued for a theory of meaning rather
than a theory of truth. He sought a philosophy that was interpersonal and
objective rather than individualist and subjective. His pragmaticism manifests
itself clearly in his view that an idea is true so long as it is profitable to our lives:
"What is true is what works," and "if the hypothesis of God works satisfactorily
in the widest sense of the word, it is true."[49] James insists this does not deny
objective reality; reality and truth differ from each other. Things have reality,
whereas ideas and beliefs are true *of* them. James argues that we are aware of
a "wider self from which saving experiences flow in" and of a "mother sea of
consciousness."[50] Suffering, however, precludes belief in an infinite, absolute
divinity so that the superhuman consciousness is limited in either knowledge
or power. Here again, as with Kant, Fichte, and Romanticism, we see a reach-
ing for an ultimate *arché* outside of human experience, but, as with Kant, the
divine is something that is required but not necessarily true or knowable.

47. Quoted in West, *American Evasion*, 48.
48. Swedenborgianism is an offshoot of Christianity that developed from the writings of
Emmanuel Swedenborg (1688–1772) who claimed new revelation from Jesus Christ.
49. William James, *Pragmatism* (Cambridge, MA: Harvard University Press, 1975), 143.
50. William James, *A Pluralistic Universe*, quoted by Kenny, *Philosophy in the Modern
World*, 46.

As we will see in the next chapter on postmodernism, in our discussion of Richard Rorty, pragmatism is beset with difficulties and dangers. Who is to determine what is "profitable" for our lives, and how do we know if something genuinely "works." American, as well as global, culture is awash with such sentiments that easily play into the worst forms of individualism and self-centeredness.

Gottlob Frege

Gottlob Frege (1848–1925) and Edmund Husserl are considered the fathers of the two most influential streams of philosophy in the twentieth century. Frege is the father of *analytical philosophy* and Husserl of *phenomenology* (discussed below). Frege was the inventor of modern mathematical logic, and his philosophy focuses on the analysis of meaning *in language*. Frege's emphasis in this respect led to the focus on language that characterized much twentieth-century philosophy. Frege gave propositional calculus its first systematic formulation, but Frege's greatest contribution to logic is predicate calculus, by which he attends to the internal structure of propositions. He sought to establish that all the truths of arithmetic follow from truths of logic, but as Anthony Kenny comments, "We now know that the logicist programme can never be carried out."[51]

Bertrand Russell

After the death of John Stuart Mill, an idealist reaction to his empiricism arose in Britain. At the turn of the century this idealism was decisively critiqued by two young Cambridge philosophers, G. E. Moore (1873–1958) and Bertrand Russell (1872–1970), in whose work we witness a return to the nature/scientific pole of modern thought. Russell's early work was in the area of logic and mathematics, influenced inter alia by Frege. His early work is often said to have inaugurated the era of analytic philosophy in Britain. The road to truth via analysis involved taking wholes to pieces and analyzing concepts. At the time of his *Principle of Mathematics* (1910–13), Russell believed that to ensure the objectivity of concepts and judgments, it was necessary to accept the existence of propositions as subsisting independently of their expression or sentences.

Russell's 1905 paper "On Denoting" gave analysis a linguistic turn; it rests on distinguishing between symbols (such as proper names) that denote something in the world and other symbols that he described as "incomplete symbols." The latter have meaning only in the sentences in which they occur; that is, the sentences express a proposition that is true or false.

51. Kenny, *Philosophy in the Modern World*, 43.

Russell came to believe that once logic had been developed into a clear form, it would reveal the structure of the world. Logic contains individual variables and propositional functions. Correspondingly, the world contains particulars and universals. In logic, complex propositions are built up as truth-functions of simple propositions. Similarly, there are in the world independent atomic facts corresponding to the simple propositions. This theory is called logical atomism. Russell came to argue that every proposition that we can understand must be made up wholly of items with which we are acquainted—that is, items of immediate presentation, such as our own sense data.

Positivism and the Early Ludwig Wittgenstein

Through exposure to Russell's philosophy, Ludwig Wittgenstein (1889–1951), while a soldier in World War I, wrote his *Tractatus Logico-Philosophicus*. It contains only seven major numbered propositions. Wittgenstein's basic idea is that synthetic language presents a logical view of the world. Facts and their relations are represented logically by language. Wittgenstein hit upon this idea when observing how a car accident was portrayed by dolls in a courtroom. We do not deal directly with things but with "facts" stated in propositions. "The world is the totality of facts."[52] Only propositions have sense, and it is only in the nexus of a proposition that a name has a meaning. To understand a proposition is to know what is the case if it is true. Language has a tendency to disguise thought, and so philosophy must be a critique of language, enabling the logical structure of propositions to be foregrounded.

Logical truths are the only other legitimate category of meaning, but according to Wittgenstein they tell us nothing about the world. He stresses the clarity of language: "Everything that can be thought at all can be thought clearly. Everything that can be put into words can be put clearly."[53] Such clear language is univocal. Wittgenstein's more enigmatic statements in the final pages of the *Tractatus* were ignored by the Vienna circle, which we will discuss below. Despite having asserted that "*the limits of my language* mean the limits of my world,"[54] Wittgenstein nevertheless says that "we feel that even when all *possible* scientific questions have been answered, the problems of life remain completely untouched."[55] Such mystical things could be "shown" but not said.

52. Ludwig Wittgenstein, *Tractatus Logico-Philosophicus*, trans. D. F. Pears and B. F. Mc-Guinness (London: Routledge and Kegan Paul, 1961), 1.1.
53. Ibid., 4.116.
54. Ibid., 5.6.
55. Ibid., 6.52.

The *Tractatus* became the bible of the logical positivist movement that developed in Vienna. *Positivism* has come to designate a philosophical movement that was influential in all countries of the Western world in the second half of the nineteenth century and the first half of the twentieth century.

L. Kolakowski discerns four main characteristics of positivism.[56] First is phenomenalism, which opposes any distinction between substance and essence. Second is nominalism, whereby "we may not assume that any insight formulated in general terms can have any real referents other than individual concrete objects."[57] Third, positivism refuses to call value judgments and normative statements knowledge. And finally, positivism upholds the unity of the scientific method. The methods for acquiring valid knowledge and the stages of theoretical reflection are essentially the same in all spheres of experience.

Positivism thus seeks to apply its epistemology to all disciplines. This means that methods derived from the natural sciences are extended to other disciplines so that a science of literature, for example, analogous to the natural sciences, emerges. At the heart of logical positivism is the verification principle, according to which a proposition is verified if, and only if, it is empirically verified. Particularly in the later years, the logical positivists sought conclusive or absolute verification. They ruled out as cognitively meaningless any language that could not be verified. Thus religious language and beliefs, for example, are meaningless.

Positivism was, however, hoisted with its own petard: the principle of verification could not itself be verified! Karl Popper (1902–94), a philosopher on friendly terms with the positivists in Vienna, further pointed out that in science hypotheses are not so much verified as that attempts are repeatedly made to *falsify* theories. Popper was also more cautious than the positivists in extending his falsification principle beyond science. In his later work Popper developed a far more helpful view of epistemology with his contrasting images of the bucket and the torch. Acquiring knowledge is not like collecting facts in a bucket; it is deeply influenced by the torchlight shone on what is being studied.

The Late Wittgenstein and Analytic Philosophy after Wittgenstein

After finishing the *Tractatus* and leaving philosophy behind, Wittgenstein was persuaded to return to philosophy and Cambridge in the late 1920s, and he

56. L. Kolakowski, *Positivist Philosophy: From Hume to the Vienna Circle* (Middlesex, NJ: Penguin, 1972), 9–18.
57. Ibid., 13.

became very critical of his earlier views. This "late" Wittgenstein focused on redoing philosophical method so that it is nonsystematic and nonmetaphysical; on overcoming Platonic dualism, which manifests itself in mind/body dualism; on correcting faulty views of language that result from dualism, views which make us think that our words can "step back from the world and picture the world." Wittgenstein thus sought a more human way of speaking, knowing, and philosophizing.[58]

Wittgenstein became critical of the view that tied concepts to referents in the world. One of Wittgenstein's sayings that reflects his new emphasis on language use was "Back to the rough ground."[59] It is more important to see how words are used in particular contexts than to come up with a logically tight definition. Wittgenstein uses the metaphor of a game to warn against trying to define words too precisely. Failure to attend to these language issues is the source of many philosophical problems: "Philosophical problems arise when language *goes on holiday*."[60] For Wittgenstein language is public, and he argues that there is no "private language." We learn the meanings of words in the forms of life, and this is a public affair.

The use of words varies in different contexts, what Wittgenstein calls "language games." Examples are giving and obeying orders; describing the appearance of an object; reporting an event; making up a story; solving a problem in mathematics; and asking, thanking, cursing, greeting, and praying. Within a specific language game, judgments can be made. Within bricklaying, one can determine whether a brick is laid correctly. However, as Wittgenstein emphasizes in *On Certainty*, when answers to questions such as why lay bricks? why do philosophy? and why struggle to live? are sought, the fundamental assumptions behind our answers are what we judge *with*, not *what* we judge. There is justification, but at some point we "stand fast." "What has to be accepted, the given, is—so one could say—*forms of life*."[61]

The analytic tradition in philosophy was continued by philosophers such as W. V. O. Quine (1908–2000) and Donald Davidson (1917–2003) in the United States and Peter Strawson (1919–2006) in England. Indeed, it continues apace in a variety of contexts. In the meantime, however, so-called postmodern philosophy emerged from the 1980s onward and altered the philosophical landscape dramatically. Postmodern philosophy is closely related to the turn to hermeneutics in philosophy and the emergence of distinctively continental

58. We are indebted to Bruce Ashford for these insights.
59. Ludwig Wittgenstein, *Philosophical Investigations*, trans. G. E. M. Anscombe (New York: Macmillan, 1958), I, 107.
60. Ibid., I, 38.
61. Ibid., II, xi.

compared to analytic philosophy.[62] The father figure in this respect is Martin Heidegger, a student of the father of phenomenology, Edmund Husserl. Before moving on to Heidegger we need to take account of Husserl.

Edmund Husserl

Edmund Husserl (1858–1938) is the founder of the other major trend in twentieth century philosophy—phenomenology. Husserl's phenomenology is a last ditch attempt to rescue the Enlightenment project. His *transcendental idealism* emerged after a long study of Kant and represents a reversion to the freedom pole of modern thought.

Phenomenology aims to study the immediate data of consciousness without reference to the extramental world. Husserl acknowledges Descartes as the genuine patriarch of phenomenology, but in contrast to Descartes he emphasizes experience rather than logic. "Husserl sees the ego simply as the matrix of experience."[63] It is this emphasis on human experience in all its rich diversity that has made phenomenology such a fertile philosophy, producing among others profound studies of the phenomenology of religion,[64] place, and liturgy.

Unlike Kant, Husserl thinks that we can know the thing-in-itself, but in our analysis the extramental world needs to be bracketed off, a procedure he calls "epoché." We can have infallible knowledge of the objects of our consciousness but only inferred, conjectured information about the external world. It is this *immanent perception* that is the focus of phenomenology. For Husserl, only consciousness has "absolute being"; other forms of being depend on consciousness for their existence.[65] Husserl states, "Accept nothing but that which we can master with insight as it is essentially presented within pure consciousness."[66]

Intuition is central to Husserl's phenomenology. He believes that we can have an intellectual intuition of objects we can see: categorical objects, states of affairs, relationships, causal connections, and so on. Such an intuition

62. The distinction between analytic and continental philosophy is important but not always easy to define. In general, analytic philosophy has a major concern with logic whereas the range of views that developed in Europe—hence "continental"—during the twentieth century are far less concerned with logic and more suspicious of metaphysics.

63. Samuel E. Stumpf, *Socrates to Sartre: A History of Philosophy*, 6th ed. (Boston: McGraw Hill, 1999), 461.

64. See our discussion of Jean-Luc Marion in chapter 12.

65. Edmund Husserl, *Ideas Pertaining to a Pure Phenomenology and to a Phenomenological Philosophy. First Book*, trans. F. Kirsten (Dordrecht: Kluwer, 1998), § 49.

66. Quoted in D. F. M. Strauss, *Philosophy: Discipline of the Disciplines* (Grand Rapids: Paideia Press, 2009), 629.

occurs when we are able to describe an object as having particular features or relationships. Simple, material objects can be intuited emptily or when present; the former is performed by memory apart from the object being present. However, even when present, objects retain aspects that are hidden so that perception is always a mixture of empty and filled intentions.

Intentionality, another key concept in Husserl's phenomenology, refers to the relationship of consciousness toward things *as perceived by the consciousness*. Intentionality is thus very different from what we nowadays call "intention." Husserl took this term from Franz Brentano (1838–1917), who adopted it from medieval contexts in which it has the meaning of being aimed at a target. An intentional object for Husserl is thus the target of a thought.

Having overcome his adherence to Kant's distinction between the phenomenal and noumenal, Husserl came to believe that we can access intuitively the thing-in-itself. Things are presented to us in a variety of ways, and philosophy should engage in precise descriptions of these appearances. For Husserl, we should aim through our descriptions to get to the essential structures of things. We achieve this through "imaginative variation," whereby in our imagination we remove various features from the object we are analyzing until we discern the essential features, the removal of which would destroy the object. This leads to *eidetic intuition*, the view that certain features belong to the *eidos*, the essence of an object. Husserl believed that eidetic analysis leads to *apodictic truths*, truths that can be seen to be necessary.

Husserl reflected long and hard on the nature of philosophical thinking and distinguished between natural—our everyday, straightforward thinking—and phenomenological thinking: "When we enter the phenomenological attitude, we put out of action or suspend all the intentions and convictions of the natural attitude; this does not mean that we doubt or negate them, only that we take a distance from them and contemplate their structure. Husserl calls this suspension the phenomenological *epoché*."[67] D. F. M. Strauss notes of Husserl's phenomenology that "setting aside the natural attitude . . . with one stroke . . . is a matter of full freedom. . . . It is indeed through complete freedom that Husserl ensures the validity of his intuitionistic . . . phenomenological science ideal. He does not wish to return to the pre-Kantian rationalistic science ideal."[68]

In the last decade of his life, however, Husserl developed an important concept, that of the *life-world*. This refers to the prescientific world, the world of lived reality that has its own structures, appearances, and truth. The truths derived from scientific abstraction should not be set in opposition

67. Robert Sokolowski, "Husserl, Edmund," in *The Cambridge Dictionary of Philosophy*, 2nd ed., ed. Robert Audi (Cambridge: Cambridge University Press, 1999), 405.
68. Strauss, *Philosophy*, 630.

to the life-world, but rather it should be shown through analysis how philosophy is a development of appearances in that life-world. Husserl's attempt to ground knowledge in pure consciousness must ultimately be judged a failure. Once the life-world is allowed back in, so too is our historical situatedness, an element that Heidegger would exploit as he took his master's phenomenology in a hermeneutical direction.

Existentialism

As the twentieth century progressed, the great optimism at the outset of the century steadily unraveled despite all the scientific and technological progress. An expression of this crisis was existentialism. There is a theistic version of existentialism associated with philosophers such as Nikolai Berdyaev (1874–1948), Gabriel Marcel (1889–1973), Karl Jaspers (1883–1969), and Martin Buber (1878–1965), although Marcel later rejected the label *existentialist*. Undoubtedly the darker version of existentialism is the atheistic one, associated with Jean-Paul Sartre (1905–80) and Albert Camus (1913–60). Three central concerns are evident in existentialism:[69]

1. A concern with the *individual person* rather than general theories about him or her. Existentialism is concerned with the uniqueness of each individual, something that general theories omit.
2. A concern with the *meaning or purpose of human life* as opposed to scientific or metaphysical truths about the world.
3. A concern with the *freedom* of individuals as their most significant and human characteristic.

Sartre was *the* major exponent of atheistic existentialism. He denied the existence of God, and like Nietzsche he regarded this "death of God" as very important. The consequence is that there are no objective values set out for us, and there is no ultimate meaning or purpose in life, so that in this respect life is "absurd." For Sartre, human existence precedes human essence. We are not created for any purpose; we simply find ourselves existing and have to decide what to do about it. We are condemned to be free.

Unlike Freud, Sartre held that consciousness is transparent to itself so that every moment requires a new choice. Self-deception or bad faith involves the attempt to escape the anguish of our freedom by pretending we are not free. The opposite virtue—namely, sincerity—while complex, implies that it is

69. Leslie Stevenson, *Seven Theories of Human Nature* (New York and Oxford: Oxford University Press, 1987), 89.

possible to achieve authenticity. A person is a unity and thus there must be a basic, fundamental choice that gives meaning to every aspect of a person's life. Later in life, Sartre espoused Marxism and thereby enlarged his existentialism beyond the individual to group struggle.

A major problem with the atheistic existentialism of Sartre, Camus, and others is that, heroic as the choice for freedom may be, it is by definition *arbitrary*. There is nothing to constrain it in any direction. Thus it would be hard to see, for example, how the committed apartheid activist in the old South Africa or the member of the Ku Klux Klan would be judged less authentic than someone like William Wilberforce in his quest to liberate slaves.

Martin Heidegger

Martin Heidegger (1889–1976), Husserl's star student, took phenomenology in a hermeneutical direction. Heidegger's philosophy[70] is strongly ontological, and his epistemology is rooted in his ontology of Dasein. Dasein means literally "being there," referring to our uniquely human way of being in the world. It is often translated as "existence." Sein (being) can be investigated only if one begins with Dasein, which does not have a viewpoint outside history. In this sense "the phenomenology of Dasein is a hermeneutic."[71] This approach allowed Heidegger to rethink along historical lines the subject-object relationship in knowing, and it is here that his most significant hermeneutical contribution lies. "Worldhood" refers to that whole in which the human person finds oneself immersed. It is ontological and a priori, given along with Dasein and prior to all conceptualizing. To conceive of objects as merely "present-at-hand" involves secondary conceptualization. The primary relationship of humans to objects is as "ready-to-hand." This contrasts with the Cartesian scientific orientation, which makes secondary conceptualization primary.[72]

Understanding is related to interpretation in that interpretation is not the acquiring of information about what is understood but the working out of the possibilities projected in understanding. In this Heidegger opened the way for the recognition of the radical historicity of hermeneutics; indeed, in his view the question of being can only be asked within time. Hans-Georg Gadamer says of Heidegger: "He was the first to liberate Dilthey's philosophical intention."[73]

70. We focus here on Heidegger's philosophy as represented by *Being and Time*, trans. John Macquarrie and Edward Robinson (Oxford: Basil Blackwell, 1962).

71. Ibid., 62.

72. Cf. ibid., 157–61, 187–91.

73. Hans-Georg Gadamer, *Truth and Method*, 2nd ed. (London: Sheed and Ward, 1989), 242–43.

This historicity of the interpreter has radical implications for hermeneutics and is central to the hermeneutic philosophy of Gadamer.

Hans-Georg Gadamer

Hans-Georg Gadamer (1900–2002), the father of hermeneutics, ascribes primary importance to understanding and insists on the historical nature of understanding itself. For Gadamer, "any interpretations of the past, whether they were performed by an historian, philosopher, linguist, or literary scholar, are as much a creature of the interpreter's own time and place as the phenomenon under investigation was of its own time and period in history."[74]

Part 1 of Gadamer's *Truth and Method* is concerned with the question of truth as it emerges in the understanding of art. Gadamer argues that experience and dialogue, and *not* abstraction, are the key to understanding art. He attacks the Enlightenment exaltation of theoretical reason and appeals to Aristotle's notion of practical knowledge and the *sensus communis*.

In part 2 of *Truth and Method* Gadamer analyzes the hermeneutic tradition stemming from Schleiermacher and develops his own historical approach. In contrast to Enlightenment attitudes, Gadamer sees all interpretation as always guided by its own prejudice. This prejudice is not just negative, and it cannot be simply discarded: "Using Heidegger, Gadamer rejects the Enlightenment prejudice against one's having presuppositions and working prejudgements, and the concomitant Enlightenment emasculation of tradition—as if one who does not question the prejudices of his own age is therefore a model knower."[75] The Enlightenment manifests a prejudice against prejudice, whereas Gadamer refuses to set reason in opposition to tradition. Indeed, understanding takes place as an event within a tradition. In contrast to existential thinking, Gadamer tries to locate meaning in the larger context of the community, as his view of tradition demonstrates.

In the light of the historicity of all interpretation, how is understanding possible? What makes understanding possible is *Wirkungsgeschichte*, which refers to the overriding historical continuum and cultural tradition of which both interpreter and historical object are part. Thus hermeneutics aims at prejudgments that will foster a fusion of the past with the present, which facilitates the miracle of understanding—the sharing of a common meaning

74. Kurt Mueller-Vollmer, introduction to *The Hermeneutics Reader: Texts of the German Tradition from the Enlightenment to the Present*, ed. Kurt Mueller-Vollmer (New York: Continuum, 1992), 38.

75. Calvin Seerveld, "Review of H. G. Gadamer, *Truth and Method*," *Criticism* 36/4 (1978): 488.

by temporally distant consciousnesses. In this "fusing of horizons," distance and critical tension are never completely obliterated; indeed, the hermeneutic task is to foreground the tensions. Nevertheless, interpretation always involves application.

Interpretation proceeds through a dialectical process of question and answer. Gadamer is opposed to trying to fix once and for all the meaning of a text. Our interpretation is only one actualization of the historical potential of a text, so that correct interpretation will be characterized by unending dialogue. Knowledge is inherently dialectical, and we humans are conversations. This does not mean that the interpreter is free to simply dominate the text with imposed meanings. The good interpreter lets the text speak and convince the receiving interpreter.

In part 3 of *Truth and Method* Gadamer offers a draft for an ontology of language-in-action. He proposes an ontology in which all understanding rests in language itself and seeks to explore systematically the universal conditions for just interpretation, which will not presume interpretation can be ahistorical.

Since Gadamer's approach, no other really groundbreaking hermeneutical innovations have appeared, but his hermeneutics has generated numerous debates, as we will see in the next chapter. Indeed, Gadamer is a pivotal figure between modern and postmodern paradigms of philosophy.

Conclusion

It is not by chance that most of the key philosophers we examined in this chapter were not Christians or were strongly opposed to Christianity. Most modern philosophies are immanent in the sense of trying to ground knowledge on some sure place *within* creation. This will never suffice, and so, as we have seen, they oscillate between privileging the pole of freedom and then, in reaction, privileging nature/science, and vice versa. Against this backdrop, Kierkegaard shines like a star in a dark firmament. In chapter 8 we saw how early modern philosophers still took Christianity seriously amid the developing focus on epistemology and humanity rather than God and ontology. During the period explored in this chapter, the residue of faith was largely cast aside, and the major philosophies developed were mainly anti-Christian. We also witnessed the divergence of Continental and analytic philosophy, but as they develop both strands leave little or no respectable room for faith. Phenomenology is particularly interesting with its focus on human experience, of which religion is a significant part. Philosophers continue to debate the extent to which phenomenology can do justice to Christian revelation. During much of the twentieth century, Christian philosophers were on the defensive and at best sought to correlate Christian thought with contemporary philosophy. Generally this involved conceding the epistemic starting point to philosophy and then seeking to find points of correlation with Christian faith—on the whole a vacuous enterprise.

From: abby@longobedience.edu
To: percy@secular.edu
Subject: Kierkegaard

Hey Perc,
I think you are right—modern philosophy is awash with Genesis 3 and human autonomy, *the* great temptation. And yet it's been encouraging to see Christian philosophers in the midst of this. I have really enjoyed our work on Kierkegaard: such interesting, creative, and definitely missional work. I wonder what an equivalent philosophy would look like today? Any thoughts?

Yours, as ever,
Abby

11

Postmodernism and Philosophy Today

We need to distinguish the increasingly convincing critique of the modern at the level of theory . . . from the fact that, at a practical level, we remain thoroughly enmeshed in modernity, largely because of the stranglehold that technology, the stepchild of modernity, has on our daily lives.[1]

Introduction

Perhaps *the* voice in philosophy that most of us are aware of is postmodernism, but it is important also to be aware that postmodernism is a minority view among philosophers. Despite its high profile, a multitude of alternative

1. Edward S. Casey, *Getting Back into Place: Toward a Renewed Understanding of the Place-World* (Bloomington and Indianapolis: Indiana University Press, 2009), 389–90.

traditions in philosophy continue to be practiced. It is also probable that postmodernism is now in decline. Postmodern movements have been passé in France, from where many of them originated, for some time now. Tony Judt notes that

> thus it comes about that French scholars who travel in Britain, the United States, or elsewhere today sometimes have the uncomfortable sense that they have flown back into their own past, as they encounter critics for whom Sartre was the "conscience of his age," hear historians deconstructing the Middle Ages, meet literary theorists disquisitioning upon the death of the text and late-structuralist feminists sorting society into linguistically gendered spheres. But it is a two-dimensional past, where time and place have disappeared, where the body of French cultural and political life has faded away, and all that is left is a postmodern Cheshire cat with a PhD, grinning.[2]

If there is a dominant philosophy in North America today, it would probably be either naturalism or pragmatism. James Sire argues that on university campuses across North America naturalism remains dominant: "Today naturalism is dominant. There is simply no academic discipline—whether in the arts and humanities, the social sciences or the natural sciences—that takes as its starting assumption the notion of a God who has created both the scholars and the world they are studying."[3]

Metaphysical naturalism is the view that only natural objects and properties are real. In such a philosophy there is no place for the God whom C. S. Lewis describes as the hunter, the warrior, the king—the God who approaches at infinite speed. In intellectual circles in North America some version of naturalism is indeed dominant. As Peter Berger so aptly describes America, it is a nation of Indians ruled by an elite of Swedes. India is the most religious society in the world; Sweden is the most secular. Despite the flourishing of religious beliefs among Americans, the elite, who are trained by the top universities, are highly secular and largely determine the direction of the country.

A good question is how pragmatism and postmodernism relate to naturalism. They seem poles apart but, we would argue, are in fact close cousins if not triplets. Modernity, and thus naturalism, took a severe beating in the twentieth century, so that the very notion of the "real," let alone the possibility of our knowing it, has come into question. The twentieth century began with immense hubris and optimism that reason and science would lead us to

---

2. Tony Judt, *Past Imperfect: French Intellectuals, 1945–1956* (Berkeley: University of California Press, 1992), 300; cf. 293–319.

3. James W. Sire, *Naming the Elephant: Worldview as a Concept* (Downers Grove, IL: InterVarsity, 2004), 157.

a utopia. Such ill-grounded hope has been trashed again and again: World War I, Stalinism, the Great Depression, World War II, the nuclear threat, the ecological threat, terrorism, and so we could continue. So devastating has this attack on modernity been that to some it appears that modernity itself has come to an end. According to John Carroll, "We live amidst the ruins of the great, five-hundred-year epoch of Humanism. Around us is that 'colossal wreck.' Our culture is a flat expanse of rubble."[4]

As we will see below, many of the foundational *beliefs* of modernity have indeed taken a beating, but, as the quote from Edward Casey at the outset of this chapter rightly notes, we should be careful of thinking we have moved beyond modernity to a new postmodern era. David Harvey, in his *Condition of Postmodernity*, provides an insightful, overarching way to think about postmodern philosophy. Modernity largely rejected tradition—including religion—as the route to truth. Reason and science were the royal road to truth about the world. Postmodernism rejects this royal route but does not recover religion and tradition. "True truth," as Francis Schaeffer called it, is no longer available, so that we are left with a multitude of views of the world without any one being able to claim to be the true view of the world. As a movement, postmodernism is thus akin to the period of the judges, when everyone did what was right "in their own eyes" (cf. Judg. 17:6; 21:25). Of course, in Judges this is a damning judgment, whereas postmodernists celebrate such diversity.

Casey furthermore reminds us quite correctly that even while criticism of modernity has been gaining ground, technology is triumphing. We would state the case even more strongly. Ironically, the postmodern critique of modernity has developed even as global consumerism has spread its tentacles around the world. The notions of the market and capitalism that underlie global consumerism are quintessentially modern, as is the dominance of technology, so that from this perspective, far from living amid the demise of modernity, we are living amid its apparent triumph. An important question is whether postmodernism has, however unintentionally, facilitated this triumph.

If you are an atheist and naturalism has been mauled, as it has been over the last hundred years, where do you go from there?

a. One route, of course, would be back to Christian theism, but for many contemporary philosophers this route no longer exists. If one rejects Christian theism, what then?

b. One might try to get modernity back on track while taking account of the critique that has developed. This, as we will see below, is the approach of the German philosopher Jürgen Habermas.

4. John Carroll, *Humanism: The Wreck of Western Culture* (London: Fontana, 1993), 1.

c. One might embrace the sort of postmodern critique of modernity already present in Nietzsche—in so many ways the father of postmodernism—and seek to defuse its radical implications of nihilism and meaninglessness. This indeed is the route that most postmodern philosophers have taken. As we will see below, Richard Rorty's pragmatic postmodernism, for example, is a variant of this approach.

It is important to note that we can learn from all of these approaches; they all have insights that Christians ignore to their detriment. But what must be noted about both b and c is that they are internal reactions to modernity without abandoning the basic humanistic religious orientation of modernity. As the British philosopher of science Mary Hesse so aptly points out, "The liberal consensus has so successfully established itself as the ideology of Western intellectual culture, that it has become almost invisible as the presupposition of every postmodern debate."[5] Postmodernism is a thoroughly Western phenomenon, and despite its many insights it remains thoroughly humanist in its basic orientation.

Take religion for example. A major contribution of postmodern philosophy has been to get religion back on philosophical agendas, and at first glance this might appear to contradict our statement above. Craig attended a roundtable discussion with Jacques Derrida about prayer with some five thousand people in attendance. The Italian postmodern philosopher Gianni Vattimo (1936–) declared at the outset of a three-hour seminar that he could now no longer see any reason to keep religion out of philosophy.

Similarly the Slovenian philosopher and Lacanian psychoanalyst Slavoj Žižek (1949–) manifests a growing interest in Christianity and theology in his published works, with provocative titles such as *The Fragile Absolute: Or, Why Is the Christian Legacy Worth Fighting For?*; *On Belief*; *The Puppet and the Dwarf: The Perverse Core of Christianity*; and *Living in the End Times*. For Žižek the perverse core of Christianity is the view of Christ's death as a substitutionary sacrifice. He rejects this but thinks we can recover a form of Christianity apart from it. Žižek's reconstruction of Christianity is complex and strange. Christ's divinity is related to the excess of life that makes us human: "The Divine is nothing more and nothing less than that which makes us human beings instead of mere animals and this is what has been revealed by Christ."[6] Christ reveals God to be imperfect and weak. The fall is not a tragedy but the first act of redemption, and Christ came not to remove the effects

5. Mary Hesse, "How to Be Postmodern Without Being a Feminist," *The Monist* 77/4 (1994): 457.

6. Frederiek Depoortere, *Christ in Postmodern Philosophy: Gianni Vattimo, René Girard, and Slavoj Žižek* (London: T&T Clark, 2008), 112.

of the curse but to fulfill the fall! The fall is a stage on the way from human animal to full humanity, and Christ came to fulfill this. Christ's death does not pay our debt but provides us with a chance to appropriate our freedom and responsibility as humans. For Žižek, Christ's incarnation means the end of God as transcendent; there is no longer a transcendent God with whom we can communicate.

Žižek is strongly influenced by Hegel, and he argues that God has passed into the Holy Spirit as the community of believers. Žižek envisages this community as one of outcasts who have "uncoupled" themselves from the social order of the day and are characterized by love. The major target of Žižek's philosophy is consumer capitalism, and in his work Christianity is embraced as a tool to buttress the possibility of an anticapitalist praxis. God as transcendent is, however, gone; and as Frederiek Depoortere perceptively asks, "Are we, therefore, not in need of a truly superior transcendence in order to heal our desire and our world from the onslaught of capitalism?"[7]

Instead of engaging with the phenomenal resurgence of orthodox religion throughout the world today, postmodernists generally agree with Gadamer that we cannot retrieve the old doctrines of the church because we are all Kantian or post-Kantian now.[8] Vattimo seeks to recover religion, but it is of a post-Nietzschean, post-Heideggerian sort that amounts, in his own words, to loving people and keeping the traffic regulations: "I always say that ethics is merely charity plus the traffic regulations. I respect the rules of the road because I don't want to cause the death of my neighbor and because I ought to love him. . . . All this is just charity plus the traffic rules: ethics is just that."[9] This bears no resemblance to the sort of Christianity (or Islam) resurgent today, especially in the two-thirds world. Instead, it is a thoroughly liberal, post-Enlightenment version of Christianity.

Indeed, in our view, the sort of cheerful nihilism so dominant in postmodernism could only take root in the flabby, comfortable West, where one can play around with everything, including God, justice, marriage, society, truth, and so on, without having to worry about the consequences. Western postmodernism could never thrive in genocidal Rwanda, Sudan, or Iraq today. Historian Gertrude Himmelfarb, who has a profound sense of how dangerous such "play" can be, is devastating in her critique of postmodernism: "Postmodernism entices us with the siren call of liberation and creativity, but it may

7. Ibid., 138.

8. Hans-Georg Gadamer, "Dialogues in Capri," in *Religion: Cultural Memory in the Present*, ed. Jacques Derrida and Gianni Vattimo (Stanford, CA: Stanford University Press, 1998).

9. Gianni Vattimo and René Girard, *Christianity, Truth, and Weakening Faith: A Dialogue*, ed. Pierpaolo Antonello, trans. William McCuaig (New York: Columbia University Press, 2010), 34–35.

be an invitation to intellectual and moral suicide."[10] Below we will explore some of the major views articulated by postmodern philosophers and develop a nuanced analysis of their work.

Postmodernity: The Debate

The contemporary debate about postmodernism began in the 1950s and 1960s as a reaction to modernism in the arts. This reaction was soon extended to a critique of modern culture as a whole. This does not, of course, mean that the postmodern debate has no earlier roots. A cursory reading of key postmodern philosophers makes clear their dependence on earlier philosophers like Nietzsche and Heidegger. Little is new in postmodern theories, but it is the widespread disillusionment with modernity and the widespread embrace of previously minority antimodern positions that makes the present different, at least philosophically. In postmodernism, we might say, Nietzsche's time has arrived.

The influence of the German philosopher Edmund Husserl, the father of phenomenology, on philosophical postmodernism should not be underestimated; indeed, to a significant extent postmodern philosophy amounts to *postphenomenology*. Husserl's phenomenology was, as we noted in chapter 10, a last-ditch attempt to secure the scientific nature of knowledge in human autonomy. Significant tensions appear in his work as a result, and it fell to his student Heidegger to turn phenomenology in a hermeneutic direction, also as noted in chapter 10, thereby subverting the strong Enlightenment character of Husserl's philosophy. Contra Husserl's privileging of intuition as the means to true knowledge, Heidegger asserted that we are always already thrown into the world so that we explore it out of this thrown-ness, which he called Dasein, rather than from a neutral, objective position. In this way Heidegger brought to fruition Dilthey's emphasis on history and understanding: central to postmodernism is a profound sense that both knower and that which is known are historically embedded, so that there is no neutral vantage point from which objective, neutral analysis is possible.

At the end of the 1980s and the beginning of the 1990s the postmodern debate was increasingly bounded on the one side by Habermas and on the other by Jean-François Lyotard (1924–98). Lyotard's *The Postmodern Condition* is a study of "the condition of knowledge in the most highly developed societies."[11] Knowledge has been profoundly affected by the replacement of

10. Gertrude Himmelfarb, *On Looking into the Abyss: Untimely Thoughts on Culture and Society* (New York: Vintage, 1994), 160.

11. Jean-François Lyotard, *The Postmodern Condition: A Report on Knowledge*, Theory and History of Literature 10 (Manchester: Manchester University Press, 1984), xxiii.

the production of material goods with information as the central concern in advanced societies. Society has become computerized, and performativity dominates other forms of reason. The resulting postmodern condition is characterized by *"incredulity towards metanarratives."*[12] Lyotard strikes at the heart of the possibility of objective legitimation of knowledge. Language games have replaced metanarratives or worldviews, and these always have only local and limited validity. In his opposition to metanarratives and worldviews Lyotard has modern science particularly in mind.

Jürgen Habermas (1929–) has reacted strongly to the postmodern notion of the end of modernity, proposing instead that we think of modernity as an unfinished project. Modernity is in crisis, but the answer is to get it back on track, not to abandon it. Habermas has strongly criticized Gadamer's understanding of hermeneutics as a fusion of horizons leading to consensus because, in Habermas's view, it fails to take account of the possibility of systematic distortion in the communication process. This led to an ongoing debate between Habermas and Gadamer that has highlighted the meta-critical (or lack thereof) dimension of Gadamer's hermeneutic. Habermas proposes a project of universal pragmatics, in which he seeks to establish that the possibility of ideal speech is implied in the structure of language. In appealing to reason, speakers assume that their claims could be substantiated through rational discourse alone. Thus communication in general points to something like Habermas's ideal speech situation.[13]

Jean Baudrillard's (1929–2007) grim analysis is deeply pessimistic about Western society. In his view, consumerism has come to dominate our social order, and, especially through electronic media, this shift has been accompanied in what he calls the third simulacra by the hyperreal replacing and being indistinguishable from the real. Disneyland, for example, is there to conceal the fact that the real Disneyland is America. Baudrillard sees everything in terms of cybernetic control, so that we are helpless victims of technological control. Even the masses are the product of information, and the only response is to "join the objects," since thinking and action have become impossible from the perspective of the subject. This is a bleak picture indeed:

We are left with a hyperreal that has escaped our control and that is beyond conceptualization in spite of the "obscene" visibility of every single detail. . . . Baudrillard, however, leaves all other theorists far behind in the nightmarish character of his conclusions. . . . For Baudrillard that [electronic] revolution

12. Ibid., xxiv (italics added).
13. Habermas's philosophy of the ideal speech situation reached its most mature presentation in the 1970s, after which he abandoned the concept but not the centrality of reasoned debate and argumentation.

has effectively made us the helpless victims of a technological determinism that through its unassailable code serves the interests of a hyperreal, meaningless capitalist order.[14]   ς

In his understanding of consumerism as central to our social order, and in his notion of the hyperreal, Baudrillard has made an important contribution to the debate about postmodernity. However, this "apostle of unreason" shows scant regard for facts and paints with a large brush. His analysis of the decay of so much contemporary culture may well be correct, but this diagnosis makes truth more, rather than less, important.

Richard Rorty (1931–2007) has expounded a pragmatic version of postmodernity. What is required is not a new quest for finding ways to validate knowledge but a detheoreticized sense of community. From such a position one could accept Habermas's privileging of undistorted communication without needing to ground it in a theory of communicative competence. Thus for Rorty postmodern bourgeois liberalism is "the Hegelian attempt to defend the institutions and practices of the rich North Atlantic democracies without using [the traditional Kantian] buttresses."[15] For such postmodern liberalism, morality is stripped of its transcendent grounding and becomes equivalent to loyalty to a society. Rational behavior is simply behavior that conforms to that of other members of a society.

Rorty uses Gadamer to support his view that all knowledge is traditioned and that the idea of the accurate representation of reality that underlies the Western concern with epistemology is a myth. All forms of knowledge are closer to making than to finding and have this in common with creative enterprises in general. Consequently the obsession of Western epistemology with legitimation is irrelevant and wedded to an outmoded metaphysic. In place of the epistemological concerns of the Western tradition, Rorty proposes the goal of "edification." Rather than trying to justify our beliefs, we should foster conversations in which we are exposed to and can explore other options and thus find better ways of coping with life.

Jacques Derrida's (1930–2004) type of postmodernism, which also developed out of phenomenology, is called deconstruction. A response to Husserl and modernity, Derrida's great contribution is to have dismantled the fortress of consciousness through his close analysis of texts, whereby he exposes in aporia the ever-present metaphysics of presence. For Derrida we cannot ultimately escape metaphysics, and his hermeneutic of deconstruction always therefore

14. Johannes W. Bertens, *The Idea of the Postmodern: A History* (London and New York: Routledge, 1995), 156.

15. Richard Rorty, "Postmodernist Bourgeois Liberalism," *Journal of Philosophy* 80/10 (1983): 584–85.

operates in two modes at the same time. This is clear with Derrida's textual strategies. On the one hand, the guardrail of authorial intention is indispensable for interpretation. On the other hand, the aporias in texts enable us to prod them into play, with the result that the texts are set in motion and flux so that textual meaning can never be saturated or finally constrained.

Paul Ricoeur (1913–2005), theologian and philosopher, represents a far more constructive version of postmodernism. He has written in depth about a wide range of issues: Freud, politics and justice, biblical interpretation, literary interpretation and metaphor, hermeneutics, history and memory, and so on. Ricoeur is particularly significant for his understanding of interpretation of a text as a semantic event, that is, of the fusion of text and interpreter through the interplay of metaphor and symbol in a reading along the lines of a second naïveté.[16] In contrast to Gadamer, Ricoeur seeks to bring together explanation and understanding. For Gadamer, in Ricoeur's view, the two collapse into each other so that there tends to be no space for critical testing of understandings. For Ricoeur "explanation" embodies a hermeneutic of suspicion: the willingness to expose and to abolish idols that are mere projections of the human will. Ricoeur is critical of the Enlightenment insofar as it locates meaning in the subject; he professes

> a permanent mistrust of the pretensions of the subject in posing itself as the foundation of its own meaning. The reflective philosophy to which I appeal is at the outset opposed to any philosophy of the Cartesian type. . . . The understanding of the self is always indirect and proceeds from the interpretation of signs given outside me in culture and history. . . . The self of self-understanding is a gift of understanding itself and of the invitation from the meaning inscribed in the text.[17]

However, Ricoeur has no desire to be premodern. We cannot, nor should we try to, escape the lessons of the masters of suspicion: Nietzsche, Marx, and Freud. Hence "explanation" is an imperative part of interpretation. But explanation alone is inadequate: "To smash the idols is also to let symbols speak."[18] An effect of Cartesian epistemology is that Western civilization has lost sensitivity to symbolic language. Secularization has led to an estrangement from the kerygmatic situation so that we need to move beyond suspicion to recover this sensitivity: "Myth's literal function must be suspended, but its

16. A helpful survey of Ricoeur's thought is Steven H. Clark, *Paul Ricoeur* (London and New York: Routledge, 1990).

17. Paul Ricoeur, preface to *Hermeneutic Phenomenology: The Philosophy of Paul Ricoeur*, by Don Ihde (Evanston, IL: Northwestern University Press, 1971), xv. Note here the phenomenological rooting of Ricoeur's philosophy.

18. Quoted in ibid., 219.

symbolic function must be affirmed."[19] "Understanding" entails a willingness to listen with openness to symbols and to indirect language in such a way that we experience being called again.

In his later writings Ricoeur focuses particularly on metaphor and narrative. His more innovative and influential contribution emerges in the way he connects metaphor with narrative. For Ricoeur the synthesis of the heterogeneous brings narrative close to metaphor. Narrative orders scattered sequential experiences and events into a coherent structure of human time. This refigured world becomes revelatory and transformative. Narrative constructs a world of the possible.

There is good reason for the positive appropriation of Ricoeur by theologians. Ricoeur's positive stance toward symbol makes him open to religious experience, and although Ricoeur retains a commitment to the autonomy of philosophy, he also wants to secure a place for religion and theology. Not only has Ricoeur written extensively about literary theory and hermeneutical issues, but he has also focused on biblical interpretation.[20] Remarkably, Ricoeur specifically addresses the issue of a hermeneutic of Scripture as revelation.[21] He recognizes that revelation is the first and last word for faith and seeks to develop a hermeneutic of revelation that overcomes the opposition between an authoritative understanding of revelation and an autonomous view of reason.

All these thinkers acknowledge the crisis of modernity, but their responses differ. What we should note from them is that postmodern philosophy challenges many of the foundations of modernity.

1. Postmodern philosophy has raised all sorts of questions about our capacity to know and whether we can accurately represent reality—that is, questions about epistemology. The possibility of universal objective knowledge is considered by many to be impossible. Much postmodern theory is strongly anti-realist and considers all knowledge to be local, communal, and a human construct. Such epistemological skepticism is captured very clearly in Lyotard's notion of "incredulity towards metanarratives." The corollary of this skepticism has been a profound suspicion of the hidden agendas of "neutral" modern knowledge; what claimed to be objective and value free has come to be seen by many as a mask for powerful ideologies. The consequence of this skepticism is an awareness of inevitable pluralism in knowledge and consequent fragmentation. Certainty and truth are regarded by many with great suspicion; paradoxically, the one thing that radical postmodern thinkers seem *quite* sure of is that there are no true metanarratives or worldviews. There is widespread disagreement about the role of rationality and whether

19. Ibid., 8.
20. See Paul Ricoeur, *Essays on Biblical Interpretation* (Philadelphia: Fortress, 1980).
21. Ibid., 73–118.

or not knowledge can be grounded. Some, like Christopher Norris (1947–), Jürgen Habermas, and Ernest Gellner (1925–95) seek to reconstruct the project of modernity. Others would seek a genuinely postmodern position in which rationality is always perspectival.

2. Epistemology is closely related to ontology, and here too postmodernity has undermined the broad consensus of modernity. One would expect that incredulity toward metanarratives would leave little room for much ontological reflection, but of course this is unavoidable. A common ontological presupposition in postmodern theory is that language is the most fundamental aspect of reality. Derrida is a good example of this view. Much postmodern theory works with a view of history as flux and change and has little room for any notion of an order in reality existing apart from human construction. Ironically, skepticism about human knowing goes hand in hand with a high view of the human community as constructing the worlds in which we live. This too reflects a particular ontology.

3. Epistemology and ontology are inseparable from anthropology in the sense of the nature of humankind. The rationalistic autonomous view of the human that was so dominant in modernity has been undermined and a plurality of alternatives proposed. Rorty, for example, suggests that we should think of the moral self as "a network of beliefs, desires, and emotions with nothing behind it—no substrate behind the attributes. For purposes of moral and political deliberation and conversation, a person just is that network."[22] Michel Foucault (1926–84) stresses the extent to which our view of the human person is a construct when he asserts that "man is only a recent invention, a figure not yet two centuries old, a new wrinkle in our knowledge . . . that will disappear as soon as that knowledge has discovered a new form."[23] In several postmodern thinkers, Freud's anthropology has been revised and renewed. If thinkers like Baudrillard play down the possibility of the human subject acting in any significant way, others stress the possibility of human *self*-creation.

Epistemology, ontology, anthropology. That so much postmodern philosophy is related to these areas indicates the extent to which the philosophical foundations of modernity are in crisis. Postmodern philosophy is characterized by pluralism, uncertainty, instability, and fragmentation. The old certainties seem to have gone, with no unified vision to replace them. It is important to note, however, that although many of the roots of modernity have been called into question by postmodern philosophers, the underlying humanist religious orientation has not been abandoned. Human autonomy, for example, tends to

22. Rorty, "Postmodernist Bourgeois Liberalism," 585–86.
23. Michel Foucault, *The Order of Things: An Archeology of the Human Sciences* (London: Tavistock, 1970), xxiii.

remain as firmly entrenched as ever, the difference being that we now simply have to learn to live with the uncertainties.

It should not be forgotten that the nihilistic and relativistic side of postmodern theory is only one aspect of the contemporary situation. As we noted above, other modern types of philosophy such as phenomenology and metaphysics continue to flourish. If modernity is a reaction to and immanentizing of a Christian worldview, then postmodernity shows little sign of openness to recovering Christian perspectives on reality. However, as Alvin Plantinga notes from a Christian point of view, what he calls the creative anti-realism of postmodernism is laughable:

> Creative anti-realism is presently popular among philosophers; this is the view that it is human behavior—in particular, human thought and language—that is somehow responsible for the fundamental structure of the world and for the fundamental kinds of entities there are. From a theistic point of view, however, universal creative anti-realism is at best a piece of laughable bravado. For God, of course, owes neither his existence nor his properties to us and our ways of thinking; the truth is just the reverse. And so far as the created universe is concerned, while it indeed owes its existence and character to activity on the part of a person, that person is certainly not a human person.[24]

Thus, within the pluralistic world of philosophy a plethora of worldviews compete for attention. Postmodernism rightly alerts us to the fact that important shifts *are* taking place. Postmodernism is influential way beyond philosophy. Whatever subject you are studying, you will find that there is now available a body of literature on postmodernism and your particular subject. Postmodernism has also had a huge impact on popular culture. It is an idea that has captured the imagination of thousands in Western culture and in one form or another is found all over the place.

Thus, while recognizing that postmodernism is one trend among many in philosophy today, it must be taken seriously. As David Lyon notes, the concept of postmodernity is a valuable "problematic" that alerts us to key questions concerning our age:[25] "The question of postmodernity offers an opportunity to reappraise modernity, to read the signs of the times as indicators that modernity itself is unstable, unpredictable, and to forsake the foreclosed future that it once seemed to promise."[26] How should Christians respond to postmodernism in philosophy?

24. Alvin Plantinga, "Advice to Christian Philosophers," *Faith and Philosophy* 1/3 (1984): 269.
25. David Lyon, *Postmodernity*, Concepts in the Social Sciences (Buckingham: Open University Press, 1994), 84–85.
26. Ibid., 70.

1. We should, in many respects, recognize and welcome postmodernism's trenchant critique of the philosophies underlying modernity. A major characteristic of modernity has been the relocation of authority from God to humankind, whether in the form of reason, science, intuition, or other such things. Humankind is an inadequate base for culture and philosophy, and the postmodern exposure of the fragility of the foundations of much modern philosophy is welcome. As George Steiner notes in his superb critique of Derrida, Derrida confronts us with the choice of nihilism or "In the beginning was the Word."[27]

2. Steiner alerts us to the need for a grammar of creation if we are to do justice to the real presences we encounter in the world and in culture. This, however, is precisely the sort of direction that most postmodernists reject. Postmodernists do not in general wish to recover that Word which was in the beginning. Postmodernism is a Western, liberal movement, and it will not go back behind Kant to recover tradition and Christian theism. Indeed, it is perfectly obvious that belief in a Creator God who has revealed himself in Christ would radically transform all the major postmodern philosophies. What we are left with in postmodernism, therefore, is the outworking of the inherently unstable DNA of humanistic modernity without any constructive project to put in its place. We thus prefer to think of postmodernism as late or ultra modernity. So much postmodern philosophy, however creative and playful, leaves us with very little to work with. You can deconstruct the very notion of the book, as Derrida attempts, but this is simply not how books work. The result is that disciples of Derrida continue to write well-crafted books about Derrida's deconstructive philosophy!

Contra most postmodernism, Steiner is absolutely right: culture needs a transcendent base, and to move forward philosophy and modern culture will need to go behind (and beyond) Kant to recover (Christian) theism. Two sociologists who have focused on this are the non-Christian Australian John Carroll (1944–) and the Jewish American Philip Rieff (1922–2006).

Carroll's critique of modernity is insightful. He perceptively argues that "humanism failed because man is not the centre of creation, in the sense of being creature and creator in one."[28] He also rightly recognizes the need to go behind Kant: "The restoration of Western culture will again have to draw on the great sources of authority in its own past. It will have to bring about a Second Reformation."[29] However, we should not misunderstand Carroll's call for a Second Reformation. His diagnosis of the problem with

27. George Steiner, *Real Presences* (London: Faber and Faber, 1989), 120.
28. Carroll, *Humanism*, 228.
29. Ibid., 229.

the church is acute: "The waning of Christianity as practiced in the West is easy to explain. The Christian churches have comprehensively failed in their one central task—to retell their foundation story in a way that might speak to the times."[30] However, Carroll is not optimistic about the church containing resources for the renewal we so urgently need. In a discussion of the university, he notes that "the humanist university has run down. The Christian university, founded in medieval form, is too culturally alien to the contemporary West to be revived. Likewise the church, the one institution that could replace the university as the master teacher of eternal truths, is in a state of hopeless despair."[31] Carroll's diagnosis is spot-on, but his proposals for recovery are inadequate.

Rieff's analysis of our contemporary situation is devastating. In his remarkable trilogy titled *Sacred Order/Social Order*, he likens our time to one of "deathworks." Rieff argues that the well-being of any society depends on a strong sense of the vertical in authority; order that in its vertical structure is immutable. He playfully labels this "via"—*vertical in authority*.[32] Rieff discerns three eras of humankind. In our third era, the sacred has been abolished, and "where there is nothing sacred, there is nothing."[33] Central to a solution is a recovery of via: "Our own motions in sacred order are locable once each of us has restored to himself the notion of sacred order. The basic restorative is to understand the purity and inviolate nature of the vertical in authority. Those arbitrary meanings warranted not by any man, but by the one God, are necessary if we are to find some safety in any world."[34]

Conclusion

Philosophically, we thus regard postmodernism as helpful as a sign of the crisis of modernity and, to an extent, in its critique of modernity. Alas, in some ways we think it does not go far enough in its refusal to challenge human autonomy and to take seriously the possibilities of Christian theism, or any other brand of theism for that matter. In other ways we think it goes too far, for if one takes seriously that Word which was in the beginning and espouses a grammar of creation, then one will be far more positive about the potential of truth, logic, and so on.

30. John Carroll, *The Existential Jesus* (Berkeley, CA: Counterpoint, 2007), 7.
31. John Carroll, *Ego and Soul: The Modern West in Search of Meaning* (Berkeley: Counterpoint, 2008), 155.
32. Philip Rieff, *My Life among the Deathworks: Illustrations of the Aesthetics of Authority*, Sacred Order/Social Order 1 (Charlottesville: University of Virginia Press, 2006), 12–13.
33. Ibid., 12.
34. Ibid., 13.

Interestingly, even as postmodernists recover some kind of religiosity, we are living amid a major resurgence of theism worldwide, particularly Christianity and Islam. Typical of Western liberalism, this does not feature on the postmodern agenda. Amid orthodox Christianity, we are also witnessing a major resurgence of Christian philosophy, which in our opinion offers far more constructive possibilities than attempting to synthesize a diluted Christianity with postmodernism, as some Western Christians do. It is to this resurgence that we now turn.

Part 3

Christian Philosophy Today

12

Christian Philosophy Today

The Remarkable Renaissance of Christian Philosophy

In our exploration of the story of Western philosophy, we have noted several times that how we tell the story is never neutral. A further example of this is that books continue to be published about the history of philosophy without any account of the remarkable renaissance of Christian philosophy over the last thirty to forty years.

In the first half of the twentieth century, positivism and a renascent empiricism put Christian philosophers on the defensive. Both trends in philosophy were thought to mark the demise of religious belief, and Christian philosophers devoted much of their energy to defending the meaningfulness of religious language and belief in God. The second half of the century witnessed a remarkable change. From having been in reaction to positivism and empiricism, Christian philosophy began a major resurgence that continues to this day.

In preparation for a meeting of the American Philosophical Association in Cincinnati, Ohio, held in April 1978, a letter was sent out from Alvin Plantinga, Robert and Marilyn Adams, Arthur Holmes, and Bill Alston to see if there was any interest in a meeting of philosophers to work together on issues of importance to the Christian community. Remarkably, some seventy Christian philosophers showed up at that meeting, and the resulting Society of Christian Philosophers has since grown to well over one thousand members and is now the largest special interest group among American philosophers.

A second major factor in the renaissance of Christian philosophy was the reception of Alvin Plantinga's inaugural as John A. O'Brien Professor of Philosophy at the University of Notre Dame, titled "Advice to Christian

Philosophers."[1] Plantinga sums up his advice to Christian philosophers in three exhortations:

1. Christian philosophers must display more autonomy, more independence, from the rest of the philosophical world. Plantinga is not for a moment suggesting that Christian philosophers should not be deeply engaged in the mainstream discussions of the day. However, we cannot spend our energies always reacting to others' agendas, especially when the intellectual culture of our day is "animated by a spirit wholly foreign to that of Christian theism."[2] The Christian community has its own concerns, and Christian philosophers need to attend to these too.

2. Christian philosophers must display more integrality, more wholeness, in their work. Plantinga imagines a student going to study at Harvard under Willard Van Orman Quine, a wonderfully gifted philosopher. However, as Plantinga rightly notes,

   [Quine's] fundamental commitments, his fundamental projects and concerns, are wholly different from those of the Christian community—wholly different and, indeed, antithetical to them. And the result of attempting to graft Christian thought onto his basic view of the world will be at best an unintegral pastiche; at worst it will seriously compromise, or distort, or trivialize the claims of Christian theism. What is needed here is more wholeness, more integrality.[3]

3. Christian philosophers need to be bold and unashamed about their Christian convictions.

In his inaugural, Plantinga explores what such an approach would mean for three areas: verifiability, epistemology, and persons (anthropology). In his discussion of theism and persons he notes that "we come to philosophy with philosophical opinions; we can do no other. And the point is: the Christian has as much right to his prephilosophical opinions as others have to theirs. He needn't try first to prove them from propositions accepted by, say, the bulk of the non-Christian philosophical community."[4]

Plantinga's inaugural has been a catalyst in the emergence of a springtime in Christian philosophy. Christian philosophers have been emboldened to rise to his challenge, and the major resurgence of Christian philosophy is now bearing considerable fruit. A whole new generation of Christian philosophers has emerged and continues to emerge, and this movement has produced a substantial body of philosophy that is hard to ignore.

1. See www.faithandphilosophy.com/article_advice.php for the article.
2. Ibid.
3. Ibid.
4. Ibid.

Alvin Plantinga and Nicholas Wolterstorff are among the most prominent Christian philosophers who work in the Kuyperian tradition today. For now, it should be noted that the Society of Christian Philosophers is a diverse group and includes philosophers from a range of Christian traditions.

Catholic Philosophy

Christian philosophy comes in many shapes and sizes. There is a rich, deep tradition of Catholic philosophy, and this tradition continues to produce outstanding work.

Alasdair MacIntyre

Alasdair MacIntyre (1929–) of the University of Notre Dame is most well known for his work in ethics, but he has also done major work in political philosophy and the history of philosophy and theology. His major works in ethics are *Three Rival Versions of Moral Enquiry: Encyclopaedia, Genealogy, and Tradition*; *After Virtue: A Study in Moral Theory*; and *Whose Justice? Which Rationality?*

MacIntyre was born in Glasgow, Scotland, in 1929, the son of physicians. He grew up shaped by two traditions: that of the local, old Gaelic culture with its stories and practices, and that of the Enlightenment theories of Kant and Mill. In MacIntyre's mature work the relationship between narrative and concept takes center stage.

As a Christian student in London, MacIntyre discovered Marxism, which provided him with the tools to critique individualistic, Western liberalism *and* contemporary Christianity. In his 1952 book, *Marxism: An Interpretation*, MacIntyre delivers a devastating critique of Western Christianity: "Religion as an activity divorced from other activities is without point. If religion is only a part of life, then religion has become optional. Only a religion which is a way of living in every sphere either deserves to or can hope to survive."[5] However, Marxism is the most developed expression of this dichotomy, for it sees the whole of life apart from its God-given character. MacIntyre came to distance himself from Marxism but struggled to find adequate grounding for moral critique.

MacIntyre trained to be a Presbyterian minister and sought to combine his sociological and historical understanding of religion with his faith. Combining the thought of scholars such as Wittgenstein with Barth's theology, he sought to demarcate a place for faith impervious to critique. As Kelvin Knight notes,

5. Alasdair MacIntyre, *Marxism: An Interpretation* (London: SCM, 1953), 9.

Faith lost out. *After Virtue* was the result of a long period of reflection upon how morality might best be justified apart from faith. This aspect of his argument has convinced some notable theorists but not MacIntyre himself. Reflection upon the inadequacies of the argument's premises has led him back to faith, albeit not the Protestant faith of his youth but a faith confirmed by the metaphysical reasoning of the Thomist tradition and sustained by the institution of the Roman Catholic Church. This, he has concluded, is the most rigorous way to respond to Nietzsche's attempt to kill off the popular belief in truth by proclaiming the death of God.[6]

Central to MacIntyre's moral philosophy is a critique of our contemporary situation. At the outset of his *After Virtue* he imagines a scenario in which for various reasons the natural sciences suffer a catastrophe.[7] Laboratories are burned down, books and libraries of science burned, and scientists eliminated from society. Later, a reaction sets in and people try to recover science, "but all they possess are fragments: a knowledge of experiments detached from any knowledge of the theoretical context which gave them significance; parts of theories unrelated either to the other bits and pieces of theory which they possess or to experiment; instruments whose use has been forgotten; half-chapters from books, single pages from articles, not always fully legible because torn and charred."[8]

Nonetheless, the fragments are reassembled and the resulting body of knowledge is taught and learned. People continue to use the vocabulary of science, but the contexts of such knowledge have been lost so that their use of the reassembled knowledge is arbitrary and random. For MacIntyre this is an apt description of the situation of the world today in terms of morality: "The hypothesis which I wish to advance is that in the actual world which we inhabit the language of morality is in the same state of grave disorder as the language of natural science in the imaginary world which I described. What we possess . . . are the fragments of a conceptual scheme. . . . But we have—very largely, if not entirely—lost our comprehension, both theoretical and practical, of morality."[9]

How have we arrived at this grave situation? According to MacIntyre, the failed attempt by Enlightenment thinkers to furnish a universal account of moral rationality led to the rejection of moral rationality altogether by subsequent thinkers such as Jean-Paul Sartre and Friedrich Nietzsche. For MacIntyre,

6. Kelvin Knight, introduction to *The MacIntyre Reader*, ed. Kelvin Knight (Notre Dame, IN: University of Notre Dame Press, 1998), 24–25.
7. Alasdair MacIntyre, *After Virtue: A Study in Moral Theory*, 2nd ed. (London: Duckworth, 1985), 1–3.
8. Ibid., 1.
9. Ibid., 2.

Nietzsche's repudiation of the possibility of moral rationality embodies the consequence of the Enlightenment's mistaken quest for final and definitive arguments that will settle moral disputes through calculative reason alone and without use of teleology.

In this context—he describes his own account as a "peculiarly modern understanding" of the task—MacIntyre is concerned with reclaiming various forms of moral rationality and argumentation that do not claim utter finality and certainty (the mistaken project of the Enlightenment) but nevertheless do not simply bottom out into relativistic or emotivistic denials of any moral rationality whatsoever (the mistaken conclusion of Nietzsche and Sartre). MacIntyre argues that it is the case that moral disputes always take place within and between rival traditions of thought. Such traditions make recourse to a store of ideas, presuppositions, types of arguments, and shared understandings and approaches that have been inherited from the past. At base such traditions have a narrative shape, so that we always understand our lives and the world in the context of a particular grand narrative or story. Thus even though there is no definitive way for one tradition in moral philosophy to vanquish and exclude the possibility of another, nevertheless opposing views can call one another into question by various means, including issues of internal coherence, imaginative reconstruction of dilemmas, epistemic crisis, and fruitfulness.

For MacIntyre *rationality* refers to the resources by which a community or individual assesses the truth or falsity of philosophical claims. MacIntyre defines *truth* as the adequation of the mind's judgment of a thing to its reality. He distinguishes formal and substantive rationality. The former includes the basic logical rules on which most philosophers agree. The latter refers to those assessments of good reasons and evidence that arise through tradition and custom and about which there is serious disagreement. The plurality of traditions in this respect is unavoidable, but this does not lead to relativism.

For MacIntyre the three major traditions available to us are the Enlightenment tradition, the Augustinian tradition, and the Aristotelian-Thomistic tradition. The Aristotelian-Thomistic tradition holds most promise for us today, and MacIntyre develops his ethics by retrieving the tradition of Aristotelian ethics, with its teleological account of the good, and of moral persons, which reached a fuller articulation in the writings of Thomas Aquinas. This Aristotelian-Thomistic tradition, he proposes, presents "the best theory so far" both of how things are and how we ought to act. Since *After Virtue*, MacIntyre's thought has developed, and more recently he has argued that we need a robust metaphysics that includes an Augustinian conception of the will and a Thomist view of truth.[10]

10. See Knight, "Guide to Further Reading," in *The MacIntyre Reader*, 282.

MacIntyre's conception of *tradition* and *narrative* is a crucial insight. It gets at the heart of the problem of the Enlightenment legacy in modernity that continues to dominate most philosophical and academic discourse. As MacIntyre perceptively notes,

> Our education in and about philosophy has by and large presupposed what is in fact not true, that there are standards of rationality, adequate for the evaluation of rival answers to such questions, equally available, at least in principle, to all persons, whatever tradition they may happen to find themselves in and whether or not they inhabit any tradition. When this false belief is rejected, it becomes clear that the problems of justice and practical rationality . . . are not one and the same set of problems for all persons. . . . What each person is confronted with is at once a set of rival intellectual positions, a set of rival traditions embodied more or less imperfectly in contemporary forms of social relationship and a set of rival communities of discourse, each with its own specific modes of speech, argument, and debate, each making a claim upon the individual's allegiance. . . . Genuine intellectual encounter does not and cannot take place in some generalized, abstract way.[11]

In opposition to the Enlightenment postulate of neutral, objective knowledge, MacIntyre shows that such an approach is *itself* traditioned, now bankrupt, and only one tradition among several. If one is therefore going to continue to inhabit this tradition, then one will need to argue for it and not just assume it to be true. MacIntyre thus exposes the basic plurality in traditions in which philosophies operate and indicates how formative is the narrative or tradition in which a philosophy operates. Far from closing down discussion, this presents the possibility of real discussions beginning, as philosophers own up to the tradition in which they work, rather than, as is so often the case, concealing their prephilosophical understanding beneath the cloak of the myth of neutrality. As MacIntyre rightly insists, "There are no tradition-independent standards of argument by appeal to which [rival traditions of inquiry] can be shown to be in error."[12]

MacIntyre's emphasis on story and virtue has been very influential. Central to MacIntyre's philosophy of virtues is his concept of *practices*. Standards emerge from practices, but practices are rooted in narratives, and narratives are rooted in communities. MacIntyre concludes *After Virtue* on this note:

> What matters at this stage is the construction of local forms of community within which civility and the intellectual and moral life can be sustained through the new dark ages which are already upon us. And if the tradition of the

11. Alasdair MacIntyre, *Whose Justice? Which Rationality?* (London: Duckworth, 1988), 393.
12. Ibid., 403.

virtues was able to survive the horrors of the last dark ages, we are not entirely without grounds for hope. This time however the barbarians are not wait-ing beyond the frontiers; they have already been governing us for quite some time. And it is our lack of consciousness of this that constitutes part of our predicament. We are waiting not for a Godot, but for another—doubtless very different—St. Benedict.[13]

MacIntyre's work has generated a range of responses. Martha Nussbaum, who remains wedded to the Enlightenment tradition, labels it "antitheoreti-cal" and appears unable to recognize the legitimacy of any other tradition of rationality than her own.[14] MacIntyre also has been accused of espousing relativism, of not being true to the Thomistic tradition, and of doing theology rather than philosophy. For our purposes, the most interesting critique relates to MacIntyre's form of Thomism: how does the traditioned nature of all knowledge relate to Thomas's view of the natural law and unaided human reason? MacIntyre argues that in this respect Thomas and Augustine are closer than is often recognized, a debate that will no doubt continue.

Charles Taylor

Charles Taylor (1931–) has done seminal work in anthropology, philosophy of language, and many other areas. Taylor's work on the nature of modernity alerts us to the important contribution that philosophy of culture makes to mission today. At an introductory level, Taylor's Massey Lectures, published as *The Malaise of Modernity*,[15] are a helpful, creative summary of his work on modernity. Western culture is widely viewed as in crisis nowadays, and by *malaise* Taylor means features of our culture that we experience as a loss or decline. He identifies three malaises.

INDIVIDUALISM

Modern freedom has brought many benefits, but often at the cost of see-ing ourselves as part of a larger order. With individualism has come a loss of meaning, and many today experience the world as disenchanted: "The dark side of individualism is a centering on the self, which both flattens and narrows our lives, makes them poorer in meaning, and less concerned with others in society."[16]

---

13. Ibid., 263.
14. Martha C. Nussbaum, *The Fragility of Goodness: Luck and Ethics in Greek Tragedy and Philosophy,* 2nd ed. (Cambridge: Cambridge University Press, 2001), xxvi.
15. Charles Taylor, *The Malaise of Modernity* (Concord, ON: Anansi, 1991).
16. Ibid., 4.

The Primacy of Instrumental Reason and the Pervasiveness of Technology

Instrumental reason refers to the kind of rationality at work when we calculate the means to an end in terms of *maximum efficiency*. Such a rationality, particularly at home in the modern economy, has extended its reach way beyond economic issues, invading other domains. Taylor uses medicine as an example, in which a real danger is that an instrumental, technological approach marginalizes the kind of care that real, embodied humans need.

The increasing dominance of technology in our lives has led many to note a corresponding diminishment of the richness of our lives. In *The Communist Manifesto* Marx noted that a result of capitalism is that "all that is solid melts in the air." Many feel that the lasting, expressive objects we had in the past are being replaced with cheap, shoddy, disposable items with which we surround ourselves. Albert Borgman (1937–) speaks in this respect of the "device paradigm," whereby we withdraw from "manifold engagement" with our environment and instead seek and attain products to deliver some benefit.[17] Since *Malaise* was published, this scenario has become only too real with globalization. Max Weber (1864–1920) spoke of the "iron cage" that the impersonal mechanisms of the market generate, and globalization has intensified this danger.

The Danger of a Loss of Political Freedom and the Emergence of a "Soft" Despotism

Individualism and the application of instrumental reason across our societies result in a loss of freedom even while freedom of choice is celebrated. Politically this is in danger of generating what Tocqueville called a "soft" despotism: the forms of democracy may remain, but in practice people feel disempowered and have little control over their lives.

Taylor sums up his three malaises as follows: "The first fear is about what we might call a loss of meaning, the fading of moral horizons. The second concerns the eclipse of ends, in the face of rampant instrumental reason. And the third is about a loss of freedom."[18] Throughout his *Malaise*, Taylor notes that responses to these three issues are often polarized between "knockers and boosters." His plea and practice is for a more nuanced examination of the issues, aimed at a retrieval of moral resources that underlie all three of these problems: "It suggests that we undertake a work of retrieval, that we identify and articulate the higher ideal behind the more or less debased practices, and

---

17. Albert Borgman, *Technology and the Character of Contemporary Life* (Chicago: University of Chicago Press, 1984), 41–42.
18. Taylor, *Malaise*, 10.

then criticize these practices from the standpoint of their own motivating ideal. In other words, instead of dismissing this culture altogether, or just endorsing it as it is, we ought to attempt to raise its practice by making more palpable to its participants what the ethic they subscribe to really involves."[19]

Taylor explains how the authentic self underlies modern individualism and how it developed from Romanticism in particular. Taylor rightly argues that this development is not all bad; it entails very real dangers, but it also represents real gains, and our strategy ought to be one of fighting over what authenticity entails rather than bashing it per se. Taylor is throughout concerned to make his case "in reason" (that is, in ways that will make sense to readers from many different backgrounds), and in his discussion of the growing focus on the subject (that is, the individual) he makes an important distinction between the *manner* and the *matter* of action. Authenticity is clearly about my self and its orientation, but this does not for a moment mean that the content or matter of action has also to originate from my self. "To confuse these two kinds of self-referentiality is catastrophic."[20] My goals can relate to something beyond my self: to God, to a political cause, to environmentalism. Indeed, for Taylor, this is precisely the battle we ought to be engaged in: to persuade people that self-fulfillment *requires* relationships and moral demands beyond the self.[21]

In terms of the dominance of instrumental reason and technology, Taylor is rightly sympathetic to Weber's analysis of this as generating an iron cage. However, Taylor insightfully insists that "we are not, indeed, locked in."[22] Taylor relates instrumental rationality, with its doctrine of optimal efficiency, to the disengaged self that emerged with Descartes. He encourages us to struggle against this and to retrieve the affirmation of the ordinary that Reformed thinkers contributed to modernity. "Runaway extensions of instrumental reason, such as the medical practice that forgets the patient as a person, that takes no account of how the treatment relates to his or her story and thus of the determinants of hope and despair, that neglects the essential rapport between cure-giver and patient—all these have to be resisted in the name of the moral background in benevolence that justifies these applications of instrumental reason themselves."[23]

According to Taylor, we should look for an alternative "enframing" of technology in the context of practical benevolence. Technology is decidedly not all bad. We should resist a determinist view of the triumph of instrumental rationality as inevitable; its role is open to being contested, and we need to

19. Ibid., 72.
20. Ibid., 82.
21. Ibid., 72–73.
22. Ibid., 101.
23. Ibid., 106.

find appropriate points of resistance, to become part of a growing *political* opposition to its defects.

Attention to politics and the structures of society is indispensable if we are to heal the malaise of modernity, and this relates to Taylor's third malaise. He perceptively notes that

> what should have died along with communism is the belief that modern societies can be run on a single principle, whether that of planning under the general will or that of free-market allocations. Our challenge is actually to combine in some non-self-stultifying fashion a number of ways of operating, which are jointly necessary to a free and prosperous society but which also tend to impede each other: market allocations, state planning, collective provision for need, the defense of individual rights, and effective democratic initiative and control.[24]

Taylor refers to these five aspects as "modes" and notes that in the short run they would restrict the negative effects of market efficiency, and that perhaps in the long run even economic performance would suffer from their denigration. We have to live with markets, but we need to do so in the context of a politically empowered democracy. Taylor is rightly alert to the need for a common good and for citizens who contribute to that good. He resists seeing modernity as good or bad; it has its *grandeur* as well as its *misère*.

Catholic philosophers come in many shapes and sizes, and there are far too many excellent ones to discuss them in any detail. To conclude this section on contemporary Catholic philosophy we mention two very different yet significant scholars.

René Girard

René Girard (1923–) is an emeritus professor of language, literature, and civilization at Stanford University. A French Catholic philosopher and sociologist, Girard "is the world's premier thinker about the role of violence in cultural origins, and about the Bible's illumination of these origins and our present human condition."[25] Published in France in 1978, Girard's *Things Hidden Since the Foundation of the World* caused intense debate among French clergy and intellectuals. His *I See Satan Fall Like Lightning* was continually on the best-seller list in France after its publication in 1999. Girard's philosophy focuses on anthropology and yields a fascinating philosophy of culture.

24. Ibid., 110.
25. James G. Williams, foreword to *I See Satan Fall Like Lightning*, by René Girard, trans. James G. Williams (Maryknoll, NY: Orbis, 2001), ix.

For Girard, we must begin with ourselves. Central to human being is desire and its consequences, or what Girard calls "mimetic desire." Desire originates through imitating others, who act as agents or mediators between us and the world. This is natural enough, and we can easily imagine how a child develops in this way. For Girard, however, mimetic desire almost always leads to conflict and frequently to violence. Mimesis can lead to rivalry, and if this is not contained, it can spiral into violence. When individual or group mimetic desire is blocked, a scapegoat is sought and the frustrated desire is turned against the scapegoat.

Girard argues that such violence is central to mythology, and he discerns great value in comparing the ancient myths to the "mythology" of the Bible. In the process, the radical answer of Christianity to mimetic desire is revealed. Girard's *I See Satan Fall Like Lightning* opens with a discussion of the tenth commandment, which Girard notes is unique in terms of if its length and its object; instead of forbidding an object it forbids a desire—mimetic desire. It thus manifests an awareness of the danger of the double idolatry of self and neighbor and the potential for this to lead to violence. In this way, "the tenth commandment signals a revolution and prepares the way for it. This revolution comes to fruition in the New Testament."[26] Jesus invites us to imitate his desire, which is to imitate the "detached generosity"[27] of God.

Girard's philosophy is far more detailed and extensive than this brief description. We include this brief exposition as an indication of the rich resources of Christian philosophy for contemporary cultural analysis. Our global world is increasingly characterized by consumerism, and it is not hard to see how mimetic desire can generate (and has generated) violence in a world divided between the haves and the have-nots.

Jean-Luc Marion

In an earlier chapter we discussed Husserl's phenomenology, and much excellent work continues to be done in the phenomenological tradition.[28] The French Catholic philosopher Jean-Luc Marion (1946–) is widely regarded as the most prominent phenomenologist alive today.

Marion was born in Meudon, Hauts-de-Seine. He did graduate work in philosophy at the École Normale Supérieure in Paris, where he studied with Jacques Derrida and Louis Althusser. Marion's deep interest in theology was privately cultivated under the personal influence of theologians such as Louis

26. Girard, *I See Satan Fall Like Lightning*, 13.
27. Ibid., 14.
28. Readers should note in particular the "theological turn" in phenomenology evident in the rich works of Jean-Luc Marion, Jean-Yves Lacoste, Michael Henry, and Jean-Louis Chrétien.

Bouyer, Jean Daniélou, Henri de Lubac, and Hans Urs von Balthasar. In 1996 he became director of philosophy at the University of Paris IV (Sorbonne). Although much of Marion's academic work has dealt with Descartes and phenomenologists such as Husserl and Heidegger, it is his explicitly religious works that have received much recent attention. *God Without Being*, for example, is concerned with an analysis of idolatry, a theme linked in Marion's work with love and the gift.

In 2002 the English translation of Marion's *Being Given: Toward a Phenomenology of Givenness* was published. Marion deals in this book with the phenomenon of revelation as found in Christ. He notes that "in terms of modality, finally, Christ appears as an irregardable phenomenon precisely because as icon he regards me in such a way that He constitutes me as his witness rather than some transcendental I constituting Him to its own liking. . . . The saturated phenomenon comes from the counter-gaze of the Other (Christ) such that it constitutes me its witness."[29]

Phenomenology has a complex technical vocabulary, and we cannot here unpack Marion's rich phenomenology. Suffice it to say that his work is yet another example of the rich Catholic work being done in philosophy at present.

Catholic Philosophy and Christian Philosophy?

A challenge for Catholic philosophers remains the extent to which the very concept of "*Christian* philosophy" is a non sequitur. The Catholic historian James Turner, in his dialogue with Mark Noll, argues that one thing he has learned from Thomism is that "faith gives no *epistemological* edge."[30] Charles Taylor similarly argues that it is the nature of philosophical discourse to "try to persuade honest thinkers of any and all metaphysical or theological commitments."[31] Not surprisingly, therefore, Alvin Plantinga's inaugural and the renaissance of Christian philosophy have generated a variety of responses from Catholic philosophers.

Linda Zagzebski, a prominent Catholic philosopher, has edited a collection of Catholic responses to *Reformed epistemology*, the name commonly given to the approach to epistemology developed by Plantinga, Wolterstorff, and others. Zagzebski rightly notes that central to the debate between Catholic philosophers and Reformed epistemologists is the issue of natural theology.

29. Jean-Luc Marion, *Being Given: Toward a Phenomenology of Givenness*, trans. Jeffrey L. Kosky (Stanford, CA: Stanford University Press, 2002), 240.

30. Mark A. Noll and James Turner, *The Future of Christian Learning: An Evangelical and Catholic Dialogue*, ed. Thomas A. Howard (Grand Rapids: Brazos, 2008), 106.

31. James L. Heft, ed., *A Catholic Modernity? Charles Taylor's Marianist Award Lecture* (New York: Oxford University Press, 1999), 13.

Historically, Catholics have affirmed the view that revealed theology rests on *natural theology*—that is, on the work of philosophers—and this view was officially enshrined in Pope Leo XIII's encyclical *Aeterni Patris* (1879), which declared Thomistic philosophy to be the basis of church theology. Natural theology and natural law retain a high view of what is possible for "unaided human reason," as is reflected in James Turner's quote above. Again, Zagzebski rightly notes that underlying the Catholic uneasiness with—if not opposition to—Reformed epistemology is the issue of the effect of the fall on human reason.

> Although both traditions agree that natural human faculties have suffered damage as a result of original sin, Catholic theology has commonly maintained that the will suffered more than the intellect, and that our powers of reasoning can still hope to achieve much that points the way to Christian belief. Catholic philosophy also has a long tradition of natural law, which implies that our reason is a potent source of knowledge about moral matters. The extension to matters metaphysical is relatively easy. The idea is that both moral and metaphysical knowledge have important underpinnings in the knowledge of human nature, and the knowledge of human nature is within the reach of ordinary human reason.[32]

In the collection Zagzebski brings together, the evidentialist position is presented by Hugo Meynell.[33] He argues that Aquinas is among the most obsessive of evidentialists and concludes his chapter with the confession: "I have to admit that my own view on this matter amounts to a very crass form of what Reformed philosophers are wont to denounce as 'evidentialism.'"[34] Other responses are more moderate, and a feature of several chapters is the view that Reformed epistemology does not take adequate account of the will; indeed most of the contributors to *Rational Faith* support some version of cognitive voluntarism. Sullivan draws on, in this respect, John Henry Newman, who argued that faith is not a conclusion from premises but an act of the will.[35] Related to this is the distinction between *internalist* and *externalist* epistemology; the former stresses that the conditions for justification are accessible to the consciousness of the believer, something that the latter denies. Plantinga's epistemology is basically externalist, as we will see in the

32. Linda Zagzebski, introduction to *Rational Faith: Catholic Responses to Reformed Epistemology*, ed. Linda Zagzebski, Library of Religious Philosophy 10 (Notre Dame, IN: University of Notre Dame Press, 1993), 3–4.

33. On evidentialism see page 217.

34. Hugo Meynell, "Faith, Foundationalism, and Nicholas Wolterstorff," in Zagzebski, *Rational Faith*, 105.

35. Thomas D. Sullivan, "Resolute Belief and the Problem of Objectivity, in Zagzebski, *Rational Faith*.

next chapter, and many of the contributors to *Rational Faith* argue for an internalist epistemology.

Ralph McInerny's concluding chapter is interesting in that it sets this renewed debate in historical context by taking account of a controversy among Catholics in the 1930s as to whether or not there is such a thing as Christian philosophy. McInerny engages irenically with Plantinga and finds his approach helpful in alerting Christian scholars where to do their work, in the sense of which projects they engage in and why. "Thus, Christian philosophizing does not result in an amalgam of faith and knowledge, but in a gain in knowledge that might never have been made without the prompting of faith."[36]

McInerny's irenic dialogue with Reformed epistemology nevertheless reveals the gap between many Catholic philosophers and the sort of "inner reformation" of philosophy proposed by Reformed epistemologists. No doubt the debate will continue.

Neocalvinism and Philosophy

Alvin Plantinga and Nicholas Wolterstorff are among the most prominent Christian philosophers today. Both have their roots in the tradition stemming from Abraham Kuyper, who fought against the neutrality postulate throughout his adult life. The Reformed epistemology developed by Plantinga, Wolterstorff, and others is one of two major philosophical developments in the neocalvinist tradition. The lesser known one is that developed by Herman Dooyeweerd, particularly in his multivolume *A New Critique of Theoretical Thought*. Plantinga notes that

> the main positive development in Christian philosophy during the first half of [the twentieth] century must surely be the work of the man whose 100th birthday we are presently celebrating. Dooyeweerd's work was comprehensive, insightful, profound, courageous, and quite properly influential. . . . Let us simply note the sheer size of Dooyeweerd's accomplishment, remembering that it took place in a context going back to Abraham Kuyper and indeed back all the way to Bonaventura, Augustine and Tertullian.[37]

Philosophy in Dooyeweerd's line is commonly known as *Reformational philosophy*, whereas that of Plantinga and Wolterstorff is commonly called

---

36. Ralph McInerny, "Reflections on Christian Philosophy," in Zagzebski, *Rational Faith*, 275.
37. James F. Sennett, ed., *The Analytic Theist: An Alvin Plantinga Reader* (Grand Rapids: Eerdmans, 1998), 329.

Reformed epistemology. The former is Continental in flavor, the latter tends to be more analytic.

When Plantinga and Wolterstorff were philosophy majors at Calvin College, there was acrimony between the more analytical style of William Harry Jellema and the overtly Reformational philosophy of H. Evan Runner. As the years have gone by, tensions have diminished and Reformed epistemology has emerged as a major player on the philosophical stage. In our opinion, both streams have crucial insights to offer to the practice of Christian philosophy today, and an advantage of the passing of the years is that we can now see more clearly the major areas of overlap between the two streams. In the following chapters we will explore Reformed epistemology and Reformational philosophy as fruitful avenues for Christian philosophy today.

From: abby@longobedience.edu
To: percy@secular.edu
Subject: Amazing

Hey Perc,
I am SURE you haven't done this in your course on philosophy. We have been discussing the remarkable renaissance of Christian philosophy over the past thirty years, especially in North America. I had no idea! I *really* want to be part of this—will see the registrar tomorrow to see about adding a minor in philosophy to my program!

Abby

13

Reformed Epistemology

From: percy@secular.edu
To: abby@longobedience.edu
Subject: Really?

Hey Abby,
No, nothing has been said about such a renaissance of Christian philosophy in our course—it would appear not to exist! Do send me details; I will have to explore this.

Introduction

In 1980 *Time* magazine reported that in a "quiet revolution in thought and arguments that hardly anyone could have foreseen only two decades ago, God is making a comeback. Most intriguingly, this is happening not among theologians or ordinary believers . . . but in the crisp, intellectual circles of academic philosophers, where the consensus had long banished the Almighty from fruitful discourse."[1]

Time identified Alvin Plantinga, then professor of philosophy at Calvin College, as a leader in this revolution and described him as the "world's leading Protestant philosopher of God." The book *Faith and Rationality*, edited by Plantinga and Nicholas Wolterstorff, was the first comprehensive account of the project of Reformed epistemology.

1. "Modernizing the Case for God," *Time*, April 7, 1980.

Metaepistemology and Classical Foundationalism

Wolterstorff notes how helpful has been the emergence of what is called *meta-epistemology.*[2] He explains this as follows: "Rather than just plunging ahead and developing epistemological theories, philosophers have stood back and reflected seriously on the structural options available to them in their construction of such theories."[3]

One theory—namely, classical foundationalism—has long been dominant. Classical foundationalism is "a picture or total way of looking at faith, knowledge, justified belief, rationality, and allied topics. This picture has been enormously popular in Western thought; and despite a substantial opposing groundswell, I think it remains the dominant way of thinking about these topics."[4]

It is important to distinguish foundationalism from classical foundationalism. The latter is a variant of the former. Both view the acquisition of knowledge as akin to building a house and stress the need for a firm *foundation* upon which the house of theory can be built. Foundationalism has been the dominant epistemology since the High Middle Ages.

In foundationalism, the foundation of the house of theoretical knowledge contains a set of basic beliefs that one is justified in believing *without* the support of other beliefs—that is, they are properly basic. If the foundation

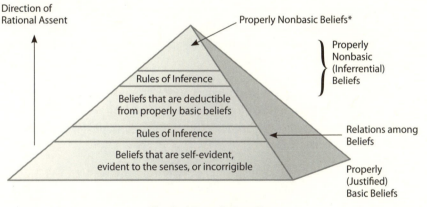

Classical Foundationalism

2. See Nicholas Wolterstorff, introduction to *Faith and Rationality: Reason and Belief in God*, ed. Alvin Plantinga and Nicholas Wolterstorff (Notre Dame, IN: University of Notre Dame Press, 1983), 1–15.

3. Ibid., 1.

4. James F. Sennett, ed., *The Analytic Theist: An Alvin Plantinga Reader* (Grand Rapids: Eerdmans, 1998), 129. Diagrams from Kelly J. Clark, *Return to Reason: A Critique of Enlightenment Evidentialism and a Defense of Reason and Belief in God* (Grand Rapids: Eerdmans, 1990), 134, 137.

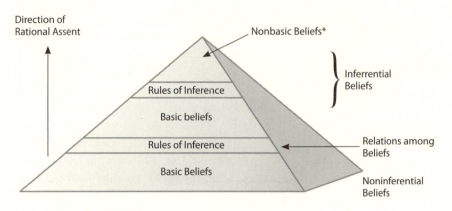

Foundationalism

is solid, then one can build upper-level beliefs upon it, using the appropriate methods (rules of inference). Rational assent moves only upward as warrant for beliefs is transferred from the lower levels to the higher levels by the rules of inference. The crucial question is *which* beliefs are properly basic; that is, which beliefs may legitimately occupy the foundation?

Classical foundationalism is foundationalist in its assertion that our beliefs are of two sorts:

1. Those that are foundational; these do not require arguments or evidence for one to rationally believe them. In this sense they are basic.
2. Those that are not foundational but are believed on the basis of other beliefs that are foundational.

Basic beliefs do not require evidence, while nonbasic beliefs do. Where classical foundationalism develops foundationalism is in its specification of which beliefs may function as properly basic. According to classical foundationalists, basic beliefs are:

1. Self-evident beliefs—that is, beliefs that are seen to be true simply by understanding them. An example of a self-evident belief is $2 + 1 = 3$; you only have to understand it to see that it is true.
2. Incorrigible beliefs—that is, beliefs that one could not be mistaken in holding.
3. Beliefs formed on the basis of sense experience (some classical foundationalists have held that these are basic).

Classical foundationalism has been bad news for Christian scholarship. W. K. Clifford, for example, states that "it is wrong always, everywhere, and for anyone to believe anything upon insufficient evidence."[5] Similarly, Bertrand Russell replied when asked what he would say if he got to heaven to discover that Christianity was true: "I'd say, 'Not enough evidence, God. Not enough evidence!'"[6] This sounds impressive until one realizes that Clifford and Russell are operating within a classical foundationalism framework, which defines in a narrow way what can and cannot be accepted as evidence. For classical foundationalism it is illegitimate to take belief in God as properly basic, and thus one would only be justified in believing in God if his existence could be proved on the basis of the foundational beliefs.

The challenge this presents to belief in God is known as evidentialism: belief in God is only justified on the basis of adequate "evidence." Some evangelical apologists have sought to prove that Christian belief is up to that challenge. Examples are Norman Geisler, Henry Morris, R. C. Sproul, and John Gerstner. In his analysis of this approach Kelly James Clark notes that "the failure of evangelical evidentialism is its uncritical commitment to Enlightenment evidentialism. . . . They . . . are unduly wedded to modern thought in their commitment to classical natural theology and its assumption of Enlightenment evidentialism. . . . They fall short of their own standards."[7]

Indeed, "most philosophers who have seen clearly the structure of this particular option [classical foundationalism] have rejected it. On close scrutiny they have found classical foundationalism untenable."[8] Plantinga and Wolterstorff have played no small role in the critique and demise of classical foundationalism. However, if this is the wrong way to construe the acquisition of reliable knowledge, what is the right way? Both Plantinga and Wolterstorff, as well as other Protestant philosophers such as William Alston, have devoted considerable energy to developing alternative models of epistemology.

Reason within the Bounds of Religion

In 1976, Wolterstorff published his *Reason within the Bounds of Religion*, a turning on its head of Kant's *Religion within the Limits of Reason*. As we have seen, Tertullian posed the question "What does Jerusalem have to do with Athens?" Wolterstorff notes that "without a doubt a person can simply live in the two different communities, doing as the Athenians do when in Athens and as the Jerusalemites when in Jerusalem. But if one who is a scholar as well as a Christian wants coherence in life . . . he cannot help asking, how does my

---

5. W. K. Clifford, *The Ethics of Belief and Other Essays* (New York: Prometheus, 1999), ix.

6. Sennett, *Analytic Theist*, 104.

7. Clark, *Return to Reason*, 46–53, here 53.

8. Ibid., 4.

membership in these two communities fit together?"[9] In *Reason within the Bounds of Religion* Wolterstorff attends creatively to the role of Christian commitment in the practice of scholarship.

Much of the first half of the book is a critique of foundationalism and classical foundationalism. Wolterstorff identifies two main problems with foundationalism. First, there is the problem with explaining the relationship of a theory to the foundation.[10] He notes that "even if there is a set of foundational propositions, no one has yet succeeded in stating what relation the theories that we are warranted in accepting or rejecting bear to the members of that set. Even if there is a set of foundational propositions, we are without a general logic of the sciences, and hence without a general rule for warranted theory acceptance and rejection."[11]

Second, there is the difficulty in finding enough propositions to belong to the foundation.[12] From his examination of foundationalism Wolterstorff concludes that "the proposed rule for warranted theory acceptance is untenable. It is not the case that one is warranted in accepting some theory if and only if one is warranted in believing that it is justified by propositions knowable noninferentially and with certitude. . . . Our future theories of theorizing will have to be nonfoundationalist ones."[13]

Wolterstorff is adamant that the Bible cannot save foundationalism. Scripture, as he rightly points out, does not provide us with a set of "indubitably known propositions"[14] that can function as a foundation for our theorizing.

In working toward an alternative epistemology—an alternative "theory of theorizing"[15]—Wolterstorff focuses on how scholars go about "weighing" theories. He notes that in weighing theories scholars inevitably carry with them the entire complex of their beliefs so that "one remains cloaked in belief."[16] In the complicated "web of theory," *data-background beliefs* influence what one does and does not accept as data. *Control beliefs* relate to what one believes constitutes an acceptable theory for the subject being studied. Control beliefs include beliefs about the logical or imaginative structure of a theory, the entities to whose existence a theory may commit us, and so on. Negatively, control beliefs lead one to reject certain theories,

9. Nicholas Wolterstorff, *Reason within the Bounds of Religion*, 2nd ed. (Grand Rapids: Eerdmans, 1984), 21.

10. Ibid., 35–45. Wolterstorff notes how *deductivism* was followed by *probabilism* and then *falsification*, none of which are adequate epistemologies.

11. Ibid., 45.

12. Ibid., 46–55.

13. Ibid., 56–57.

14. Ibid., 62.

15. Ibid., 21.

16. Ibid., 66.

whereas positively they provide the basis for constructing theories. In this way Wolterstorff discerns in a scholar's weighing of a theory three levels of belief:

1. data beliefs,
2. data-background beliefs, and
3. control beliefs.

The radicality of Wolterstorff's proposal emerges with his argument that for Christian scholars their religious beliefs should function as control beliefs in their construction of theories. Christian scholarship ought to emerge from *authentic Christian commitment*, that commitment of Christ-followers that involves responding to God's call to be a witness, agent, and evidence of the coming of the kingdom of God. Authentic Christian commitment is far more than belief, but it certainly includes belief, not just about God but also about the world. As Plantinga emphasizes in his inaugural, so too does Wolterstorff insist that Christian scholars ought to seek *integrality* in their scholarship; it should be of one piece with their faith commitment. This will mean rejecting theories that conflict with this commitment and developing theories that comport with it.

Wolterstorff develops seven corollaries of this argument:

1. By and large the faith commitment of Christian scholars will not contain their theories. The Bible is not a book of theories, and it is fatal to expect Scripture to provide what it never was intended to offer.
2. In many areas more than one theory will comport with the belief content of a scholar's faith commitment.
3. By and large the data for Christian scholars' theory weighing are not derived from their faith commitment but, like all other scholars, from observing and reflecting on the world around them.
4. Faith commitment ought to function internally to the theorizing of Christian scholars. This excludes the harmonizing or correlation approach that characterizes so much Christian scholarship. The problem with such an approach is that it assumes that science is okay and then seeks to correlate Christian belief with it.
5. Generally not all Christian scholars' control beliefs will be contained within their faith commitment.
6. In some cases Christian scholars and non-Christian scholars may well accept the same theory.
7. In line with rejecting foundationalism, neither the data nor the controls in our theorizing can be developed from a foundation of certitudes.

Wolterstorff's theory of theorizing privileges authentic Christian commitment, but he rightly notes that theory can also raise questions about the precise nature of Christian commitment and lead to revisions of it. His vision is a creative one: "Christian scholarship will be a poor and paltry thing, worth little attention, until the Christian scholar, under the control of his authentic commitment, devises theories that lead to promising, interesting, fruitful, challenging lines of research."[17]

Christian scholarship is not for hacks. It requires competence, imagination, and courage. Nor should the Christian scholar conceive of authentic commitment as simple: "The belief-content of one's authentic Christian commitment is a wonderfully rich and complex structure, and ever again one discovers that some connection of commitment to theory has been missed by oneself as well as by one's predecessors."[18]

In our twenty-first-century Western culture we need to make a *conscious* decision to see the world through Christian lenses. We also need to be intimately acquainted with Christian theology and philosophy if we are to see the relevance of authentic commitment for theorizing. Wolterstorff notes perceptively that "where Christian theology and Christian philosophy are not in a healthy and robust state, or where their results are not widely diffused among scholars, I see little hope that the rest of Christian scholarship can be solid and vigorous. Christian philosophy and theology are at the center, not because they are infallible . . . but because it is in these two disciplines that the Christian scholar engages in systematic self-examination."[19]

Among philosophers there is a debate over whether scholarship should be "pure" or be praxis oriented, aimed at transforming the world. Wolterstorff explores this issue under the rubric of the biblical concept of *shalom*, a rich term referring to the flourishing of all of creation as God intends for it. He rightly resists the view that all scholarship should be praxis oriented; the Christian scholar will have to assess the priority, in her context, of the value of pure knowledge and praxis-oriented scholarship.

Wolterstorff's *Reason within the Bounds of Religion* exemplifies the creative, foundational role that philosophy can play in the service of all academic disciplines. Indeed, in his own scholarship Wolterstorff has used his philosophical expertise to explore a wide range of disciplines. He has a long-standing interest in education and has also written two books on the philosophy of art, as well as two groundbreaking books on justice (political philosophy). His earlier book *Until Justice and Peace Embrace*[20] is a wonderful book dealing

17. Ibid., 106.
18. Ibid., 107.
19. Ibid., 108.
20. Nicholas Wolterstorff, *Until Justice and Peace Embrace* (Grand Rapids: Eerdmans, 1983).

with Calvinism as world-formative and includes discussions of liberation theology, liturgy, and the aesthetics of the city.

Alvin Plantinga and Warranted Christian Belief

Alvin Plantinga has had a long-standing concern with epistemology and the status of religious beliefs. This concern came to fruition in his acclaimed three-volume work on warrant and epistemology.[21] Central to debates in epistemology has been the issue of what changes a *true belief* into *reliable knowledge*. One may hold the belief that it will snow tomorrow, and this may turn out to be a true belief, but what is the x factor that turns a true belief into knowledge? Traditionally scholars have spoken of *justified* true belief, but Plantinga prefers the term *warrant*.

Plantinga uses the term *warrant* to refer to that property enough of which makes the difference between knowledge and true belief. For a true belief to count as knowledge it must "have more going for it than truth."[22] Warrant is the additional factor that transforms true belief into knowledge, and Plantinga locates warrant in *proper function*. In *Warrant: The Current Debate* and *Warrant and Proper Function*, Plantinga examines the current alternatives in epistemology—namely, internalism (the grounds for counting a belief as knowledge are internal to one's mind), coherentism (beliefs are warranted as knowledge by their coherence with the network of one's beliefs), reliabilism (for a belief to count as knowledge it must be produced by a reliable belief-forming process), and externalism (the grounds for counting a belief as knowledge are external to the mind). In *Warrant and Proper Function* Plantinga argues for an externalist epistemology[23] that locates warrant in proper function: "A belief has warrant just if it is produced by cognitive processes or faculties that are functioning properly, in a cognitive environment that is propitious for that exercise of cognitive powers, according to a design plan that is successfully aimed at the production of true belief."[24]

Five key elements are discernible in Plantinga's view of warranted belief:[25]

21. Alvin Plantinga, *Warrant: The Current Debate* (New York: Oxford University Press, 1993); Alvin Plantinga, *Warrant and Proper Function* (New York: Oxford University Press, 1993); Alvin Plantinga, *Warranted Christian Belief* (New York: Oxford University Press, 2000).

22. Plantinga, *Warranted Christian Belief*, xi. Plantinga uses the example of an ardent fan of the Detroit Tigers, who through her loyalty to the team believes they will win the pennant, despite their poor performances in the previous year. Contrary to all expectations, they do! Nevertheless, her belief was a lucky guess, not knowledge. Knowledge is more than true belief.

23. See C. Stephen Evans, *Faith Beyond Reason* (Edinburgh: Edinburgh University Press, 1998), 41–43.

24. Plantinga, *Warranted Christian Belief*, xi.

25. Ibid., 153–56.

1. A belief has warrant only if it is produced by cognitive faculties functioning properly.
2. Warranted belief is inextricably bound up with the view that this involves functioning in accordance with a design plan.
3. Cognitive faculties will achieve their purpose only if they function in an environment for which they were designed.
4. The design plan must be a good one—that is, one that is successfully aimed at producing true belief.
5. When a belief meets the above conditions and is thus warranted, its degree of warrant will depend on the strength of the belief—that is, on the firmness with which it is held.

In Plantinga's epistemology these elements describe the core of his concept of warrant. He recognizes that there are areas surrounding the core whose extremities will involve cases in which it is unclear whether a case is or is not a case of warrant.

In *Warranted Christian Belief* Plantinga brings his epistemology to bear on Christian belief. He develops a model—the Aquinas/Calvin model—for theistic beliefs that have warrant. Drawing on Calvin's notion of the *sensus divinitatis*, Plantinga argues that humans have a natural tendency to form beliefs about God: "The *sensus divinitatis* is a disposition or set of dispositions to form theistic beliefs in various circumstances, in response to the sorts of conditions or stimuli that trigger the working of this sense of divinity."[26] Theistic beliefs are occasioned by such circumstances but are *not* conclusions drawn from them. Plantinga argues that theistic belief produced by the *sensus divinitatis* is properly basic.

Plantinga extends the Aquinas/Calvin model to cover specifically Christian belief and argues that Christian belief is warranted; it is not just true belief but is in fact knowledge. But what of the effects of sin on knowledge? As Plantinga rightly notes, this is a major difference between theism and Christianity.[27] To take account of this, Plantinga develops his extended Aquinas/Calvin model, in which he unapologetically discusses the role of faith and the work of the Holy Spirit. As he notes, "Some may find it scandalous that theological ideas should be taken seriously in a book on philosophy; I find it no more scandalous than the ingression into philosophy of scientific ideas from (for example) quantum mechanics, cosmology, and evolutionary biology."[28]

The extended Aquinas/Calvin model claims that God has made us in his image; we are persons with intellect and will. Part of this image is the *sensus*

26. Ibid., 173.
27. Ibid., 201.
28. Ibid., 200.

divinitatis. Our fall into sin has had cataclysmic effects, affective and cognitive. By his redemptive acts, climaxing in Jesus, God has provided the remedy for sin, a way for us to be restored to God and to become what God intended us to be. At the cognitive level God informs human beings of his salvation in two ways: first, through Scripture, a collection of human writings inspired by God so that he is its primary author, and second, through the work of the Spirit who produces in us the gift of faith and through his "instigation" assures us that the central Christian affirmations are true. According to Plantinga, "The internal invitation of the Holy Spirit is therefore a source of belief, a cognitive process that produces in us belief in the main lines of the Christian story. Still further, according to the model, the beliefs thus produced in us meet the conditions necessary and sufficient for warrant. . . . If they are held with sufficient firmness, these beliefs qualify as *knowledge*, just as Calvin's definition of faith has it."[29]

On the back of the refutation of classical foundationalism, Plantinga and others have argued that belief in God is a properly basic belief that, like other properly basic beliefs, does not require evidence before it can be taken as properly basic. Plantinga is not saying that there are no good arguments for belief in God, but that we must not make belief in God dependent for its *warrant* on such evidence. This is what C. Stephen Evans is getting at when he characterizes Plantinga's view of the faith/reason relationship as "faith without reasons."[30]

Plantinga does agree with classical foundationalism that not just any belief can be properly basic, but he does not offer criteria for proper basicality. He argues that we must proceed *inductively* in this respect and "assemble examples of beliefs and conditions such that the former are obviously properly basic in the latter, and examples of beliefs and conditions such that the former are obviously not properly basic in the latter."[31] We must proceed in this regard from below rather than from above. But we should not assume that everyone will agree on the relevant examples.

> The Christian will of course suppose that belief in God is entirely proper and rational; if he does not accept this belief on the basis of other propositions, he will certainly conclude that it is basic for him and quite properly so. Followers of Bertrand Russell and Madelyn Murray O'Hare may disagree; but how is that relevant? Must my criteria or those of the Christian community, conform to their examples? Surely not. The Christian community is responsible to its set of examples, not to theirs.

29. Ibid., 206.
30. Evans, *Faith Beyond Reason*, chapter 3.
31. Sennett, *Analytic Theist*, 151.

So, the Reformed epistemologist can properly hold that belief in the Great Pumpkin is not properly basic, even though he holds that belief in God is properly basic and even if he has no full-fledged criterion of proper basicality.[32]

Belief in God is properly basic, but this does not mean it is groundless. Such an approach is not a form of fideism, which ignores reason or plays it down in the interests of faith. Belief in God, for Plantinga, *is* a deliverance of reason, just as much as any other properly basic belief is.[33] Furthermore, belief in God as basic does not mean that it might not be wrong or that it cannot be disputed. Part 4 of Plantinga's *Warranted Christian Belief* is devoted to possible defeaters of Christian belief.[34] Plantinga attends to the following defeaters:

1. The explanation of religious beliefs as our projecting into the heavens a being like an idealized father (e.g., Freud, Marx, Émile Durkheim).
2. Historical biblical criticism. In a brilliant chapter on biblical interpretation, Plantinga makes the case for what he calls "traditional biblical commentary," which assumes the inspiration of the Bible.
3. Postmodernism and pluralism. Plantinga traces the laughable bravado of the creative anti-realism of postmodernism back to Kant and is highly critical of the view that we and not God create our world.
4. Suffering and evil. Plantinga's free-will defense is well known and has been described by a non-Christian philosopher as a thing of beauty that cannot be ignored.

Conclusion

In our conclusion to the chapter on postmodernism we argued that in some respects it goes too far and in others not far enough. Against that backdrop, the genius of Reformed epistemology is apparent in that it rightly goes behind and beyond Kant in asserting the legitimacy of taking Christian belief as foundational for philosophy. At the same time, this enables it to hold on to a commitment to truth and a form of realism so that it remains positively engaged with the best of modern philosophy. In the latter respect, a kindred spirit in the Catholic world is Charles Taylor. His work is characterized by a sustained attempt to retrieve the good in modern thought and philosophy. In our view, this is vital if we are to contribute today to the healing of modernity.

32. Ibid.
33. See ibid., 157–61.
34. See Plantinga, *Warranted Christian Belief*, 359–66, for Plantinga's analysis of the nature of defeaters.

There is much in modernity worth holding on to, and we need the sort of nuanced critique represented by Plantinga, Wolterstorff, Taylor, and others.

In arguing that Christian belief may legitimately be taken as properly basic without evidence, Plantinga and Wolterstorff have truly gone for the jugular of the religious dimension of much modern philosophy. As Plantinga notes, one can climb a mountain with one's feet chained, but why do that when you don't need to? If Christ is the true revelation of God, that Word which was in the beginning, and if Scripture tells the true story of the whole world, then why on earth would one want to bracket out such insights when seeking to analyze the structure of God's world? Reformed epistemology confronts us with what in Reformed circles is called the *antithesis* and resolutely will not let us off the hook of choosing one of two ways: that of wisdom or that of folly. In its own way, Reformed epistemology is a contemporary embodiment of that ancient insight that the fear of the Lord is the beginning—both starting point and foundation—of knowledge. As such, it is profoundly refreshing and is to be welcomed for the space it has created for work to be done which is genuinely Christian philosophy.

14

Reformed Epistemology Applied

Reformed epistemology has developed in the Calvinist tradition, but it is Calvinism influenced by or read through the lens of the Kuyperian tradition. The opening chapter of Nicholas Wolterstorff's brilliant *Until Justice and Peace Embrace* references "world-formative" Christianity.[1] In a succinct articulation of philosophy of religion, Wolterstorff distinguishes between *avertive* and *formative* religions as two types of salvation religions. Both types anticipate liberation from that which is inferior in our existence, but in avertive Christianity the focus is away from ordinary earthly life, whereas in formative Christianity the focus is on the re-formation of earthly life as the sphere of God's saving activity. "Original Calvinism represented, then, a passionate desire to reshape the social world so that it would no longer be alienated from God. Thereby it would also no longer be alienated from mankind, for the will of God is that society be an ordered 'brotherhood' serving the common good."[2]

A strength of this type of world-formative Calvinism is that it takes all of life seriously as the theater of God's glory. Christian life and thought cannot be confined to church and theology; it extends to the whole range of God's good creation. The range of Wolterstorff's and Plantinga's work embodies this comprehensive vision. Both have written on a wide range of issues. Some scholars make a distinction between first-order philosophy—ontology, epistemology, anthropology—and second-order philosophy, such as philosophy of art, of politics, of science, of education, and so on. Wolterstorff and Plantinga, with many others, have made a seminal contribution to first-order philosophy, but they have also

1. Nicholas Wolterstorff, *Until Justice and Peace Embrace* (Grand Rapids: Eerdmans, 1983), 3–22.
2. Ibid., 21–22.

written extensively about second-order topics. In this chapter we will examine
some of the second-order areas in which they have made significant contributions.

The Grand Evolutionary Story

In recent years evolution has reemerged as a hot-button issue. This is related
to the "New Atheism" of our day and the often virulent reaction to intelligent
design, which has publicly challenged Darwinism. Evolution is a highly emotive
issue, and positions on it are deeply entrenched and often characterized by a
lack of grace and nuance. The sanity and clarity of Alvin Plantinga's work in
this area is a refreshing contribution to this volatile debate.[3]

In his essay "When Faith and Reason Clash: Evolution and the Bible,"[4]
Plantinga starts by acknowledging the clear, apparent clash between evolution
and the biblical account of origins in Genesis. He explores different historical
approaches to this apparent clash between faith and reason and concludes that
"we must do our best to apprehend both the teachings of Scripture and the
deliverances of reason; in either case we will have much more warrant for some
apparent teachings than for others."[5] A contribution of Plantinga's approach
is to recognize that different aspects in the Christian view of creation—and in
the theory of evolution—have more probability than others. Thus it is most
clear that God created the world so that everything depends on him for its
existence and nothing has existed for eternity apart from God. Next clearest
is that there was an original human pair who rebelled against God and whose
fall was disastrous for both humankind and nature. That the earth is young
is far less clearly taught, whereas, from Plantinga's perspective, the longevity
of the earth has strong scientific warrant, so that it is probable.

Plantinga rightly argues that the theory of evolution is by no means religiously neutral. He discerns three basic, current Western ways of viewing reality:

1. perennial naturalism, which argues that nature is all there is and humans
   are part of nature;
2. Enlightenment humanism/subjectivism/anti-realism, which can be traced
   back to Immanuel Kant and which views humans as the real authors of
   the structures of our world; and
3. Christian theism.

3. Plantinga has made several forays into this debate. The most recent is his *Where the Conflict Really Lies: Science, Religion, and Naturalism* (Oxford: Oxford University Press, 2011).
4. Alvin Plantinga, "When Faith and Reason Clash: Evolution and the Bible," (Ancaster:
Redeemer College, 1991).
5. Ibid., 12.

All three options are *religious* worldviews, and the stakes could not be higher; "this is a battle for men's souls."[6] Indeed the religious dimension of these views goes a long way toward explaining why the debate is so virulent; the theory of evolution has become, at least in academia, "an idol of the contemporary tribe,"[7] and it relates to how we understand ourselves and our world at the most basic level. As Richard Dawkins has asserted, evolution enables one to be a fulfilled atheist.[8]

Plantinga discerns five theses that constitute the "Grand Evolutionary Story":

1. the ancient earth thesis, which claims that the earth is very old;
2. the progress thesis, which claims that life has progressed from relatively simple to relatively complex forms, in particular the human;
3. the common ancestry thesis, which asserts that life originated at only one place on earth and all subsequent life is descended from these original living creatures;
4. Darwinism, according to which the evolutionary mechanism is natural selection operating on random genetic mutation; and
5. the naturalistic origins thesis, which claims that life itself developed from nonliving matter without any special creative activity from God.

Here again the nuance in Plantinga's approach is helpful. As he rightly notes, the scientific evidence for these theses varies enormously. The evidence for thesis 1 is very strong. There is less evidence for 2 but still good evidence in the fossil record. Thesis 5 is, for the most part, "mere arrogant bluster."[9] Theses 3 and 4 are central to evolution, more narrowly defined.

Stephen Jay Gould presents three arguments for thesis 4:

1. observational evidence;
2. homologies, in which a common ancestry explains why a rat runs, why a bat flies, why a porpoise swims, and why we type at our computers, and all with structures built of the same bones; and
3. the fossil record.

Plantinga notes regarding 1 that while there is widespread evidence for microevolution, the key question is whether we can extrapolate from this to macroevolution. "As plants or animals are bred in a certain direction, a sort

6. Ibid., 15.
7. Ibid., 16.
8. Ibid., 17–18.
9. Ibid., 21.

of barrier is encountered; further selective breeding brings about sterility or a reversion to earlier forms."[10] With respect to the fossil record the problem is that it shows very few transitional forms. The argument from homologies is suggestive but certainly not decisive. Universal common descent is possible, but it is ridiculous to regard it as certain.

Plantinga takes as an example the mammalian eye:

> And here is the problem: how does the lens, e.g., get developed by the proposed means—e.g., random genetic variation and natural selection—when at the same time there has to be development of the optic nerve, the relevant muscles, the retina, the rods and cones, and many other delicate and complicated structures, all of which have to be adjusted to each other in such a way that they can work together? . . . Imagine starting with a population of animals without eyes, and trace through the space in question all the paths that lead from this form to forms with eyes.[11]

The amount of variables required to explain such a process by random mutation is high, and we do not know what they are. Epistemically evolution may have occurred, but biologically we don't even know if it is possible.

The certainty with which evolution is trumpeted nowadays is at best a gross exaggeration. The problem is that for a nontheist evolution is the only game in town. Furthermore, from a naturalistic perspective evolution will be more probable than alternatives. But a naturalistic perspective is far from unproblematic. In *Warranted Christian Belief* Plantinga develops his courageous critique of naturalism. He argues that the person who denies the existence of God and accepts contemporary evolutionary theory is irrational. More precisely, Plantinga argues that accepting both metaphysical naturalism—the view that only natural objects, kinds, and properties are real—and evolution is self-defeating. The defeater lies in the fact that such a view makes belief in the reliability of human cognition very difficult, if not impossible, because there is no reason why adaptation for survival should produce reliable cognitive equipment in humans.

The Christian, Plantinga argues, has far more freedom than the nontheist. The Christian knows that creation is the Lord's, but has room for differences of opinion in terms of how God brought about this creation. Plantinga himself is wary of the semi-deistic approach that some Christians adopt in their embrace of theistic evolution:

> It is important to remember, however, that the Lord has not merely left the Cosmos to develop according to an initial creation and an initial set of physical laws. According to Scripture he has often intervened in the workings of his

10. Ibid., 26.
11. Ibid., 27.

cosmos. . . . Towering above all, there is the unthinkable gift of salvation for
humankind by way of the life, death, and resurrection of Jesus Christ, his son.
. . . There is therefore no initial edge to the idea that he would be more likely
to have created life in all its variety in the broadly deistic way.[12]

Plantinga thinks that the view that God created humankind, as well as many
plants and animals, separately and specially is more probable than the common ancestry view.

How should Christian intellectuals contribute to this debate? One thing
we should do is avoid rejecting evolution for unfounded reasons. But more
than this we need to do cultural analysis and "theistic science." Evolution as
propagated in the academy today is not religiously neutral, and we need to
test the spirits of our day no matter how prestigious or acclaimed they are. In
addition to such cultural analysis, we need answers to the question of origins
from all we know, that is, with our faith fully engaged. Such work "is worthy
of the very best we can muster; it demands powerful, patient, unstinting and
tireless effort but its rewards match its demands; it is exciting, absorbing and
crucially important. Most of all, however, it needs to be done. I therefore
commend it to you."[13]

Art

Nicholas Wolterstorff has published an interlocking pair of works on aesthetics,
or philosophy of art: his more philosophical *Works and Worlds of Art* and the
more accessible and openly Christian *Art in Action*. Art—which Wolterstorff
defines simply as a product of the fine arts—is universal in that it is found
in every culture. But a unique development in Western culture has been the
institution of high art with its museums, galleries, and concert halls.[14] "It is
this institution—fallen but pretentious, secular but mystical—that confronts
us all."[15] The result is that a chasm has opened up between elite high art and
popular art. In high art, generally, the art object's sole or primary function
is to act as the object of aesthetic contemplation. Even the anti-art of people
like Marcel Duchamp and John Cage works with—albeit in reaction to—this
view of art as being for disinterested contemplation.

Duchamp notoriously presented an ordinary urinal for display in a museum.
As Wolterstorff notes, "Duchamp's *Fountain* is an example of *anti-art*—an

12. Ibid., 23.
13. Ibid., 37.
14. See Nicholas Wolterstorff, *Art in Action* (Grand Rapids: Eerdmans, 1980), especially 19–63.
15. Ibid., 193.

object presented to us not that we should find it satisfying to contemplate but rather that we should find it interesting *that it is presented* as if for contemplation, and for the reasons that it is. What counts is the *gesture* along with the reasons for the gesture, not the object with which the gesture is made. In such gestures there is a repudiation of the aesthetic."[16]

A comparable example is John Cage's composition for piano, 4'33". A pianist comes on stage and sits at the piano, opens the score, and holds his hands suspended above the keyboard for four minutes and thirty-three seconds, hence the title. He shuts the score, rises, and leaves the stage!

According to Wolterstorff, the result of the development of high art is not only the unhealthy separation of high art from popular art but also the way that we are blinded to the myriad ways in which people use art to act. In the West up until the seventeenth century, liturgical art was the art of the tribe, but pop art is now that of the marketplace and is thoroughly commercialized.[17]

Wolterstorff does not argue that we should ignore or abandon the institutions of high art. Alluding playfully to Tertullian's "What does Jerusalem have to do with Athens?" he poses the question "What does Jerusalem have to do with New York?"[18] His answer: a great deal. After all, art for the sake of contemplation has its place, but only amidst the many other roles art plays. At the end of *Art in Action* he argues for both *liberation from* and *participation in* high art. We need to extend its limited vision to take in the aesthetics of the city, the church, and so many other contexts in which art can play a vital, humanizing role. And for those of us actively engaged in the institutions of high art, we must not do so at the cost of avoiding responsibility or integrality, and we must resist the claims of ultimacy made by too much modern art. Following on from Kant and Hume, the idea of the artist as creator akin to God as Creator took hold. From this perspective the arts become the place where meaning can be created and discovered in a meaningless world; such an idolatrous approach must be avoided.

Wolterstorff argues provocatively that art objects are objects and instruments of action, hence his title *Art in Action*. Art objects are embedded in the fabric of human intention and thus in life. It is therefore a major mistake to seek one purpose for art; it serves a great diversity of roles, and we use artworks to perform a variety of actions. "*Artistically man acts.*"[19]

In part 3 of *Art in Action*, Wolterstorff develops a Christian aesthetic. He argues that art must be understood with the Christian framework of creation, fall, and redemption. He proposes that we think of the artist as a responsible

16. Ibid., 62.
17. Ibid., 23.
18. Ibid., 192.
19. Ibid., 5 (italics in the original).

servant amid God's glorious creation. A biblical view of what it means to be human and a biblical doctrine of creation are essential to a correct understanding of art as action. "Man's *embeddedness* in the physical creation, and his creaturely *vocation* and creaturely *end* within that creation, are where we must begin if we are to describe how the Christian sees the arts, provided, in turn, that the arts are seen as instruments and objects of action."[20] Wolterstorff rightly notes that devaluation of the materiality of creation flies in the face of God's affirmation of creation. We are interwoven into the creation so that in art we work with things that bear an intimate relationship to us. Our uniqueness lies in our responsibility; dominion involves imposing order for the sake of serving human livelihood and delight. "Man's vocation is to be the world's gardener."[21] Humans have a triadic responsibility: to God to subdue the earth, to God for loving our neighbor, to God for acknowledging him.

It is not hard to see how humankind's vocation of subduer, of humanizer of the world, of one who imposes order for the sake of benefiting mankind or honoring God, applies to the artist. "The artist takes an amorphous pile of bits of colored glass and orders them upon the wall of the basilica so that the liturgy can take place in the splendor of flickering colored light and in the presence of the invoked saints. He takes a blob of clay and orders it into a pot of benefit and delight."[22]

"Responsibility," according to Wolterstorff, needs to be complemented with the biblical notion of *shalom*, lest we conceive of the arts as stern and overly serious: "Responsible action is the vocation of man, shalom is his end."[23] Art is not exempt from the fall; indeed it is too often an instrument of the fallenness of the world. But art can also be an instrument of renewal in our fallen but being-redeemed world. What might such art look like?

The artist works with various mediums given in God's creation. Familiarity with the medium with which one works is indispensable. "The stage of actuality is God's structured creation."[24] The Christian view thus places the artist's working with materials at the heart of the artistic enterprise.

Wolterstorff discerns *fittingness*, which he defines as cross-modal similarity, as a central characteristic of art. Expressiveness, about which so much is made nowadays, is itself grounded in fittingness. Every artist is in fact a worker in fittingness.

- The artist's work will inescapably be an expression of a state of consciousness, of self-expression.

20. Ibid., 69 (italics in the original).
21. Ibid., 76.
22. Ibid., 77.
23. Ibid., 79.
24. Ibid., 92.

- The character of a work of art may bear relations of fittingness not only to a state of consciousness but to many other qualities as well.
- Often there will be close fittingness between the character of a work and things outside the work.
- The internal unity of a work of art is related in various ways to fittingness, to the unity of the work in terms of its coherence and/or completeness.

In terms of the many actions performed by art and artists, Wolterstorff focuses on one in particular—the action of world projection. Although world projection is only one of the actions the artist performs by means of his artwork, Wolterstorff argues that it is perhaps the most pervasive and important of the actions that artists perform. "The projected world of a work of art is a state of affairs—usually a rather complex state of affairs, sometimes an extraordinarily complex one."[25] Intriguingly, Wolterstorff argues that if a state of affairs ever exists, it always exists.[26] This relates back to his point about the artist working with the givenness of creation; artistic work in this respect involves selection rather than creation, although this still leaves ample room for creativity. Wolterstorff also notes that there is always a world behind the work, but—and this is an important point—the work by no means always fully reveals the world behind it. To assess an artist's work, one needs to attend to the corpus as a whole.

One of the great attractions of approaching art as action is that it enables one to answer the question, what does art do? Hans Rookmaaker rightly argued that art needs no justification; its justification is the way God made the world.[27] Well and good! But this still leaves dangling the benefits of art. Wolterstorff discerns seven benefits in the action of world projection by artists.

1. Confirmation. By projecting a world, an artist may confirm our view of the world. This is far more common than is often realized.
2. Illumination. World projection may illuminate a part of the world in fresh ways.
3. A means of escape. It can be false to our actuality and provide a means for us to enter into a very different world.
4. Evocation of emotions.
5. Modeling of ways of living and orienting ourselves in the world.
6. Communication of a message.
7. Consolation.

25. Ibid., 131.
26. Ibid.
27. Hans R. Rookmaaker, *Art Needs No Justification* (Vancouver: Regent College Publishing, 2010).

What are the norms for art? This is a vexed question, and Wolterstorff explores some of the traditional answers. Art should be excellent, and he further suggests three norms: an artwork should be unified in character; it should be internally rich, varied, and complex; and there should be a fittingness-intensity of characters where appropriate to the medium.

Political Philosophy: Justice and Human Rights

Injustice—in particular, the injustice of apartheid in South Africa and the oppression of the Palestinians—impelled Wolterstorff to think about justice. In the name of Christ, South Africa was structured around racism (apartheid) and the—often brutal—oppression of the black majority by the white minority. Wolterstorff first visited South Africa in 1976. He says of his visit, "I saw, as never before, the good overwhelming the just, and benevolence and the appeal to love being used as instruments of oppression."[28] Thus began his ongoing engagement with South Africa and the struggle for liberation. In May 1978 Wolterstorff attended a conference in Chicago on Palestinian rights; once again he felt a powerful call to speak up for the oppressed and soon became chairman of the Palestine Human Rights Campaign.

Such experiences were formative for Wolterstorff in terms of both his scholarly focus and his view of Christian scholarship. Justice and human rights have remained major concerns of his at both the practical and theoretical levels, and he has published three major books on justice—*Until Justice and Peace Embrace* in 1983 and, more recently, *Justice: Rights and Wrongs* and *Love and Justice*. In the former, Wolterstorff took for granted a certain view of justice and applied it to various circumstances; the latter are his philosophical attempts to account for his view of justice.

Justice: A Philosophical Account

South Africa under apartheid was—and the Palestinian situation is—characterized by horrific human rights abuses, and not surprisingly Wolterstorff focuses his philosophical treatment of justice on human rights. Indeed, he thinks of justice as constituted by rights: "A society is just insofar as its members enjoy the goods to which they have a right."[29] In *Justice: Rights and Wrongs* he focuses on primary, as opposed to rectifying, justice and seeks to articulate a Christian, theistic, philosophical account of it. As a Christian

28. Nicholas Wolterstorff, *Justice: Rights and Wrongs* (Princeton and Oxford: Princeton University Press, 2008), vii.
29. Ibid., xii.

he believes that God and justice are intertwined, and "if one believes in God then not to bring God into the picture, when relevant, is to defect from the philosopher's calling. It would be like a Platonist refraining from mentioning the Forms."[30]

Wolterstorff discerns two competing accounts of primary justice in the Western tradition: that of *inherent rights* and that of *right order*. Part of the argument against inherent rights is that this concept is a late development emerging from philosophers such as Hobbes and Locke. Wolterstorff challenges this narrative head-on. The idea of natural rights was common among twelfth-century canon lawyers, and even among the church fathers such rights were recognized. How, Wolterstorff asks, did the church fathers come to this recognition? It had to have come from either their classical or their biblical inheritance.

Among the Greeks, the key concept in this respect is *eudaimonism*, or the good life, of which the Stoics and Aristotle are the major exponents. Wolterstorff argues that eudaimonism cannot account for the fathers' understanding of rights. Does the Bible then provide an adequate resource for rights? Wolterstorff argues that indeed it does, with the Old Testament and New Testament affirmation of inherent human worth. In a remarkable element of his argument, Wolterstorff says that "had the spell of ancient eudaimonism not been broken, an adequate theory of rights would have been impossible."[31] He credits Augustine with breaking this spell as his understanding of love was reshaped over his lifetime by Scripture.[32] In his early work Augustine argues that *love* should be reserved for God alone and *enjoyment* for excellent created goods. By the end of his career Augustine had come to see that love was also appropriate for one's neighbor and oneself. "It was Christ's injunction to love not only God but one's neighbor as oneself that roiled the water of Augustine's eudaimonism."[33] Unlike God, one's neighbor and oneself are mutable, and Augustine's shift in his understanding of love radically alters his view of the tranquility that was the goal of eudaimonism.

Wolterstorff's argument for rights is complex and detailed, and here we can only outline its major elements. A *right* is a good in one's life or in history that contributes positively to one's existence. There are goods that are not part of the experientially satisfying life, and to some of these we have rights. Wolterstorff argues in detail that rights cannot be adequately grounded in desire, proper function, or duty; they are normative social relationships, and the only adequate grounding is respect for the worth of a human being.

30. Ibid., x.
31. Ibid., 180.
32. See ibid., 180–206.
33. Ibid., 194.

Wolterstorff examines secular attempts to ground human rights, most
of which locate human dignity in certain capacities. He rightly notes that a
focus on capacities is inadequate, since it leaves the most vulnerable without
protection. This leaves us with four options:

1. We can continue to believe in natural rights and hope that a secular
   grounding will turn up.
2. We can provide a theistic grounding for human rights.
3. We can give up on the existence of inherent human rights.
4. We can deny that there are any inherent natural rights whatsoever.

Wolterstorff opts for option 2. He is open to grounding human rights in
the *imago dei* but wary of a reading of it along the lines of human capacities, which would get us back into the same problems of secular groundings.
An interpretation of the *imago dei* along the lines of our resembling God
uniquely by our human nature is more helpful, but "the image of God is not
adequate, all by itself, for grounding natural human rights."[34] Wolterstorff
finds adequate grounding in the fact that every human is loved by God, a relation that bestows great worth on human beings: "And if God loves equally
and permanently each and every creature who bears the *imago dei*, then the
relational property of being loved by God is what we have been looking for.
Bearing that property gives to each human being who bears it the worth in
which natural human rights inhere."[35]

Wolterstorff extends his account of rights to include social entities, as well
as cultural artifacts—such as works of art, and animals, and plants. Of animal
rights he notes that "if animals have rights, then they can be wronged. The role
that being wronged plays in their lives is only a pale imitation, however, of the
role it plays in the lives of persons. . . . They cannot perform the (illocution-
ary) action of claiming their rights; *you and I must do that on their behalf.*"[36]

Wolterstorff notes that the recognition of human rights since World War II
is an extraordinary achievement since we are by nature tribalists. Christian
theism is the rich soil in which human rights have come to the fore, and a
danger of secularization is to deny this soil and to reap the consequences.
We would add that not only is the Judeo-Christian soil of rights in danger
of being ignored, but so too is the remarkable contribution of Christians to
human and animal rights. William Wilberforce and the Clapham Sect not
only spearheaded the drive to abolish slavery, but they also led the movement

34. Ibid., 352.
35. Ibid.
36. Ibid., 370 (italics added).

for the protection of animals from rampant abuse, which led to the founding of the Society for the Prevention of Cruelty to Animals (SPCA) and then to the Royal Society for the Prevention of Cruelty to Animals (RSPCA) under Queen Victoria's reign. Similarly, although it is often downplayed or denied, Christians played a crucial role in facilitating the United Nations Declaration on Human Rights.

Justice in Action: Philosophy of Society

God's Word always comes to us and calls us to action in our particular historical contexts, and our practice of mission will be woefully inadequate if not downright dangerous if we fail to understand our times. Philosophy of culture is a major help in this respect, and *Until Justice and Peace Embrace* is a great example of what such work might look like. Wolterstorff rightly asserts the need for an architectonic analysis of our society, an analysis of our social institutions and practices that constitute our social world.

There are two major approaches to the modern world-system: that of modernization theorists and that of world-system theorists. Modernization theory conceives of our world as made up of many different societies all at certain points of development in the process of modernization. Modernization, characterized by such features as a high degree of differentiation, adaptive upgrading, a forming of the differentiated parts into an integrated whole, and value generalization, is viewed by such theorists as a good thing, and in principle all societies could and should reach a high level of modernization. Most modernization theorists identify technology as the driving force behind modernization. Causes of low levels of modernization are located in individual societies and not in the system as a whole or in highly developed societies.

Wolterstorff rightly argues that this approach is bankrupt. Some thirty years since *Until Justice and Peace Embrace* was published, the injustices of modernization have gotten worse and not better. This is not to say that modernization theory contains no important insights. However, for Wolterstorff we need a world-systems approach, not least because of the interconnectedness of the world today and the global dominance of capitalism: "I have made clear my conviction that we must see ourselves as living today in a global society that combines an integrated capitalist economy with a multiplicity of states and a diversity of peoples. I have argued that we must prefer the basic picture offered by the world-system theorist over that offered by the modernization theorist."[37]

A world-systems approach enables us to get at the realities of our day in a far more nuanced way than does modernization theory. As Wolterstorff

---

37. Wolterstorff, *Until Justice and Peace Embrace*, 33.

238 Christian Philosophy Today

notes, if we distinguish between social groups on the basis of their (1) having a single economy, (2) being a distinct political nation, and (3) being distinct as a nation/people, we can start to see that a variety of possible combinations among these units exist.

A major asset of this type of approach is that it enables us to see just how dominant global consumer capitalism has become. Wolterstorff discerns six criteria that enable us to see if an economy is more capitalist than not:

1. If it distributes goods by means of a market system. A market system is far more than a means for exchanging goods; it is a mechanism for maintaining an entire society.
2. If the goal of economic enterprises is to make a profit.
3. If labor has become an item of the market system.
4. If more capital[38] enters into the production and distribution processes of the economy.
5. If more participants in an economy use their income derived from capital to achieve title to items used in turn as capital.
6. When more capital is owned by private parties than by the public.

Thus defined, the global economy is clearly capitalist, but it is important to distinguish between the capitalist core, periphery, and semi-periphery. Economically, the core dominates and controls the periphery and semi-periphery so that the world-system is characterized by major economic injustice.

The great attraction of the modern world-system lies in its expansion of freedom by mastery and its freedom of self-direction. Negatively, it has led to chronic inequality across the globe and has spawned tyranny. Clearly modernity has brought both gift and toxin, and this sort of analysis is crucial if we are to contribute to the healing of modernity. How should world-formative Christianity respond missionally to the modern world-system?

In response, Wolterstorff opens up a dialogue between Lima and Amsterdam, between Gustavo Gutierrez's liberation theology and Herman Dooyeweerd's neocalvinist philosophy. Wolterstorff rightly affirms Gutierrez's desire to give the wretched of the world their voice. What he finds questionable is the goal of liberation according to Gutierrez; it is freedom, but what exactly does this freedom constitute? Wolterstorff perceptively notes the lack of a robust doctrine of creation in Gutierrez's theology; creation is viewed as a salvific act, with the result that salvation and history remain unlinked.

---

38. Wolterstorff defines capital as "consisting of items to which persons (or corporate entities) have title, that are used in the production or marketing of goods or services, and whose use therein entitles the owner to income on account of the (purported) utility of those items in that process" (ibid., 30).

In contrast to liberation theology, the concern of Dooyeweerd is with authority, and in his philosophy one does not find the cries of the wretched given voice. However, Wolterstorff does find very insightful the approach of the Dutch economist Bob Goudzwaard in his *Capitalism and Progress*. Goudzwaard, using the insights of Reformational philosophy, argues that in the West we have embraced economic growth and technological development as the ultimate good, with the result that we have birthed a "tunnel society." Using the Reformational idea of sphere sovereignty, Goudzwaard argues that we have allowed the economic sphere to dominate the other spheres of society, thereby subverting the normative stewardship of economics and preventing "disclosure"—that is, the opening up of the economic sphere in relation to the norms of other spheres.

Wolterstorff likes Goudzwaard's analysis but questions whether it needs the baggage of Dooyeweerd's ontology. In his view, "we do not have to adopt this ontology in order to preserve the core of Goudzwaard's contribution."[39] As an alternative, Wolterstorff proposes as the guiding principle what best serves justice and *shalom*.

If one has any doubts about the practical relevance of good Christian philosophy, then the chapters that follow in *Until Justice and Peace Embrace* should once and for all dispel such doubts. Wolterstorff writes penetratingly about poverty, nationalism, the aesthetics of the city, and justice and liturgy. Wolterstorff's work bridges the far-too-common gap between philosophy and life and does so in exemplary fashion. In our words, his work embodies a *missional philosophy*; it is both rigorous and contextual.

Warranted Biblical Interpretation?

Does philosophy have anything to do with how we interpret the Bible? In this section we will focus on Plantinga's insightful comments in this respect. Plantinga notes that rigorous, academic biblical interpretation has a long and prestigious tradition in Christianity, aimed at discerning what the Lord says to us through the Bible. Plantinga calls this traditional biblical commentary. However, out of the Enlightenment came another type of biblical interpretation, which Plantinga describes as historical biblical criticism. Anyone who has done biblical studies at a mainstream university will know just how confusing and challenging it is when you are inducted into historical biblical criticism as *the* way to read the Bible scientifically.

The defining characteristic of historical biblical criticism, according to Plantinga, is that it insists on reading the Bible according to reason alone; it specifically

39. Ibid., 62.

excludes employing theological assumptions in its epistemology. One may argue toward, but not from, theological beliefs. Plantinga discerns three types of historical biblical criticism: Troeltschian, which interprets Troeltsch's principles to preclude direct divine action in the world; Duhemian, which aims to avoid all assumptions that are not common to parties in the dialogue; and Spinozistic, which uses principles of reason that may not be agreed upon by all participants.

Plantinga examines Troeltschian historical biblical criticism in particular. Arguments for its principles are noticeable by their absence, and yet one finds these sorts of assumption all over the literature. Perhaps everyone "in the know" accepts Troeltschian principles, but this arrogantly ignores the millions of contemporary Christians. Van A. Harvey argues that *morally* we are compelled to accept these principles, but as Plantinga discerns, "what lies at the bottom of this moral claim is really a philosophical-theological judgment: that traditional Christian belief is completely mistaken in taking it that faith is, in fact, a reliable source of true and warranted belief on these topics."[40] Plantinga is unable to find any compelling arguments for historical biblical criticism as opposed to traditional biblical commentary.

These types of historical biblical criticism raise the important epistemological question of why one should avoid employing *all* one's resources in the search for truth. Unlike physics or chemistry, according to Plantinga, the very foundations of biblical scholarship are deeply influenced by theological issues.[41] In a review of Thomas Sheehan's *The First Coming: How the Kingdom of God Became Christianity*, Plantinga presents a strong case for utilizing *all* of our theological resources in the quest for true knowledge of the Bible:

> Isn't it simple common sense that a Christian scholar . . . should use everything she knows in pursuing her discipline? . . . If your aim is to reach as much as you can of the full-fledged, full-orbed truth about the matter at hand, then presumably the right way to proceed is to use all of your resources, everything you know, including what you know by faith. . . .
>
> This claim—that one ought not to employ the view that Jesus was (is) divine in scholarship—rests on the assumption that the only way in which we could properly come to characteristically Christian beliefs is by way of ordinary scientific or historical investigation. But this assumption is dubious *in excelsis*; it is part and parcel of classical Foundationalism and shares its liabilities. . . .
>
> What really is at issue here is a philosophical (epistemological) view about what constitutes correct or reasonable belief, about what constitutes proper or real knowledge.[42]

40. Plantinga, *Warranted Christian Belief*, 407.
41. Ibid., 414.
42. James F. Sennett, ed., *The Analytic Theist: An Alvin Plantinga Reader* (Grand Rapids: Eerdmans, 1998), 325–27.

Plantinga here applies to biblical interpretation his critique of classical foundationalism and his assertion of the Christian's right to take belief in God as properly basic. If Plantinga is right—and we think he most definitely is—then we should not be afraid of putting our Christian beliefs to work in biblical studies, even though such an approach will inevitably draw forth the dreaded f-word![43]

Take the Ten Commandments, for example. David Clines says of them, "Did God (if there is a God) actually speak audible words out of the sky over a mountain in the Arabian peninsula in the late second millennium BCE? . . . It will not shock many readers of these pages if I say I do not believe that any such thing ever happened, and that I would be surprised if any scholarly reader did either."[44] Clines presents no arguments for this view but clearly is deeply influenced by a *belief* that excludes the possibility of God acting and speaking in the world. Without for a moment trying to argue that there is a one-to-one correspondence between the telling of the giving of the commandments in Exodus 20 and Deuteronomy 5 and what actually happened, from a theistic perspective there is nothing unbelievable about God speaking to a particular group in history, so the possibility of God speaking the Ten Commandments to the Israelites should not be ruled out. Indeed, we take it from Plantinga's epistemology that we don't need evidence of a foundationalist sort for such a belief to be accepted as true knowledge, and that we may be warranted in taking this belief as knowledge.

Conclusion

The fertility of Reformed epistemology is obvious from our examination of some of the areas to which Plantinga and Wolterstorff have applied themselves. However, in his *Reason within the Bounds of Religion* Wolterstorff notes that he does not see himself alone in his attempt to construct a theory of theorizing: "I do not see myself as a lonely pioneer on the far side of the mountains from civilization. In the twentieth century especially Herman Dooyeweerd has seen the need for such a theory and has tried to construct one."[45] Similarly, we noted in chapter 12 Plantinga's positive comment about Dooyeweerd.

Despite these affirmations, Reformed epistemology and the Reformational philosophy of Herman Dooyeweerd, Dirk Vollenhoven, and their successors cross like ships in the dark. How do we account for their lack of interaction?

43. That is, fundamentalism! See Plantinga, *Warranted Christian Belief*, 244–46.
44. David Clines, "The Ten Commandments, Reading from Left to Right," chapter 2 in *Interested Parties: The Ideology of Writers and Readers of the Hebrew Bible* (Sheffield: Sheffield Academic Press, 1995), 27, 28.
45. Wolterstorff, *Reason within the Bounds of Religion*, 22.

First, although they share a common parentage, Reformed epistemology has developed in the analytic tradition, whereas Reformation philosophy is Continental. As we will see in the next chapter, the result is very different types of philosophy. Second, Reformed epistemology has been far more successful as a movement in philosophy than has the Reformational tradition. Such has been the success of Reformed epistemology that it is impossible to ignore, whereas Reformational philosophy still remains largely unknown.

Our own orientation is closer to Reformational philosophy than Reformed epistemology, and the good news is that one is now able to stand back and observe the myriad common emphases between them. As we attend to Reformational philosophy and all it has to offer in the next chapter and in the conclusion, we will draw attention to the common ground as well as highlighting the differences.

From: abby@longobedience.edu
To: percy@secular.edu
Subject: Two types, so exciting!

Hey Perc, hope you received all my notes on Reformed epistemology that I sent you. Apparently within the Reformed tradition there is also another type of Christian philosophy, more Continental, I understand. What blows me away is the relevance of this stuff. I know our prof said early on that Christian philosophy is missional, but I had no idea!

Abby

NB: My minor in philosophy is confirmed.

15

Reformational Philosophy

Introduction

Although Reformed epistemology is far better known than Reformational philosophy, both developed out of neocalvinism. Reformational philosophy actually preceded Reformed epistemology, originating in Holland in the first half of the twentieth century. Abraham Kuyper stressed the importance of a Reformed worldview, and the great Dutch theologian Herman Bavinck (1854–1921) recognized the need for a Christian philosophy, but it fell to their successors Herman Dooyeweerd, his brother-in-law Dirk Vollenhoven, and an expanding team of scholars to develop this worldview into a full-blown Christian philosophy. Dooyeweerd argued that an integral Christian philosophy could only develop in the tradition of John Calvin with his religious starting point,[1] and a contemporary proponent of this philosophy, aesthetician Calvin Seerveld, coined the term *Reformational philosophy*, which has stuck.

The great influences on Dooyeweerd were neo-Kantians, Heidegger, and Husserl. Although Dooyeweerd's philosophy has a definite place for logic, it is not nearly as central as it is in Reformed epistemology.[2] As René van Woudenberg rightly notes,

the philosophical tradition behind analytic epistemology is, broadly speaking, Anglo-American empiricism and rationalism. . . . The philosophical tradition

---

1. Herman Dooyeweerd, *A New Critique of Theoretical Thought*, trans. David H. Freeman and William S. Young, 4 vols. (Jordan Station, ON: Paideia, 1984), 1:515–18.
2. See Albert M. Wolters, "The Intellectual Milieu of Herman Dooyeweerd," in *The Legacy of Herman Dooyeweerd*, ed. Carl T. McIntire (Lanham, MD: University Press of America, 1985), 1–19.

behind Dooyeweerd, however, is German transcendental idealism, with its towering figures, Kant, the neokantians . . . and Husserl. The differences between these
traditions are enormous: there are differences in style, differences as to the role
the history of philosophy is assigned in the actual doing of philosophy, differences as to the methods of philosophy, and differences as to the conceptuality
in which philosophical problems are couched.[3]

In recent decades we have witnessed something of a rapprochement between analytic and Continental philosophy, and now, as we look back at the
achievements of Reformed epistemology and Reformational philosophy, it is
possible to see important areas of agreement between them.

Dooyeweerd's Epiphany

Philosophy often develops in surprising ways through epiphanic moments that
are far more than rational. Dooyeweerd describes his epiphany as follows:

> Originally I was strongly under the influence first of the Neo-Kantian philosophy,
> later on of Husserl's phenomenology. The great turning point in my thought was
> marked by the discovery of the religious root of thought itself, whereby a new
> light was shed on the failure of all attempts, including my own, to bring about
> an inner synthesis between the Christian faith and a philosophy which is rooted
> in the self-sufficiency of human reason. . . . From a Christian point of view, the
> whole attitude of philosophical thought which proclaims the self-sufficiency of
> the latter, turns out to be unacceptable, because it withdraws human thought
> from the divine revelation in Christ Jesus.[4]

Central to Dooyeweerd's philosophy is his view of the human person. Especially in Old Testament wisdom literature, we find the concept of the *heart* as
the center of the person, and this emphasis is closely related to Dooyeweerd's
turning point. For Dooyeweerd, the heart is the religious center of the person,
and it is always religiously directed, either toward the true God or toward an
idol. The heart and its religious direction influence the whole of the person,
including theoretical thought.

A central tenet in neocalvinism is the *antithesis*, that battle between good
and evil, between the kingdom of God and that of darkness, which runs
through every aspect of life, through believer and unbeliever. Dooyeweerd's
epiphany involves the insight that theoretical thought—both philosophical

---

3. René van Woudenberg, "Two Very Different Analyses of Knowledge," in *Ways of Knowing
in Concert*, ed. John H. Kok (Sioux Center, IA: Dordt College Press, 2005), 103.
    4. Dooyeweerd, *New Critique*, 1:v.

and scientific—is not exempt from the antithesis. As Herman Bavinck notes, "Revelation, while having its centre in the Person of Christ, in its periphery extends to the uttermost ends of creation. It does not stand isolated in nature and history, does not resemble an island in the ocean, nor a drop of oil upon water. With the whole of nature, with the whole of history, with the whole of humanity, with the family and society, with science and art it is intimately connected."[5] Dooyeweerd's turning point came with the realization that this is as true of theory and of philosophy as of any other aspect of human life.

Because of when he lived, it is not hard to imagine the radicality of such a view and the difficulty of gaining an audience for it. Nowadays, with the onset of so-called postmodernism, it is far easier to get religion on philosophical agendas. Dooyeweerd lived in a very different context, and a result is that he first needed to clear the ground by demonstrating that all theoretical thought is irretrievably rooted in religion before proceeding to develop a systematic Christian philosophy. The former he does under the title of his *transcendental critique*, and it is to this that we first turn.

The Transcendental Critique

Dooyeweerd takes over the word *transcendental* from Kant with the connotation of "the conditions that make thought possible." Dooyeweerd expresses this as follows: "By this we understand a critical inquiry . . . into the *universally valid conditions which alone make theoretical thought possible, and which are required by the immanent structure of this thought itself.*"[6] Through an examination of the conditions for thought to function, Dooyeweerd aims to show that all thinking is rooted in religion—that is, in the heart of the knower. Not surprisingly, therefore, he often referred to the transcendental critique as the "entrance" to his philosophy. However, for Dooyeweerd there is a significant difference between ordinary, everyday thinking and logical, theoretical thought of the sort that characterizes the disciplines of the university; hence his emphasis on "theoretical thought" in the quote above.

Dooyeweerd has two major elements in mind with his transcendental critique: the nature of theoretical thinking and the inner connection between theoretical thought and religion.[7] The first relates to how we think about theoretical thought. Theoretical thought is characterized by *abstracting* from

5. Herman Bavinck, *The Philosophy of Revelation* (Grand Rapids: Baker, 1979), 27.

6. Dooyeweerd, *New Critique*, 1:37 (italics in the original).

7. Henk Geertsema, "Dooyeweerd's Transcendental Critique: Transforming It Hermeneutically," in *Contemporary Reflections on the Philosophy of Herman Dooyeweerd*, ed. D. F. M. Strauss and Michelle Botting (Lewiston, NY: Edwin Mellen, 2000), 85.

the fullness of lived experience, and for Dooyeweerd this process of theoretical abstraction is very different from how we think and know in daily, concrete life. For Dooyeweerd, many philosophies have gone wrong from the outset by failing to identify the crucial difference between everyday knowing and theoretical abstraction.

Abstraction involves separating off part of reality from its connectedness with all of reality and analyzing it independently. Dooyeweerd refers to this as the *Gegenstand* relationship. *Gegenstand* means "to stand or set against," and from this perspective, when we engage in theoretical analysis, we set our logical way of functioning as humans against another aspect of created reality. Crucially for Dooyeweerd, even as we do this, we continue to function as full, religious human beings so that theoretical analysis remains deeply influenced by the direction of our hearts.

But how exactly does the direction of the heart influence theoretical analysis? Dooyeweerd articulates this through his concept of the *transcendental ground idea*. Every philosophy, from his perspective, has at its root a basic ground idea that directs the emerging philosophy and shapes it integrally. For Dooyeweerd the transcendental ground idea answers three questions.

1. What is the *Archimedean point* from which a philosopher gains a sense of the whole of reality? In 250 BC, Archimedes made levers with which he was able to do extraordinary feats. He even said that he could raise the earth from its foundation if he was given a fixed point of support—an Archimedean point. By its very nature, philosophy is concerned with the whole of reality, and every philosopher assumes, even if not consciously, a certain place to stand from which to obtain a view of the whole. This remains true, as we saw in chapter 11, even of postmodern philosophers who deny the possibility of such an Archimedean point, because they have to stand *somewhere* to be able to see that there is no such point. The supposed humility of many postmodernists conceals a profound hubris. As Henk Geertsema notes, "Being human implies an understanding of self and of the world and related to both is some idea of an ultimate horizon from which reality is understood in its nature and meaning. It makes a radical difference if time and chance are considered as that ultimate horizon as is the case with Richard Rorty . . . or if we believe in a personal God who created both man and world with love and wisdom."[8]

Christianity is radically different from modern paganism, and thus Dooyeweerd distinguishes carefully between the Archimedean point—common to all philosophies—and the *Archē*, the origin upon which the Archimedean point depends in a Christian philosophy. From a Christian perspective, the only adequate place to stand in order to get a true sense of the whole of reality is "in

8. Ibid., 98.

Christ," because from here we have revealed to us a true sense of the creation as creation, fallen but redeemed and being redeemed in Christ. "In Christ," it is not possible to view the cosmos as self-sustaining and self-sufficient. It is dependent, creaturely being and refers beyond itself to the *Archē*, to God, from whom and through whom and to whom are all things. Karl Barth uses the adjective "contingent" to describe this dependent, creaturely mode of the creation; Dooyeweerd gets at the same truth by saying that creaturely being does not *have* meaning, it *is* meaning.

2. How does a philosophy explain and deal with the *diversity* in creation? A great concern of Dooyeweerd's is reductionism, in which different aspects of the creation are reduced into another aspect. For Dooyeweerd immanent philosophies are perennially guilty of this move. It is only as we are liberated to understand the whole of creation as contingent, as "meaning," that we are liberated from reductionism and are able to do justice to the *irreducible diversity* in the creation.

3. Having abstracted a part of the creation for analysis, how does a theorist bring the different parts together again? That is, how does a theorist account for the unity of creation? Dooyeweerd has a rather unusual concept of the transcendental heart, which we will not elaborate on since it has been heavily critiqued and we find it unhelpful.[9] Geertsema is right to note that the unity of creation lies in its relationship to God as the Creator and, we would add, Redeemer.[10]

Dooyeweerd uses as a synonym for the transcendental ground idea, the Dutch term *wetsidee*, or law-idea. He notes that "this term was favored by me, when I was particularly struck by the fact that different systems of ancient, medieval, and modern philosophy (like that of Leibniz) *expressly* oriented philosophic thought to the Idea of a divine world-order, which was qualified as lex naturalis, lex aeterna, harmonia praestabilia etc. . . . A cosmonomic Idea is actually at the base of every philosophical system."[11]

One might imagine that such an approach to philosophy would close down discussion between Dooyeweerd's approach and that of others. In Dooyeweerd's view, the result is quite the opposite; as long as forces shaping a philosophy are obscured or concealed, it is impossible for real dialogue to take place.[12] Once the whole is in view, including the pretheoretical forces shaping a philosophy, the stage is set for real comparisons and genuine dialogue.

---

9. Basically Dooyeweerd turns Kant's transcendental ego into a transcendental heart. This revolutionizes Kant's philosophy but introduces serious problems since Dooyeweerd argues that the heart is supratemporal.

10. Geertsema, "Dooyeweerd's Transcendental Critique," 99.

11. Ibid., 94–95.

12. Ibid., 1, 70.

Thus, for Dooyeweerd *every* philosophy is based on a transcendental ground idea. Being aware of the transcendental ground idea enables us to get at what is really going on in any philosophy—it enables us, as it were, to open its suitcases and see what ideological and religious baggage it is carrying. Dooyeweerd asserts that

> philosophy is theoretical, and in its constitution it remains bound to the relativity of all human thought. As such, philosophy itself needs an absolute starting point. It derives this exclusively from religion. Religion grants stability and anchorage even to theoretical thought. Those who think they find an absolute starting point in theoretical thought itself come to this belief through an essentially religious drive. Because of a lack of true self-knowledge, however, they remain oblivious to their own religious motivation.[13]

This has major implications for the history of philosophy and was exploited by Dooyeweerd and his brother-in-law Dirk Vollenhoven, who developed a complex analysis of the history of philosophy by means of his problem-historical method.

The History of Philosophy

History is inseparably related to time, and before examining Reformational approaches to the history of philosophy, we should note that for Dooyeweerd history and time are distinct. We will see below that the historical is one of his fifteen modal aspects, but time is not. For Dooyeweerd time is more basic than these aspects, and he develops a complex view of time, which he calls "cosmic time." His theory of time is controversial, and it has few followers nowadays. Suffice it to say that an important insight of his view is that all of creation is *temporal*—it is timed. This is an integral part of the way God has made his world.

Ground Motives: Dooyeweerd

Apart from his transcendental ground idea, Dooyeweerd also used the concepts of *ground motives* to get at the religious dimension of all philosophic thought, and indeed of cultural development. As noted in earlier chapters of this book, anyone telling the story of Western philosophy is faced with identifying the overarching themes and the key thinkers. Dooyeweerd argues that

---

13. Herman Dooyeweerd, *Roots of Western Culture: Pagan, Secular, and Christian Options*, trans. John Kraay (Toronto: Wedge, 1979), 8.

beneath the cultural and spiritual development of the West, one can identify deep driving forces, and he calls these ground motives.

> In every religion one can point to a ground-motive having such a force. It is a force that acts as a spiritual mainspring in human society. It is an absolutely central driving force because, from the religious center of life, it governs temporal expressions and points towards the real or supposed origin of all existence. In the profoundest sense it determines a society's entire life- and world-view. It puts its indelible stamp on the culture, science, and the social structure of a given period. This applies so long as a leading cultural power can be identified as giving clear direction to the historical development of society. If such ceases to be the case, then a real crisis emerges at the foundations of that society's culture. Such a crisis is always accompanied by spiritual uprootedness.[14]

Ground motives are communal and never just individual and may govern the life of an individual even when he or she is unconscious of it.[15] Dooyeweerd identifies four major ground motives in the history of Western philosophy and culture. It is important to note that the emergence of a new ground motive does not displace the former ones; the former ones continue in tension with the new one.

THE FORM-MATTER GROUND MOTIVE

Dooyeweerd discerns the form-matter ground motive as the basic one in Greek and Roman thought. He discerns its origin in a conflict between two religions, one centered on the vital forces of life and one centered on the cultural activities of humankind. In the former the formless was deified, while in the latter the principle of form was deified.

Central to Dooyeweerd's analysis of ground motives is the view that once an aspect of the creation is absolutized, it causes its opposite pole to emerge, with the two in irreconcilable dialectical tension and with thought oscillating between the poles in an attempt to close down the tension. Dooyeweerd argues that the Greek thinkers move back and forth between matter and form, with the Sophists opting for matter, Aristotle for a harmony between the two, and so on.

THE NATURE-GRACE GROUND MOTIVE

Chronologically the nature-grace ground motive was dominant in the High and Late Middle Ages and thus follows the biblical or Christian ground motive of creation-fall-redemption, which we will discuss below. Dooyeweerd's

14. Ibid., 8–9.
15. Ibid., 9.

prime example of this ground motive at work is in the Scholastic thought of Thomas Aquinas. Through his appropriation of Aristotle, Aquinas embraced the Greek dualistic understanding of nature and sought to synthesize this with the gospel (grace). For Dooyeweerd this is an unsustainable synthesis of conflicting ground motives that inevitably led to trouble. Nature became separated from grace in the Renaissance and Enlightenment, with the upper story of grace becoming more and more marginal, until it was denied altogether.

THE NATURE-FREEDOM GROUND MOTIVE

The fruits of modern science were undeniable and seemed to affirm a mechanistic view of the world dominated by natural, scientific laws. However, this creates problems for any view of humankind as free, and thus the emphasis on nature evokes the freedom pole. Thus one finds, for example, science championed by Comte and freedom by the Romantics. Dooyeweerd refers to this nature-freedom ground motive as "humanism." It pushed Roman Catholicism and Protestantism onto the defensive for nearly three centuries.

Dooyeweerd died before the emergence of postmodernism. However, he was clear that in the final decades of the nineteenth century the emergence of Marxism, Darwinism, and Nietzscheism signaled internal disarray in the humanist worldview, and that this was further enforced after World War I. He discerned a major spiritual crisis in Western culture but was unsure where it would lead.[16]

THE CREATION-FALL-REDEMPTION GROUND MOTIVE

As noted above, this biblical or Christian ground motive comes second historically, but we treat it last because for Dooyeweerd this is the true ground motive that escapes the dialectical tensions of the other three. Dooyeweerd is adamant that this ground motive does not arise from theological reflection; it arises solely from the work of the Spirit in the hearts of believers. In our view, Reformational philosophy rightly stresses that the gospel is the power of God for salvation (Rom. 1:16) and that it alone has the capacity to redirect the heart toward the living and true God. Implicit in the faith that results from such transformation will be the concept of creation-fall-redemption, but as noted earlier in this book and in our *Living at the Crossroads*, we believe that the sort of clear reflection on this ground motive found in Dooyeweerd's *Roots of Western Culture* does involve reflection and analysis, at least of a worldviewish sort. Creation-fall-redemption is itself an abstraction from the biblical story and as such includes a view of God, his work in Christ, and the work of the Holy Spirit.

16. Ibid., 11.

The Problem-Historical Method: Dirk H. Th. Vollenhoven

Shortly after Dirk H. Th. Vollenhoven (1892–1978) completed his graduate studies, he began his search for a reliable way to approach the history of philosophy. In 1950 he designated his new approach the "problem-historical method." Vollenhoven's method is guided by the following ideas:

1. The philosophical analysis of every philosopher is bound by the same reality.
2. This reality is ordered by the Creator—a world dominated in time by fallen human beings, who, along with their activity, are able to be reconciled to God through Christ.
3. Thus, philosophers cannot but assume some stance toward the structure, origin, troubled state, and meaning of reality.
4. It is in the stand that philosophers take on these foundational issues that one finds the key to a critical understanding and comparison of their contributions.

As he worked away on the history of philosophy Vollenhoven was struck one day—his epiphany!—by the similarities in certain conceptions of Arthur Eddington, Albert Einstein, and Archimedes. As he thought about this, the idea occurred to him that perhaps there were certain *types* of philosophical approaches, certain basic patterns that kept recurring throughout the history of philosophy. So as not to be anachronistic in his approach, Vollenhoven began his exploration of this possibility with the pre-Socratics. He concluded that there is unmistakable evidence for a number of basic philosophical approaches that find adherents generation after generation since the origins of philosophy. Although these types recur, one should not simplistically think that they recur in the same form. With his concept of types, Vollenhoven also stressed *time-currents*, which embody the spirit of the age in which a philosopher works.

For example, a category that Vollenhoven found repeating itself is that of *monism and dualism*. He concluded that the materialistic monism of Thales is a philosophical approach essentially the same as that of Leucippus, Democritus, Aristippus, Epicurus, Lucretius, and many others all the way down to Pierre Gassendi and Sartre. Similarly a dualistic approach first developed by Xenophanes has been shared by such diverse thinkers as Parmenides, Marcion, Arnobius, William of Ockham, and Karl Marx. Vollenhoven worked on his problem-historical method for the remainder of his years, and several of his students have continued to pursue it.

Vollenhoven's method is meticulous, and we cannot begin to assess it in detail here. Even within Reformational circles it has not been without its critics.

Suffice it here to note the central insights of his approach. Vollenhoven was way ahead of his time in recognizing the myth of religious neutrality when it comes to examining the history of philosophy. We are now far more aware that historiography produces multiple histories of history rather than a unified, universally agreed-upon history. Bias in history writing is inevitable, and buy-in to some philosophy of history is unavoidable. Vollenhoven describes his approach as *thetical-critical*. *Thetical* refers to where one stands, alerting us to the fact that one always has to stand somewhere in order to tell the history of philosophy. For Vollenhoven the deepest and most formative level of where one stands is religious, and this should be embraced openly. If we believe that God has revealed himself in Christ, then the full light of this revelation must be brought to bear on the history of philosophy. As Calvin Seerveld notes, "As for the Christian shock in Vollenhoven's thorough method? His point is that without the forming light of God's Word-Revelation upon a person's philosophical conception, that person's philosophy always has and necessarily shall miss the glories of creation and distort reality into one of various reasonable ways."[17]

If one takes the thetical nature of history writing seriously, then one's first responsibility will be to develop a schema consistent with one's standing place as a grid through which to analyze the history of philosophy, and this is what Vollenhoven does with his types and time-currents.

This, however, is the beginning, not the end, of the hard work. One needs to explore the history of philosophy *meticulously* in the light of this schema while remaining open to the fact that what one discovers may lead to a revision of the schema and method applied. Vollenhoven's work requires contemporary evaluation and renewal, but one thing it cannot be accused of is mediocrity. He was meticulous in his examination of the history of philosophy, as his students bear witness.

Suffice it here to note a fruit that all of us can enjoy of Vollenhoven's work. We have often said in this book that the way one tells the history of philosophy is never neutral. Most textbooks on the history of philosophy assume the following four main periods: ancient, medieval, modern, and contemporary. In the light of his problem-historical method, Vollenhoven finds this division unhelpful and instead proposes three major periods: pre-synthesis (pagan), synthesis (Christian and pagan synthesized together), and anti- or post-synthesis. As readers will note, to a large extent we have followed Vollenhoven in this periodization.

17. Calvin Seerveld, "Philosophical Historiography," in *In the Fields of the Lord: A Calvin Seerveld Reader*, ed. Craig G. Bartholomew (Carlisle: Piquant; Toronto: Toronto Tuppence Press, 2000), 100.

Dooyeweerd's Ontology

Dooyeweerd identifies the following items as central to a Christian transcendental ground idea:

- *the Archimedean point* for a Christian philosophy is Christ;
- *the antithesis*: through belonging to Christ the Christian is daily engaged in spiritual warfare, and not least in philosophy;
- *the Origin*: the origin of creation law and individual subjectivity is God's holy, sovereign, creative will; for Dooyeweerd the law is the absolute boundary between God and his creation;
- *the totality of meaning*: creation *is* meaning; and
- *the coherence in the modal diversity of meaning*: Dooyeweerd identifies fifteen irreducible modalities or ways of being in his philosophy; these can be separated only through philosophical abstraction; in lived experience we experience them as a coherent whole; these modes are real (they are not a philosophical construct), sustained by God, and irreducible, pointing beyond themselves to the fullness of meaning in Christ.

Modalities

Reformational philosophy is attentive to the rich, interconnected diversity of creation. Creation consists of a myriad of concrete things, and these answer the *what* question. When we ask "What is that?" and we get the answer "That's a South African gemsbok!" then we are in touch with concrete things. The *what* question is to be carefully distinguished from the *how* question. Modes or aspects answer the *how* question. As noted, for Dooyeweerd there are fifteen modal aspects or ways of being in the world, and every concrete thing functions in *all* fifteen. These modes are not things—you cannot go outside and collect five of them—they are ways of functioning.

To illustrate the nature of a mode, a good example is this book that you are reading. As a concrete entity it functions, according to Dooyeweerd, in all fifteen modal aspects. This book is not an art object, but it does function in the *aesthetic* mode. As any reader knows, how a book functions in this mode influences our attraction to it even before we start reading. Our hope is that not only is the content exciting, accessible, and informative, but that the cover and the layout complement the content aesthetically and combine to draw the reader into the book. We all know that experience of dragging an ugly text off our shelves and struggling to get into it; it is as though the text fails to stir our imagination before we even start reading.

Nor is the book an economic object, and yet it also functions in the *economic* mode. Doubtless you checked the price before buying it, and hopefully you felt the cost was proportionate—at least!—to its value.

If you have to write an essay related to a portion of this book, you may be tempted to simply extract large parts and put them under your name—that is, until you remember that this book also functions in the *juridical* mode and such plagiarism is protected by copyright and university regulations! And so we could continue. Hopefully this provides a good example of what is involved in entities functioning in modes and just how insightful such analysis can be.

The order of the modes is not arbitrary, since the higher ones require the lower ones in order to function. Dooyeweerd calls the arithmetic and pistic modes the *terminal modes*, since the arithmetic mode is not preceded by another and the pistic mode is not followed by another. The following diagram lists the modes and indicates on the left how Dooyeweerd uses the way entities function in the modes to analyze their individuality structures (see below).

Dooyeweerd's Modal Scale

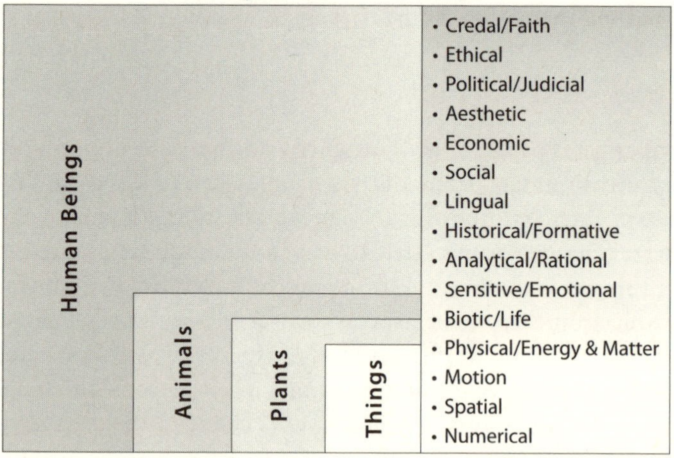

It is important to know what each mode is about. In this respect Dooyeweerd refers to the "meaning-nucleus" of each mode, and these are as follows:

Pistic—faith

Ethical—love

Political/juridical—retribution

Aesthetic—harmony

Economic—frugality

Social—social intercourse

Lingual—symbolic meaning
Historical—formative power
Analytical—distinction
Sensitive—feeling
Biotic—vitality
Physical—energy
Kinematic—motion
Spatial—continuous extension
Arithmetic—quantity

Doubtless many questions may emerge at this point. One can see how a book functions aesthetically, but how does a rock function in the lingual mode or a plant in the pistic mode? To understand this we need to introduce an important distinction Dooyeweerd makes between functioning as a *subject* (or subjectively) in a mode compared with functioning as an *object* (or objectively) in a particular mode. Indeed, for Dooyeweerd it is by attending to these distinctions that we can analyze the individuality structure of a concrete thing.

Individuality Structures

Individuality structures refer not to the structures *of* concrete things but to God's order or law *for* concrete things. You never encounter a tree in the abstract; it is always this particular, concrete tree. The individuality structure is God's order for trees. For Dooyeweerd, it is by examining *how* entities function in the modal aspects that we can arrive at their individuality structure. Let us take the examples of a large rock, a maple tree, and a horse called Bucephalus. According to Dooyeweerd the rock functions as a subject up to and including the physical modality; in the remaining eleven it functions as an object. The maple tree functions as a subject up to and including the biotic mode; in the remaining ten modes it functions as an object. Bucephalus functions as a subject up to and including the sensitive mode; in the remaining nine he functions as an object.

The highest mode in which an entity functions as a subject is called its *qualifying* mode. This mode gives the entity its particular character and colors how it functions in the other modes in which it is a subject. Thus a rock is a physical entity, a tree is a biotic entity, and a horse is a sentient entity. A horse is alive in a way that a plant is not, but whereas we would not think it immoral to cut a branch off a tree, we would rightly regard it as immoral to abuse a horse. At this simple level—Reformational analysis becomes far more complex—one can see the value of discerning God's order for his creation in this way.

It is crucial to realize that an entity does *not* cease functioning in the modes above its qualifying one. This is an important insight of Dooyeweerd's, since it resists reductionism *and* anthropomorphism at the same time. For Dooyeweerd, God has ordered the world such that all entities function in all fifteen modes. Thus, the aesthetic and spiritual dimensions of a butterfly are not imaginary but real and part of what it means for a butterfly to be a butterfly. Vladimir Nabokov's description of standing among rare butterflies fits with reality: "This is ecstasy, and behind the ecstasy is something else, which is hard to explain. It is like a momentary vacuum into which rushes all that I love. A sense of oneness with sun and stone. A thrill of gratitude to whom it may concern—to the contrapuntal genius of human fate or to tender ghosts humouring a lucky mortal."[18]

A tree is a living organism, and its qualifying mode—the biotic—gives it its distinctive character as a plant. A tree cannot speak or name other objects, but its function in the lingual mode means that part of creation is the capacity built into creation for humans to name trees. A tree will not admire the beauty of other trees, but its functioning in the aesthetic mode means that its beauty is not imaginary; it is real and able to be recognized and relished by humans.

The conception of creation order or law, which is central to Reformational philosophy, may suggest a type of determinism, as though there is no freedom within these laws. This, however, is not the case. Within Dooyeweerd's modal scale there is a crucial distinction between the first six modalities (up to and including the sensitive) and the remaining nine (the analytical and those that follow it). The former are referred to as *laws*, whereas the latter are described as *norms*. The former could be described as *natural* laws—although Dooyeweerd would not like this terminology—in the sense that they cannot not be obeyed. The latter require human response, and this responsible implementation Dooyeweerd calls "positivization." To be human is to have *response-ability*, and although we do function in all fifteen modal aspects by virtue of creation, we have freedom as to how we positivize the modalities from the analytical upward.

Take the social modality, for example. To be human is to be in relationship with other humans; we flourish in community. But of course this norm can be and has been positivized in an immense variety of ways. For some, the extended family is at the heart of social life; others live alone but have a network of close friends. For some, playing sports and having a drink in the pub is socially fulfilling, whereas for others a long walk with a friend is far

---

18. Quoted in Jeremy Mynott, *Birdscapes: Birds in Our Imagination and Experience* (Princeton: Princeton University Press, 2009), 96.

more socially renewing. If you visit friends in England, you are bound to be offered a cup of tea with milk; in Canada it is more likely that you will be offered a coffee with cream. In much of Africa the time of meeting up is far less important than the meeting, whereas in the West we tend to arrange a specific time and place to meet and expect a friend to honor that.

Norms also alert us to the fact that an implication of the fall is that we often positivize them in a way that embodies rebellion against God. An affair with another married person may be socially fulfilling, but it is a disobedient positivization of the social norm. The entertainment industry in the West is an attempt to positivize the social norm, but it doesn't take much reflection to see that large parts of it are unhealthy. Getting drunk regularly at a nightclub followed by one-night stands where you hardly ever have a real conversation is a misdirection of the social norm. Technology is also a mixed blessing in this respect. You may have hundreds of Facebook friends, but is this real friendship?

Before we move on to look at a Reformational anthropology, it is worth pausing to ask how Dooyeweerd came up with these fifteen modal aspects. There is no quick answer to this question, and the modes certainly are not referenced in the Bible. They stem in part from the neo-Kantian tradition that Dooyeweerd drew upon, as well as intense reflection on the history of philosophy and the nature of the world around us. Reformational thought stresses the need to attend to the creation in order to learn about it, and this is reflected in Dooyeweerd's development of his theory of modalities.

The Human Person: A Tin-Can Theory

In Reformational philosophy the nature of the cosmos, the view of the human person, and how we know are all of one piece. Human beings are part of God's creation and are as subject to his creation order as any other part of the creation. Calvin Seerveld, a student of Vollenhoven, has developed a creative Reformational anthropology, which he calls, disarmingly, a "tin-can theory of the human person."[19]

Reformational thinkers are wary of the common Christian view of the human person as consisting of a body and a soul. Seerveld is no exception. He stresses that each human person is a whole, a profound unity. His analysis aims at discerning the individuality structure of the human person: the human person is a creature, a temporal, identifiable, individuality-structured thing. The existence of the whole person manifests itself in a variety of ways: a

19. Calvin Seerveld, "A Christian Tin-Can Theory of the Human Creature," in Bartholomew, *In the Fields of the Lord*, 102–16.

person is a certain size, moves, breathes, feels, imagines, thinks, talks, social-
izes, loves, fights, and prays. All these manifestations of concrete existence
are an expression of the one, individual subject.

The human person functions as a subject in all fifteen modal aspects. Seerveld
stresses that we should not think of these as human *faculties*, as some sort
of autonomous human power, a common view in the modern philosophical
tradition. "No, all the discernible ways humans can act are the very defining,
cosmic, operating order of reality which each then as an individuality-structured entity enjoys."[20] Just as Dooyeweerd stresses that the modes interpen-
etrate one another, so Seerveld points out that the irreducible ways in which
a human functions are interpenetrating. For example, while a person's *feeling*
is different from his or her *thinking*, there is always emotional content in a
person's thought and there is creational pressure to have emotions thoughtful.
Indeed, for Seerveld it is precisely this cohering pattern of enduring, ordered
activities that constitutes embodiment, or what he calls *corporeality*. A person is not an animated corpse or a body/mind dichotomy but a body. "Do
not misunderstand me. Because angels are as real as cement I am not saying
prayers are like digestion and toothaches are mental. Only this: the whole
blanket of activities, all the ways a person is in concrete action is him or her
bodily, corporeally there."[21]

Although humans are unique among creatures in functioning as subjects
in all fifteen modal aspects, readers may be surprised that humans are not
qualified by the pistic mode, the highest one in which they function as a
subject. Dooyeweerd and Seerveld distinguish the pistic mode from the religious center of a person. For Seerveld what makes the embodied human
human is that he or she is designed with an openness and readiness to receive
God's Word.

> Men and women are religious creatures: individuality-structured entities called
> to act out of the self-conscious (communal-conscious) office of being coram
> Deo, serving lords of the universe. Peculiar to a woman or man's existence is
> that the whole richly concrete corporeality a human is has a thrusted bent to it.
> That person's existence is thrusted, innerly focused and intrinsically referential
> of all one does and means towards the true or some pretended Absolute Origin:
> that is woman or man's being in the image of God.[22]

The implications of this sort of anthropology are rich. Seerveld stresses
that humans are communal by nature and also notes the effect of sin on the

20. Ibid., 108.
21. Ibid., 109.
22. Ibid., 110.

Philosophy

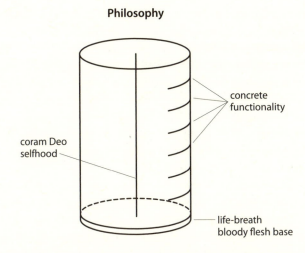

coram Deo
selfhood

concrete
functionality

life-breath
bloody flesh base

religious direction of the core of a tin-can person. As with holiness, so with sin: it manifests itself in *all* aspects of our lives. It is possible to sin emotionally, socially, aesthetically, pistically. Sin is not always best thought of as intentional; it runs deeper than this and is a profound malaise, a deep brokenness. Seerveld's model alerts us to just how complex and multifaceted such brokenness can be. Ignoring these multiple dimensions can get us into trouble in all sorts of ways. Christians with a narrow anthropology, when searching for a new pastor or president or lecturer, often focus almost exclusively on the *confession* of the person; are they orthodox pistically? While this is certainly important, we often discover to our detriment that their emotional, logical, social, and imaginative functioning may be as important for the job they are being hired for. An orthodox president without imagination or good social skills is not going to be a great asset, however orthodox he or she is. An orthodox pastor whose conservatism is tied into an undeveloped emotional life will cause havoc in a congregation.

We are far more broken than we imagine. The good—truly good—news is that it is just such broken tin cans that Christ came to save and to restore. If we pose the question, why does God save us? the answer is: to make us fully human! Sanctification, the process of becoming holy, is best understood as the process of becoming whole. The Spirit redirects our core and then sets about restoring us whole human beings, tin cans functioning in all modalities. Sanctification or holiness, from this perspective, has as much to do with a healthy emotional life, good and wholesome social interaction, and a developed imagination as it does with a truthful confessional life that affirms the fundamental of the Christian faith. In other words, holiness involves formation or re-formation, and this includes every aspect of our personhood.

Philosophy of Society

There is widespread agreement that the French Revolution marks the gateway into modern society, not least because of its commitment to restructuring society according to reason and science. Guillaume Groen van Prinsterer (1801–76), an important predecessor of Reformational thought, posed the question "Can Christianity, after the French Revolution, be revived in order to have a salutary effect on the direction of western culture?"[23] Van Prinsterer thought it could, and he devoted his life to a renewal of biblical Christianity in Holland. Van Prinsterer and Abraham Kuyper (1837–1920) recognized that societal reconstruction was not neutral and that the gospel has fundamental insights to offer in terms of a contemporary philosophy of society.

Kuyper in particular is credited with the development of the philosophy of society known as *sphere sovereignty*. According to sphere sovereignty, the sovereign God has provided each sphere within society with its own peculiar laws by which that sphere is to function. Thus, different societal spheres such as the state, the institutional church, the family, the school and university, business, and so on, are sovereign in their own spheres. God and not the state is the source of authority in each sphere, so that each sphere is directly accountable to God.

Dooyeweerd built on sphere sovereignty in his development of a Reformational philosophy of society. He recognizes the following:

1. All social institutions, whether past or contemporary, have their ultimate origin in creation. There is built into creation a dynamic to the creation order with potential to develop it.
2. God is sovereign over all creation, at its beginning and during its unfolding.
3. God's authority is a legal authority as befits a great king. The laws of creation assume a diversity of forms and govern—provide the norms for—the development of human institutions such as the family, the institutional church, and the state.
4. According to creation order each social institution has a right to exist alongside other institutions and has a God-given responsibility to fulfill its calling in history in accordance with God's laws.

The laws of creation, therefore, make possible a plurality of social institutions or spheres, each with a measure of autonomy or sovereignty, vis-à-vis

23. Quoted in Bernard Zylstra, introduction to *Contours of a Christian Philosophy: An Introduction to Herman Dooyeweerd's Thought*, by L. Kalsbeek (Amsterdam: Buitjen and Schipperheijn, 1975), 16.

all others. The sovereignty of any social sphere, however, is always limited by the sovereignty of coexisting spheres and limited to the task or function to which it is called. Moreover, this earthly sovereignty is subservient to the absolute sovereignty of God. It is delegated by God and remains ever dependent upon him.[24]

However, Dooyeweerd recognizes that insightful as this is, it leaves many questions unanswered, and he applies his ontology of modes and individuality structures to deepen his philosophy of society.

A major insight of Dooyeweerd is his notion of *the differentiation process*. Primitive societies are relatively undifferentiated; they contain no distinct spheres of the school, the government, and so on. There is nothing bad about such undifferentiation, but Dooyeweerd argues that it is normative for a society to become differentiated into a variety of spheres over time. Thus, it is normative for schools and universities to develop and for parents to hand over the substance of their children's education to such institutions. It is normative for government to become a separate sphere in society and for the institutional church to develop as the place where formal worship takes place.

As he examines the diversity of institutions, Dooyeweerd makes three careful distinctions:

1. He distinguishes natural from social institutions. Natural institutions such as marriage and the family are given with creation, and Dooyeweerd gets at this by arguing that they are founded in the biotic mode. Social institutions, by comparison, emerge in history and are founded in the historical mode. Families have always existed but governments have not; the latter emerge in the course of history and take a variety of forms, from monarchy and autocracy to democracy.

2. Dooyeweerd distinguishes between communities and intercommunal or interindividual relationships. Communities, such as the state, the family, and the church, bind people together in a more or less permanent fashion. Intercommunal or interindividual relationships are cooperative—or antagonistic—relationships between (a) two institutions, (b) two individuals, or (c) an institution and an individual. Examples are the relationship between the church and the state, between a buyer and a corporate seller, and between an individual and his or her family.

3. Dooyeweerd distinguishes authoritative social forms from free social forms. The state and the family are examples of the former; individuals are included in them nonvoluntarily. These authoritative social forms have a permanent nature. Free social forms are institutions formed and

24. John Witte Jr., introduction to *A Christian Theory of Social Institutions*, by Herman Dooyeweerd, trans. Magnus Verbrugge (La Jolla, CA: The Herman Dooyeweerd Foundation, 1986), 17.

dissolved on a voluntary basis, examples of which are labor unions, academic associations, and chess clubs.

The Reformational stress on sphere sovereignty must not be misunderstood. While it does assert the relative autonomy of each sphere, it also insists on sphere universality. Spheres are intimately connected with one another, and in daily life we will move in and out of an immense variety of them and are members of a considerable number. Dooyeweerd uses the term *enkapsis* to describe the interlaced relationships between spheres. Two institutions may interact to the extent that they give rise to a more complex social whole and the emergence of new social institutions.

In his social philosophy Dooyeweerd seeks to define the individuality structures of the spheres and social institutions. Government, for example, is founded in the historical mode but qualified by the juridical mode. Government is thus about justice for all under its jurisdiction. The church, too, is founded in the historical mode—it was initiated by Christ—but qualified by the pistic mode. It is essentially about faith and the faith-life of its members.[25]

The valuable insight in this sort of analysis is that if one can work out the telos of an institution, then one knows what to work toward (as has been said: if you aim for nothing you are bound to hit it). If, for example, we can work out what the institutional church is for, then we can focus our attention and energies in that direction and not be distracted by other possibilities.

Dooyeweerd's social philosophy has been particularly fruitfully developed in politics, and we will focus on some of these developments in the next section. In no way does his philosophy undermine the crucial, unique role of the institutional church, and thus we will also explore that below.

Politics

Politics is an area where the Reformational tradition has borne rich fruit, both at the theoretical level of political philosophy and at the practical level. One of the great challenges of our day is pluralism: how does one structure a society with so many diverse communities? The clash of such diversity is what has become known as the culture wars. Contemporary Reformational thinkers have developed Dooyeweerd's insights to propose a normative way for thinking about pluralism in a contemporary Western society.[26]

25. See Kalsbeek, *Contours of a Christian Philosophy*, 196–268.
26. A superb book on this topic is Richard J. Mouw and Sander Griffioen, *Pluralisms and Horizons: An Essay in Christian Public Philosophy* (Grand Rapids: Eerdmans, 1993).

A careful distinction is made between structural and confessional pluralism. *Structural pluralism* is a synonym for sphere sovereignty and argues against a state that controls every area of life; each sphere or societal structure is sovereign in its own area. Thus the parents are responsible to God for their family, and the state is justified in intervening only when an issue of legal justice is at stake.

Structural pluralism is distinct from *confessional pluralism*. The latter acknowledges the diversity of confessional communities in a modern state and argues that such communities need to have the freedom to let their confessions come to full fruition in the diverse structures of society. This, it is argued, is only just. Such a view is diametrically opposed to the marginalization of religion so characteristic of modernity and the ideology of the "neutral" public square. Instead, the Christian community, for example, should have the freedom to develop its confession in terms of Christian schools, in terms of family life and leisure, in terms of political involvement and labor relations, and so on. Such freedom should also be granted to Muslims and to secular humanists; the latter are, from this perspective, one confessional community among many and are often a minority.

Labor relations are notoriously nasty, and a remarkable example of confessional pluralism in practice is the Christian Labor Association of Canada. The association functions as a normal labor union, has Christian and non-Christian members, and works across Canada with some thirty thousand members. It was founded and developed in the Reformational tradition and continues to operate in this way, with offices dotted around Canada.

Few people have done as much to develop the political aspect of Reformational philosophy as has Jim Skillen, formerly executive director of the Center for Public Justice in Washington, DC. One of the areas in which Skillen and the Center for Public Justice have done extraordinary work is welfare reform in the United States. The Center for Public Justice boxed well above the weight of its small structure in the development of the Charitable Choice legislation, which allowed faith-based organizations to apply for government funding in welfare work. The significance of this should not be underestimated. Like most Western democracies, the United States has found its welfare budget expanding exponentially, while on the ground little seems to change, with far too many people trapped in cycles of poverty. Often it is precisely the local church, synagogue, or mosque that is present amid the poverty and best situated to set up programs to alleviate poverty. Charitable Choice has enabled faith-based organizations to obtain government money for such purposes and thus ensure that the poor are far better served than through "neutral" government bureaucracies who have no local, community-based knowledge of the poor.

The Institutional Church and the Sermon

Much theological ink has been spilled over the nature of the church. We find it helpful to think of the church as *the life of the people of God*. In this sense of church, Christians are engaged in all spheres of society, and the Christian family or Christian political involvement is as much part of the life of the people of God as is church attendance and worship. This broad sense of the church needs to be distinguished from what Christians do when they gather for prayer, to hear the Word, for the sacraments, for fellowship, and so on. We call the latter part of the life of the people of God *the institutional church*.

What makes the institutional church distinct from other spheres of society, and how does it relate to them? First, it should be noted that the institutional church is not better than or more important than other spheres. This may sound alarming, but who would argue that the church is more important than the family? Or that the church is more important than the state? Without the family there would be no church, and only someone who has no idea what happens in a society when government collapses would suggest that we can quite comfortably be the church without a just state. The societal spheres should not be ranked in a hierarchy; all are vital and unique, and we can discern the role of the church by attending to its unique function.

Dooyeweerd, rightly in our view, sees the institutional church as qualified by the pistic mode. This alerts us to the fact that the church is in essence about the faith-life of the community. The church is there to keep us alert to God, to feed us on Jesus through Word and sacrament, and to send us out week after week into his world as his servants. The institutional church may do many things, but this should be its focus. Indeed, in most of our churches we identify brothers and sisters with the gifts of pastoring and preaching, train them, and then set them apart to work full time in our midst as shepherds who keep us attentive to God, feed us on his Word, and journey with us through the vicissitudes of life.

Analysis of the individuality structure of the church in this way can be remarkably illuminating. There is, for example, a significant philosophical difference between a lecture and a sermon. How many of us have sat through a long, arid lecture in church, bored to tears with our hearts unmoved even while the pastor thinks he is deepening our faith life? A lecture is *logically* qualified, aimed at informing, educating, and imparting information. A sermon is *pistically* qualified. It should be informative and educational, but it primarily aims to bring God's Word to the very core of our existence—our hearts—and is the mechanism God uses above all else to draw us into relationship with him. You can taste the difference between a good sermon and a lecture, and the difference is important; our spiritual health depends on it.

Art

Within the arts, the two major Reformational thinkers are the late Hans Rookmaaker (1922–77) and Calvin Seerveld. Both have produced a rich trove for artists and Christians in general. Countless artists can testify to the saving grace of Rookmaaker's and Seerveld's work. As a Reformational philosopher, Seerveld has specialized in aesthetics. Central to his aesthetics are four claims:

1. The aesthetic is part of the fabric of created reality, and aesthetic norms can be violated or ignored only at great cost. In his *Until Justice and Peace Embrace*, Nicholas Wolterstorff has a chapter on the "City of Delight," in which he discusses the aesthetics of the city. One only needs to reflect on what the dismal state of so many cities does to its multitude of workers to see the cost of violating the aesthetic dimension of life.[27]

2. The arts, despite their variety and their continuing development, are a unified sphere distinct from other spheres of cultural endeavor, offering opportunities for vocational service to Christians today. With this claim Seerveld aligns himself with Dooyeweerd's notion of differentiation. There was, for example, a time historically when the fine arts were not distinguished from the crafts. For Seerveld the differentiation is normative, hence his caution on Wolterstorff's strong critique of the institutions of modern art. Seerveld's *Rainbows for a Fallen World* was published around the same time as Wolterstorff's *Art in Action*, and the status and role of modern artistic institutions is one of the key areas they differ on.

3. The aesthetic is not limited to the arts, just as the arts have many other facets than the aesthetic. Everything, you will recall, functions in all fifteen modal aspects, and that includes the aesthetic. Artists specialize in the aesthetic, and a gift of theirs is to open up our aesthetic, imaginative life so that how we dress, how we decorate our houses, how we write, and so on, may be aesthetically nuanced.

4. The core of meaning—the nucleus or kernel of the aesthetic, and the distinguishing character of the arts—is allusiveness and imaginativeness. Here Seerveld parts company with Dooyeweerd and Rookmaaker, who see the kernel as beauty or harmony. For Seerveld art can legitimately be ugly, provided it retains its allusive quality.

27. Seerveld offers concrete ways that the aesthetic aspect of a city might be improved in "Cities as a Place for Public Artwork: A Glocal Approach," in *The Gospel and Globalization: Exploring the Religious Roots of a Globalized World*, ed. Michael W. Goheen and Erin G. Glanville (Vancouver: Regent College and Geneva Society, 2009), 283–98.

Conclusion

In writing this chapter we have been struck again by the richness of the Reformational tradition, not least philosophically. In this conclusion we offer some proposals for the renewal of Reformational philosophy.

Reformational Philosophy as Missional

Coming to Reformational philosophy as evangelicals, we were struck by its missional potential. We would argue that Reformational philosophy is inherently missional. Dooyeweerd saw the need for a Christian philosophy while involved in cultural activism. If Reformational philosophy is inherently missional, how is it that it has been so unsuccessful in sharing its gifts across North America? In our opinion, Reformational philosophy remains as relevant to our late modern context as it was to Dooyeweerd's modern context. Naturalism remains a dominant philosophy in our day, and in this respect a Reformational critique remains relevant. With its strong doctrine of a dynamic creation order, Reformational philosophy also has the resources to combat the pervasive historicism of postmodernism without lapsing back into an uncritical realism. Dooyeweerd provides several vital contributions to Christian life and scholarship today: his nonreductionistic modal analysis, his recognition that the antithesis runs through theoretical thought, his recognition of the importance of Christian philosophy for Christian academic work and practice, his dynamic understanding of creation order and individuality structures, his notion of the inner reformation of the sciences, his dynamic philosophy of society and sphere sovereignty, and his insistence that lived experience is primary.

We urgently need to reposition Reformational philosophy in a missional context and learn how to communicate it and contextualize it in an accessible way and open up dialogue with the philosophies and cultural trends of our day. If Reformational philosophy is as insightful academically as we think, then we need to be able to show how it opens up insights in the disciplines without simply imposing the whole structure. The missional dimension will also become clearer as we attend to the issues below.

Reformational Philosophy as Orthodox, Evangelical Christianity

The early Reformational philosophers took the Reformed faith for granted as the ethos within which they worked. For example, Dooyeweerd never says so, but his philosophy, with its appeals to being "in Christ," is clearly trinitarian. Recent decades have witnessed a resurgence of trinitarian theology, and foregrounding the trinitarian nature of Reformational philosophy would provide an obvious connecting point for debate with scholarly trends in Christian thought.

An issue that we think the Reformational tradition does need to revisit is the relationship between philosophy and theology. Reformational circles have produced many philosophers but few theologians, Gordon Spykman (1926–93) being a notable exception.[28] Neocalvinism has a rich theological tradition, including the dogmatics of Herman Bavinck, and in our view the systematic reflection on the main themes of Scripture that is central to theology has, with Christian philosophy, a foundational role to play in Christian scholarship. The Reformational tradition needs to excavate and renew its rich theological resources and cultivate its dialogue with Reformational philosophy. And if the tradition is to have missional credibility in our day, then it must be seen to be normed by Scripture. Indeed, a good Christian philosophy, like a good Christian theology, will lead us deeper into the truth of Scripture and not away from it.

Reformational Philosophy and the Primacy of Lived Experience

The Reformational tradition rightly stresses the primacy of lived experience over theory, of which philosophy is part. Good philosophy will provide serviceable concepts for Christian scholarship and will deepen lived experience, life *coram Deo*. There has been a tendency in some Reformational thought and practice to downplay the roles of the institutional church and personal formation. It should be apparent from the above discussion that this runs counter to all the main streams of Reformational thought. Van Prinsterer and Kuyper recognized that a renewal of biblical Christianity in Holland must involve a renewal of the church. Philosophy is important, but from a Reformational perspective it is one among many hallowed human activities. It has its own contribution to make and when done well serves to deepen our life in Christ and our lived experience.

From: abby@longobedience.edu
To: percy@secular.edu
Subject: Certainly different!

Dear Percy,
Hope all is well on your side! Well, we have completed our introduction to that other type of Reformed philosophy. It goes by the name *Reformational philosophy*.

28. Gordon J. Spykman, *Reformational Theology: A New Paradigm for Doing Dogmatics* (Grand Rapids: Eerdmans, 1992).

Certainly different than Reformed epistemology, although I can see lots of similarities too. We will have to discuss this at length over the summer so I can work out
which side I come down on. I love Seerveld's tin-can theory of the human person
but am a bit unsure about how opposed Reformational philosophers are to a body/
soul approach to anthropology. Notes to follow.

Conclusion

As you come to the conclusion of this book, we hope it is with a sense of just what an important gift God has given us in philosophy. The early Christians engaged deeply with the philosophies of their day as they witnessed to Christ in their context. Augustine was the first major Christian philosopher, and his work continues to reverberate around the world today. Aquinas saw the challenge of Aristotelianism and worked tirelessly to relate the gospel to it. Modernity witnessed a progressive severing of philosophy from faith, and yet major philosophical work continued to be done from a Christian perspective. Postmodernity signals the unraveling of the inherently unstable secular modernity, and we are now amid an exhilarating renewal of Christian philosophy at the highest levels.

This is a fertile time in which to engage in philosophy, and much work remains to be done to secure the emerging renaissance and to build upon it. In our opinion, the crucial insight that Reformational philosophy and Reformed epistemology have foregrounded is the legitimacy—indeed imperative—of a Christian starting point for philosophy. Missionally, this cuts to the heart of the contemporary challenge of modernity without for a moment squandering the insights and contributions of modernity. Both types of Reformed philosophy we have explored have in their own ways recovered this biblical insight and have laid the basis for continuing to do Christian philosophy in the context of the biblical story and Christian worldview.

Our own preference is for the more Continental Reformational philosophy, but one cannot doubt that Reformed epistemology has been far more effective in communicating its message. Both approaches should be taken seriously today, and we urgently need dialogue and cooperation between the two. Another great need is healthy systematic theology working in dialogue with philosophy. Indeed, in our view, as a healthy cooperation develops between philosophy and theology—both working out of the biblical story—both should lead backward into deeper engagement with Scripture and forward into foundational insights for all disciplines.

Much is at stake in this endeavor. Take, for example, the desperate need for integrally Christian scholarship across the disciplines today. This will never be achieved without the sort of foundational work described above. Within our secular universities, knowledge is notoriously fragmented, and sadly it is not always that different in Christian universities. Recovery of a vibrant Christian philosophy in dialogue with theology working at the central topics in philosophy as well as the philosophy of other disciplines would make a major contribution to contemporary Western culture and beyond.

Our hope in writing this book is that for many readers this is not the end or the beginning of the end, as Winston Churchill once said, but perhaps the end of a beginning on the rich and vital journey of Christian philosophy.

The Summer

Abby and Percy are back together for the summer, working at jobs in the same city. Amidst leisurely walks, runs, meals, and numerous cups of coffee, they have debriefed extensively about their first year at university. Percy is fired up to get on with medicine, and Abby is looking forward to second-year psychology. A major topic of discussion has been philosophy and the importance of Christian philosophy for both their majors. During the summer they are reading together Richard Tarnas's *The Passion of the Western Mind* as well as Wolterstorff's *Reason within the Bounds of Religion* and Seerveld's article on the tin-can theory of the human person. Needless to say, their families and friends are surprised at how excited they both are about philosophy. As Abby keeps telling them, if we are really committed to a missional engagement with our culture, then studying philosophy is essential.

Annotated Further Reading List

Teaching resources and a more detailed bibliography for this book are available online at www.paideiacentre.ca under "Resources → Teaching Resources" as well as www.biblicaltheology.ca. Below you will find what we regard as essential and interesting reading as you explore the subject matter of this book in more detail.

Note that we have not included primary sources at every point. We regard these as essential, but they are readily available, and often one needs some sense of the thought of a philosopher before plunging into his or her work.

A good dictionary of philosophy is indispensable; get a portable one and carry it with you! One that we continue to find helpful is Peter A. Angeles, *Dictionary of Philosophy* (New York: Harper & Row, 1981).

There are a variety of histories of philosophy to choose from, but no recent, excellent Christian one. Do, however, look out for C. Stephen Evans's forthcoming history of Western philosophy from InterVarsity. The most recent history of Western philosophy, and a very good one, is Anthony Kenny, *A New History of Western Philosophy* (Oxford: Oxford University Press, 2010). Richard Tarnas's *The Passion of the Western Mind: Understanding the Ideas That Shaped Our World View* (New York: Ballantine, 1991) is a very useful and accessible overview of the history of Western thought.

A major online resource for Kuyperian philosophy is Steve Bishop's website www.allofliferedeemed.co.uk.

Chapter 1   *Why* Philosophy?

Chang, Curtis. *Engaging Unbelief: A Captivating Strategy from Augustine and Aquinas.* Eugene, OR: Wipf and Stock, 2000. In this delightful book Chang shows how important parts of Augustine's and Aquinas's work arose from the challenges of mission.

Clark, Kelly J., ed. *Philosophers Who Believe: The Spiritual Journeys of 11 Leading Thinkers.* Downers Grove, IL: InterVarsity, 1993. A great book in which major philosophers explain their intellectual journeys.

Laughery, Gregory J. "Evangelicalism and Philosophy." In *The Futures of Evangelicalism*, edited by Craig Bartholomew, Robin Parry, and Andrew West, 246–70. Leicester, UK: Inter-Varsity; Grand Rapids: Kregel, 2003. Greg heads up L'Abri in Switzerland. He begins the chapter with the important role philosophy played in Francis and Edith Schaeffer's worldwide ministry from L'Abri, and then examines the resurgence and challenges of Christian philosophy today.

Sire, James W. *A Little Primer on Humble Apologetics*. Downers Grove, IL: InterVarsity, 2006. A short, useful approach to apologetics.

Chapter 2   Faith and Philosophy

For a summary of the biblical story, see our "Story-Line of the Bible" under Drama of Scripture "Articles" on www.biblicaltheology.ca.

On worldview, see the following:

Goheen, Michael W., and Craig G. Bartholomew. *Living at the Crossroads: An Introduction to Christian Worldview*. Grand Rapids: Baker Academic; London: SPCK, 2008.

Sire, James W. *The Universe Next Door: A Basic Worldview Catalog*. 5th ed. Downers Grove, IL: InterVarsity, 2004. This is the great book that Percy refers to at the end of chapter 3.

Wolters, Albert M. *Creation Regained: Biblical Basics for a Reformational Worldview*. 2nd ed. Grand Rapids: Eerdmans, 2005. An excellent introduction to the Kuyperian worldview.

———. "Facing the Perplexing History of Philosophy." *Tydskrif vir Christelike Wetenskap* 17 (1981): 1–17. This is the article referred to by Abby at the start of chapter 5.

———. "On the Idea of Worldview and Its Relation to Philosophy." In *Stained Glass: Worldviews and Social Science*, edited by Paul Marshall et al., 14–25. Lanham, MD: University Press of America, 1983. In this chapter Wolters develops the typology of the relationship between worldview and philosophy that we use. Available online for Kuyperian philosophy at Steve Bishop's website www.allofliferedeemed.co.uk.

Chapter 3   Ancient Pagan Philosophy: The Pre-Socratics to Socrates

Kirk, G. S., J. E. Raven, and M. Schofield, eds. *The Presocratic Philosophers*. 2nd ed. Cambridge: Cambridge University Press, 1983. The major English source for the writings of the pre-Socratics.

Kok, John H. *Patterns of the Western Mind*. Sioux Center, IA: Dordt College Press, 1998, esp. 29–51. A Reformational introduction to early Greek philosophy.

Long, A. A. "The Scope of Early Greek Philosophy." In *The Cambridge Companion to Early Greek Philosophy*, edited by A. A. Long, 1–19. Cambridge: Cambridge University Press, 1999. A useful introduction to early Greek philosophy. The volume as a whole contains many good chapters for further study.

Seerveld, Calvin. "The Pedagogical Strength of a Christian Methodology in Philosophical Historiography." *Koers* 40 (1975): 269–313. We emphasize that how we tell the story of philosophy is never neutral. Seerveld is a leading Reformational philosopher, and here he makes the case for a Christian method in history of philosophy.

Chapter 4   The High Point of Greek Philosophy: Plato, Aristotle, and Their Legacy

Bett, Richard, ed. *The Cambridge Companion to Ancient Skepticism*. Cambridge: Cambridge University Press, 2010. Provides a sense of the current state of scholarship on Skepticism.

Cooper, John M., ed. *Plato: Complete Works*. Indianapolis: Hackett, 1997.

Grene, Marjorie. *A Portrait of Aristotle*. London: Faber and Faber, 1963. An important work on Aristotle with a convincing critique.

Inwood, Brad, ed. *The Cambridge Companion to Stoicism*. Cambridge: Cambridge University Press, 2003. Provides a sense of the current state of scholarship on Stoicism.

Kraut, Richard. "Introduction to the Study of Plato." In *The Cambridge Companion to Plato*, edited by Richard Kraut, 1–50. Cambridge: Cambridge University Press, 1992. A good introduction to the current state of Plato studies.

Morrow, David R., and Anthony Weston. *A Workbook for Arguments: A Complete Course in Critical Thinking*. Indianapolis: Hackett, 2011. A good introduction to logic and critical thinking. Do be aware that there is more to knowing than logic and that rationality always operates within a tradition.

Priest, Graham. *Logic: A Very Short Introduction*. Oxford: Oxford University Press, 2000. A good introduction to logic and critical thinking.

Warren, James, ed. *The Cambridge Companion to Epicureanism*. Cambridge: Cambridge University Press, 2009. Provides a sense of the current state of scholarship on Epicureanism.

Chapter 5   Medieval Synthesis Philosophy: Augustine to Abélard

Augustine. *Confessions*. A must read! Be sure to find a modern translation.

Chang, Curtis. *Engaging Unbelief: A Captivating Strategy from Augustine and Aquinas*. Eugene, OR: Wipf and Stock, 2000.

Cochrane, Charles N. *Christianity and Classical Culture: A Study of Thought and Action from Augustus to Augustine*. 2nd ed. Oxford: Oxford University Press, 1944. This remains a classic.

Fitzgerald, Allan D., ed. *Augustine Through the Ages: An Encyclopedia*. Grand Rapids: Eerdmans, 1999. A major resource on Augustine.

Gilson, Étienne. *History of Christian Philosophy in the Middle Ages*. New York: Random House, 1955. One of many useful works by this brilliant Catholic philosopher.

Marrone, Steven P. "Medieval Philosophy in Context." In *The Cambridge Companion to Medieval Philosophy*, edited by A. S. McGrade, 10–50. Cambridge: Cambridge University Press, 2003. A very insightful discussion.

Nash, Ronald H. *The Light of the Mind: St. Augustine's Theory of Knowledge*. Lima, OH: Academic Renewal Press, 2003. An insightful analysis of the shape of Augustine's philosophy.

Pieper, Josef. *Scholasticism: Personalities and Problems of Medieval Philosophy*. Translated by Richard Winston and Clara Winston. New York: McGraw-Hill, 1964. A great, accessible introduction by a prominent Catholic philosopher.

Wilken, Robert L. *The Spirit of Early Christian Thought: Seeking the Face of God*. New Haven and London: Yale University Press, 2003. A delightful assessment of the achievement of the church fathers in articulating the Christian vision in their contexts.

Chapter 6   The Middle Ages: Aristotle Rediscovered

Dooyeweerd, Herman. *Roots of Western Culture: Pagan, Secular, and Christian Options*. Translated by John Kraay. Toronto: Wedge, 1979, 117–18. This section contains Dooyeweerd's critique of medieval synthesis.

Nichols, Aidan. *Discovering Aquinas: An Introduction to His Life, Work and Influence*. London: DLT, 2002. A good introduction to Aquinas.

Pieper, Josef. *Guide to Aquinas.* Translated by Richard and Clara Winston. San Francisco: Ignatius, 1962, 1991. A good introduction to Aquinas.

Spade, Paul V., ed. *The Cambridge Companion to Ockham.* Cambridge: Cambridge University Press, 1999. Contains a multitude of useful materials on Ockham.

Vos, Arvin. *Aquinas, Calvin, and Contemporary Protestant Thought: A Critique of Protestant Views on the Thought of Thomas Aquinas.* Washington, DC: Christian University Press; Grand Rapids: Eerdmans, 1985. An important work on the relationship between Calvin and Aquinas.

Chapter 7   The Renaissance and Reformation

Cassirer, Ernst, Paul O. Kristeller, and John H. Randall, eds. *The Renaissance Philosophy of Man.* Chicago and London: Phoenix, 1948.

Hankins, James, ed. *The Cambridge Companion to Renaissance Philosophy.* Cambridge: Cambridge University Press, 2007. Provides an insight into contemporary views. Hankins is a leading authority on Renaissance philosophy today.

Hoitenga, Dewey J., Jr. *Faith and Reason from Plato to Plantinga: An Introduction to Reformed Epistemology.* Albany: SUNY, 1991. Includes a detailed examination of Calvin on philosophy.

Kristeller, Paul O. *Renaissance Concepts of Man and Other Essays.* New York: Harper & Row, 1972. Kristeller played a major role in the current explosion of work on Renaissance philosophy, and his works remain accessible and useful.

Muller, Richard. *Post-Reformation Reformed Dogmatics: The Rise and Development of Reformed Orthodoxy, ca. 1520–ca. 1575.* 2nd ed. 4 vols. Grand Rapids: Baker Academic, 2003. Muller has done seminal work on post-Reformation thought, including philosophy.

Vos, Arvin. *Aquinas, Calvin, and Contemporary Protestant Thought: A Critique of Protestant Views on the Thought of Thomas Aquinas.* Washington, DC: Christian University Press; Grand Rapids: Eerdmans, 1985.

Chapter 8   Early Modern Philosophy: Bacon to Leibniz

Bacon, Francis. *The New Organon.* Edited by Lisa Jardine and Michael Silverthorne. Cambridge Texts in the History of Philosophy. Cambridge: Cambridge University Press, 2000.

Buckley, Michael J. *At the Origins of Modern Atheism.* New Haven: Yale University Press, 1987. A very important work on the origins of modernity and mistakes Christians made.

Dooyeweerd, Herman. *Roots of Western Culture: Pagan, Secular, and Christian Options.* Translated by John Kraay. Toronto: Wedge, 1979, 149–73. A good place to explore Dooyeweerd's analysis of the nature/freedom dialectic in modern philosophy.

Nadler, Steven. *The Best of All Possible Worlds: A Story of Philosophers, God, and Evil in the Age of Reason.* Princeton and Oxford: Princeton University Press, 2010. Provides a lively account of Leibniz and his dialogue partners on this issue.

Pascal, Blaise. *Pensées.* Translated by and with an introduction by A. J. Krailsheimer. London: Penguin, 1966. One of the great Christian philosophers. Take and read!

Peters, James R. *The Logic of the Heart: Augustine, Pascal, and the Rationality of Faith.* Grand Rapids: Baker Academic, 2009. This contains a useful comparison of Pascal with Hume.

Snyder, Laura J. *The Philosophical Breakfast Club.* New York: Broadway, 2011. Provides an example of the influence of Bacon. This is the story of four friends in Cambridge in the early nineteenth century who were inspired by and worked in the tradition of Bacon and exercised an important influence on modern science.

Wolterstorff, Nicholas. *John Locke and the Ethics of Belief*. Cambridge Studies in Religion and Ethical Thought. Cambridge: Cambridge University Press, 1996.

Chapter 9   Modern Philosophy: Hume to Schleiermacher

Bayer, Oswald. *A Contemporary in Dissent: Johann Georg Hamann as a Radical Enlightener*. Translated by Roy A. Harrisville and Mark C. Mattes. Grand Rapids: Eerdmans, 2012. A detailed study of Hamann.

Beiser, Frederick C. "The Enlightenment and Idealism." In *The Cambridge Companion to German Idealism*, edited by Karl Ameriks, 18–36. Cambridge: Cambridge University Press, 2000. An excellent overview of the rise of idealism against the backdrop of the growing crisis in the Enlightenment.

———. *The Fate of Reason: German Philosophy from Kant to Fichte*. Cambridge, MA: Harvard University Press, 1987. Excellent.

Betz, John R. *After Enlightenment: The Post-Secular Vision of J. G. Hamann*. Oxford: Wiley-Blackwell, 2012. A detailed study of Hamann.

———. "Reading 'Sibylline Leaves': J. G. Hamann in the History of Ideas." *Journal of the History of Ideas* 70/1 (2009): 93–118. An excellent introduction to Hamann.

Cuneo, Terence, and René van Woudenberg, eds. *The Cambridge Companion to Thomas Reid*. Cambridge: Cambridge University Press, 2004.

Hamann, Johann Georg. *Writings on Philosophy and Language*. Edited by Kenneth Haynes. Cambridge Texts in the History of Philosophy. Cambridge: Cambridge University Press, 2007. An important primary source.

Kant, Immanuel. *An Answer to the Question: What Is Enlightenment?* Translated by H. B. Nisbet. London: Penguin, 1991. A short work useful for gaining an understanding of Kant's view of autonomy.

Kroner, Richard. *Kant's Weltanschauung*. Chicago and London: University of Chicago Press, 1956. An important work arguing that Kant's view of morality is central to his philosophy and exposing tensions in Kant's philosophy.

Penelhum, Terrence. *God and Skepticism*. Dordrecht: Reidel, 1983; *Hume*. London: Macmillan, 1975. Important works by a Christian philosopher.

Peters, James R. *The Logic of the Heart: Augustine, Pascal, and the Rationality of Faith*. Grand Rapids: Baker Academic, 2009, 103–60. Discussion of Hume and Pascal.

Chapter 10   Modern Philosophy: Romanticism to Gadamer

Arbaugh, George B., and George E. Arbaugh. *Kierkegaard's Authorship: A Guide to the Writings of Kierkegaard*. Rock Island, IL: Augustana College Library, 1967. A useful introduction to all of Kierkegaard's writings.

Ashford, Bruce R. "Wittgenstein's Theologians? A Survey of Ludwig Wittgenstein's Influence on Theology." *Journal of the Evangelical Theological Society* 50, no. 2 (June 2007): 357–75. Ashford shows the immense influence of Wittgenstein on theology.

de Lubac, Henri. *The Drama of Atheist Humanism*. Translated by Edith M. Riley, Anne Englund Nash, and Mark Sebanc. San Francisco: Ignatius, 1995. An important work by a great twentieth-century Catholic thinker.

Engels, Friedrich. Preface to the 1888 English edition of *The Communist Manifesto*. Available at http://www.marxists.org/archive/marx/works/1848/communist-manifesto/preface.htm.

Evans, C. Stephen. *Kierkegaard: An Introduction*. Cambridge: Cambridge University Press, 2009. Superb!

Gaines, James R. *Evening in the Palace of Reason: Bach Meets Frederick the Great in the Age of Enlightenment*. New York: Harper Perennial, 2005. An entertaining account of the Enlightenment.

Holmes, Richard. *The Age of Wonder: How the Romantic Generation Discovered the Beauty and Terror of Science*. London: Harper Press, 2008. An entertaining account of Romanticism and its contribution to science.

Ingraffia, Brian D. *Postmodern Theory and Biblical Theology*. Cambridge: Cambridge University Press, 1995, 17–97. An excellent Christian critique of Nietzsche.

Kierkegaard, Søren. *The Point of View of My Work as an Author: A Report to History*. Translated by Walter Lowrie. Edited by Benjamin Nelson. New York: Harper & Row, 1962.

Nietzsche, Friedrich. *Ecce Homo*. Translated by R. J. Hollingdale. London: Penguin, 1979.

Ratner-Rosenhagen, Jennifer. *American Nietzsche: A History of an Icon and His Ideas*. Chicago and London: University of Chicago Press, 2012. On the influence of Nietzsche and his reception in America.

Schirmacher, Wolfgang. "Living Disaster: Schopenhauer for the Twenty-First Century." In *The Essential Schopenhauer*, edited by Wolfgang Schirmacher, vii–xxi. New York: Harper Perennial, 2010. A good introduction by a leading authority and a fan of Schopenhauer.

Schopenhauer, Arthur. *The Horrors and Absurdities of Religion*. Translated by R. J. Hollingdale. Great Ideas. London: Penguin, 1970. Provides a sense of Schopenhauer's views of religion.

Stern, J. P. *Nietzsche*. Fontana Modern Masters. London: Fontana, 1978.

West, Cornel. *The American Evasion of Philosophy: A Genealogy of Pragmatism*. Madison: University of Wisconsin Press, 1989.

Chapter 11 Postmodernism and Philosophy Today

Bertens, Johannes W. *The Idea of the Postmodern: A History*. London and New York: Routledge, 1995. Useful for gaining a sense of the big picture.

Carroll, John. *Humanism: The Wreck of Western Culture*. London: Fontana, 1993. Penetrating analysis by a scholar who is always stimulating and raises the central questions.

Depoortere, Frederick. *Christ in Postmodern Philosophy: Gianni Vattimo, René Girard and Slavoj Žižek*. London: T&T Clark, 2008. A good introduction to these major thinkers.

Himmelfarb, Gertrude. *On Looking into the Abyss: Untimely Thoughts on Culture and Society*. New York: Vintage, 1994. A penetrating analysis of postmodernism from an outstanding historian.

Lyon, David. *Postmodernity*. Concepts in the Social Sciences. Buckingham: Open University Press, 1994. Useful for gaining a sense of the big picture. Lyon is a Christian sociologist.

Rieff, Philip. *My Life Among the Deathworks: Illustrations of the Aesthetics of Authority*. Sacred Order/Social Order 1. Charlottesville and London: University of Virginia Press, 2006. Rieff's work needs to be widely known and read.

Rose, Margaret A. *The Post-Modern and the Post-Industrial: A Critical Analysis*. Cambridge: Cambridge University Press, 1991. Useful for gaining a sense of the big picture.

Steiner, George. *Real Presences*. London: Faber and Faber, 1989. A rigorous critique of contemporary literary and philosophical theory including a call for a grammar of creation.

Chapter 12 Christian Philosophy Today

Girard, René. *I See Satan Fall Like Lightning*. Maryknoll, NY: Orbis, 2001. A phenomenal book.

Knight, Kelvin. Introduction to *The MacIntyre Reader*, edited by Kelvin Knight, 1–27. Notre Dame, IN: University of Notre Dame Press, 1998. A good introduction to MacIntyre's seminal work.

MacIntyre, Alasdair. *After Virtue: A Study in Moral Theory*. 2nd ed. London: Duckworth, 1985.

Noll, Mark A., and James Turner. *The Future of Christian Learning: An Evangelical and Catholic Dialogue*. Edited by Thomas A. Howard. Grand Rapids: Brazos, 2008. A fascinating dialogue between a Kuyperian and a Catholic.

Plantinga, Alvin. "Advice to Christian Philosophers." *Faith and Philosophy* 1/3 (1984): 253–71. See www.faithandphilosophy.com/article_advice.php for the article. One of the major stimulants for the current renaissance in Christian philosophy. You really must read it!

Taylor, Charles. "God Loveth Adverbs." In *Sources of the Self: The Making of the Modern Identity*, 211–33. Cambridge: Cambridge University Press, 1989. This delightful chapter is must reading! Taylor is a leading Catholic philosopher.

Chapter 13 Reformed Epistemology

Clark, Kelly J. *Return to Reason: A Critique of Enlightenment Evidentialism and a Defense of Reason and Belief in God*. Grand Rapids: Eerdmans, 1990. A great introduction to Reformed epistemology.

"Modernizing the Case for God." *Time*, April 7, 1980. Identifies Alvin Plantinga as the leading Protestant philosopher of God and the surprising resurgence of God in philosophy.

Plantinga, Alvin. *Warranted Christian Belief*. New York: Oxford University Press, 2000. A tour de force by one of the great (Christian) philosophers of our day.

Wolterstorff, Nicholas. Introduction to *Faith and Rationality: Reason and Belief in God*, edited by Alvin Plantinga and Nicholas Wolterstorff, 1–15. Notre Dame, IN: University of Notre Dame Press, 1983. Introduction to a book that really got Reformed epistemology going.

———. *Reason within the Bounds of Religion*. 2nd ed. Grand Rapids: Eerdmans, 1984. A classic. Accessible, clear, and short!

Chapter 14 Reformed Epistemology Applied

Plantinga, Alvin. *Where the Conflict Really Lies: Science, Religion, and Naturalism*. Oxford: Oxford University Press, 2011. Vintage Plantinga.

Wolterstorff, Nicholas. *Art in Action*. Grand Rapids: Eerdmans, 1980.

———. *Justice: Rights and Wrongs*. Princeton: Princeton University Press, 2008.

———. *Until Justice and Peace Embrace*. Grand Rapids: Eerdmans, 1983. A great vision of world-formative Christianity.

Chapter 15 Reformational Philosophy

Bartholomew, Craig G., ed. *In the Fields of the Lord: A Calvin Seerveld Reader*. Carlisle: Piquant; Toronto: Toronto Tuppence Press, 2000. A rich trove of Seerveld's work.

———. "Islam in Africa." *Journal of Interdisciplinary Studies* VI 1/2 (1994): 129–46. Explores ways in which a Reformational philosophy of pluralism can untangle the challenges of Islam today.

Dooyeweerd, Herman. *Roots of Western Culture: Pagan, Secular, and Christian Options*. Translated by John Kraay. Toronto: Wedge, 1979. A good place to start when reading Dooyeweerd.

Geertsema, Henk. "Dooyeweerd's Transcendental Critique: Transforming it Hermeneutically." In *Contemporary Reflections on the Philosophy of Herman Dooyeweerd*, edited by D. F. M. Strauss and Michelle Botting, 83–108. Lewiston, NY: Edwin Mellen, 2000. An important article by an authority on Dooyeweerd.

Kalsbeek, L. *Contours of a Christian Philosophy: An Introduction to Herman Dooyeweerd's Thought*. Toronto: Wedge, 1975. Still the best introduction to Dooyeweerd's philosophy.

Kok, John H. *Patterns of the Western Mind*. Sioux Center, IA: Dordt College Press, 1998. Provides an introduction to Vollenhoven's problem-historical method.

Mouw, Richard J., and Sander Griffioen. *Pluralisms and Horizons: An Essay in Christian Public Philosophy*. Grand Rapids: Eerdmans, 1993. Outstanding!

Seerveld, Calvin. "Biblical Wisdom Underneath Vollenhoven's Categories for Philosophical Historiography." *Philosophia Reformata* 38 (1973): 127–43. Provides an introduction to Vollenhoven's problem-historical method.

Skillen, James. *In Pursuit of Justice: Christian-Democratic Explorations*. Lanham, MD: Rowan and Littlefield, 2004.

———. *Recharging the American Experiment: Principled Pluralism for Genuine Civic Community*. Grand Rapids: Baker, 1994.

———. *With or Against the World? America's Role among the Nations*. Lanham, MD: Rowan and Littlefield, 2005.

Spykman, Gordon J. *Reformational Theology: A New Paradigm for Doing Dogmatics*. Grand Rapids: Eerdmans, 1992. A great systematic theology in the Reformational tradition.

Wolters, Albert M. "The Intellectual Milieu of Herman Dooyeweerd." In *The Legacy of Herman Dooyeweerd*, edited by Carl T. McIntire, 1–19. Lanham, MD: University Press of America, 1985.

For web resources, see www.allofliferedeemed.co.uk, www.missionworldview .com, and www.reformationalpublishingproject.com. The latter site is a major resource for Reformational philosophy.

Index

as "classical" or "pagan," 32
and Heraclitus, 34–35
importance of, 37–38
and Ionian naturalism, 33–35
and matter-form distinction, 36
ordering principle(s) of, 37–38
and Pythagoras, 35
and rationalism, 36–37
in relation to Old Testament, 38
on structure vs. genesis, 38
Principle of Mathematics (Russell), 170
Protagoras, 39–40
Proverbs, book of, 39, 42
Pyrrho, 57
Pythagoras, 35

qualities (primary vs. secondary), 128
Quine, Willard Van Orman, 199–200

Rad, Gerhard von, 15
Rainbows for a Fallen World (Seerveld), 265
Raphael, 50
Rational Faith, 211–12
rationalism, 76, 83, 115, 140, 142, 144, 149
pre-Socratic, 36–37
and Socrates, 41–42
realism vs. nominalism, 74, 89, 95–97, 124, 128, 172
Reason within the Bounds of Religion (Wolterstorff), 217–21, 241, 270
Reformation, the, 107
contra-dualism, 107
counter-Reformation, 107, 112
and relationship between theology and philosophy, 107–8, 111
and Aristotelianism, 108, 111–12
and Calvin, 109–11
and Colossians 2:8, 109
and double truth, 111–12
and instrumental view of reason, 112
Reginald of Piperno, 83–84
Reid, Thomas, 138
and Christianity, 139
on common sense, 138–39
his influence, 140
religion, and philosophy, 11, 29, 152, 184–85
Religion within the Limits of Reason Alone (Kant), 142
Renaissance, the, 99
and Aristotelianism, 104–7
and Christian orthodoxy, 106–7

humanism of, 101, 106, 183
Christian, 107
and human freedom/dignity, 103–4
and Platonism/Neoplatonism, 102–4
innovations of, 100–101
relationship to middle ages, 100
Renan, Ernest, 37
Repetition (Kierkegaard), 162
Republic, The (Plato), 46, 49, 59
Ricoeur, Paul, 189–90
Rief, Philip, 193, 194
rights, 235
animal, 236–37
Christian vs. secular grounding for, 235–36
Romans, book of, 100
romanticism, 140, 154–56
Rome, fall of, 71
Rookmaaker, Hans, 265
Roots of Western Culture (Dooyeweerd), 250
Rorty, Richard, 170, 184, 188, 191
Rousseau, Jean-Jacques, 140–41
Runner, H. Evan, 213
Russell, Bertrand, 18, 170–71, 217

Sacred Order/Social Order (Rief), 194
sapientia, 70–71
Sarte, Jean Paul, 176–77
Schaeffer, Edith, 6
Schaeffer, Francis, 6, 183
Schleiermacher, Friedrich, 152
scholarship, Christian, 7–9, 61, 216, 219–20, 270
scholasticism, 74, 78, 79–80, 100, 102, 108, 116–17
School of Athens, The (Raphael), 50
Schopenhauer, Arthur, 157–58
science, 116, 117–18
and reason, 18
and theology, 81
"science, theistic," 230
Science of Knowing, The (Fichte), 150
Science of Logic, The (Hegel), 151
scientia, 70–71
scientific method, 168–69
Scripture, 13–15, 125, 162–63, 190, 218, 219
reasoning without, 74, 77
Spinoza on, 129–30
warranted biblical interpretation, 239–41
and worldview, 16–17
Scruton, Roger, 146
Seerveld, Calvin, 38, 243, 252, 270
on aesthetics, 265
on reformational anthropology, 257–59